Migrating Shakespeare

GLOBAL SHAKESPEARE INVERTED

Global Shakespeare Inverted challenges any tendency to view Global Shakespeare from the perspective of 'centre' versus 'periphery'. Although the series may locate its critical starting point geographically, it calls into question the geographical bias that lurks within the very notion of the 'global'. It provides a timely, constructive criticism of the present state of the field and establishes new and alternative methodologies that invert the relation of Shakespeare to the supposed 'other'.

SERIES EDITORS

David Schalkwyk, Queen Mary, University of London, UK
Silvia Bigliazzi, University of Verona, Italy
Bi-qi Beatrice Lei, National Taiwan University, Taiwan

ADVISORY BOARD

Douglas Lanier, University of New Hampshire, USA
Sonia Massai, King's College London, UK
Supriya Chaudhury, Jadavpur University, India
Ian Smith, Lafayette College, USA

Eating Shakespeare: Cultural Anthropophagy as Global Methodology
Edited by Anne Sophie Refskou, Marcel Alvaro de Amorim and Vinicius Mariano de Carvalho

FORTHCOMING TITLES

Disseminating Shakespeare in the Nordic Countries: Shifting Centres and Peripheries in the Nineteenth Century
Edited by Nely Keinänen and Per Sivefors

Shakespeare's Others in 21st-century European Performance: Othello and The Merchant of Venice
Edited by Boika Sokolova and Janice Valls-Russell

Migrating Shakespeare

First European Encounters, Routes and Networks

Edited by Janet Clare and Dominique Goy-Blanquet

THE ARDEN SHAKESPEARE
LONDON • NEW YORK • OXFORD • NEW DELHI • SYDNEY

THE ARDEN SHAKESPEARE
Bloomsbury Publishing Plc
50 Bedford Square, London, WC1B 3DP, UK
1385 Broadway, New York, NY 10018, USA
29 Earlsfort Terrace, Dublin 2, Ireland

BLOOMSBURY, THE ARDEN SHAKESPEARE and the Arden Shakespeare
logo are trademarks of Bloomsbury Publishing Plc

First published in Great Britain 2021
This paperback edition published in 2022

Copyright © Janet Clare, Dominique Goy-Blanquet and contributors, 2021

Janet Clare, Dominique Goy-Blanquet and contributors have asserted their right
under the Copyright, Designs and Patents Act, 1988, to be identified as the
authors of this work.

For legal purposes the Acknowledgements on p. ix constitute an extension
of this copyright page.

Cover design: Charlotte Daniels
Cover image: *The Wild Swan* (watercolour on paper) by
William Frederick Mitchell, 1906 (© Bridgeman Images)

All rights reserved. No part of this publication may be reproduced or transmitted in
any form or by any means, electronic or mechanical, including photocopying,
recording, or any information storage or retrieval system, without prior
permission in writing from the publishers.

Bloomsbury Publishing Plc does not have any control over, or responsibility for, any
third-party websites referred to or in this book. All internet addresses given in this
book were correct at the time of going to press. The author and publisher regret
any inconvenience caused if addresses have changed or sites have ceased to
exist, but can accept no responsibility for any such changes.

A catalogue record for this book is available from the British Library.

A catalog record for this book is available from the Library of Congress.

ISBN: HB: 978-1-3501-0328-3
PB: 978-1-3502-1385-2
ePDF: 978-1-3501-0330-6
eBook: 978-1-3501-0329-0

Series: Global Shakespeare Inverted

Typeset by RefineCatch Limited, Bungay, Suffolk

To find out more about our authors and books visit www.bloomsbury.com
and sign up for our newsletters.

No worthier service can be paid to literature than to transport the masterpieces of the human mind from one language to another. There exist so few productions of the first rank; genius, of whatever kind, is such a rare phenomenon that if each modern nation were reduced to its own treasures, it would be forever poor. Indeed, the circulation of ideas is, of all the existing sorts of trade, the one which offers the most assured profits.

Germaine de Staël,
'De l'esprit des traductions', 1816

CONTENTS

Acknowledgements ix
Notes on contributors x

Introduction: 'Migrating Shakespeare' 1
  Janet Clare and Dominique Goy-Blanquet

1 'Michelangelo of tragedy': Shakespeare's tortuous Italian routes 29
   Maria Luisa De Rinaldis

2 'No stranger here': Shakespeare in Germany 55
   Wolfgang G. Müller

3 Shakespeare at cultural crossroads: Switzerland 79
   Balz Engler

4 Opening the book: The disclosure of Shakespeare in the Netherlands 95
   Detlef Wagenaar

5 Jean-François Ducis, global *passeur*: Shakespeare's migration in Continental Europe 119
   Michèle Willems

6 'No profit but the name': The Polish reception of Shakespeare's plays 145
Anna Cetera-Włodarczyk

7 From migration to naturalization: Shakespeare in Russia 167
Marina P. Kizima

8 Trade routes, politics and culture: Shakespeare in Sweden 189
Per Sivefors

9 The mirror and the razor: Shakespeare's arrival in Spain 209
Keith Gregor

10 Migrating with migrants: Shakespeare and the Armenian diaspora 233
Jasmine H. Seymour

11 Shakespeare in Greece: From Athens to Constantinople and beyond 259
Mara Yanni

Index 283

ACKNOWLEDGEMENTS

The editors are thankful to Professor Mami Adachi for her generous and stimulating contribution to the World Shakespeare Congress seminar in Stratford-upon-Avon in 2016 from which this project originally arose. We are grateful to all the participants of the seminar for initiating discussion of transcultural Shakespeare. For the editors it has been a pleasure to collaborate with each other and to work with the contributors. Janet Clare would like to record her great gratitude to Raymond Hargreaves for so willingly sharing his expertise in modern languages and literature.

NOTES ON CONTRIBUTORS

Anna Cetera-Włodarczyk is Associate Professor of English Literature at the University of Warsaw. Her research interests focus on Shakespeare and translation either in a theatrical context or within Polish cultural history. She has published extensively in the field, including three monographs on translation history and critical editions of new Polish translations of Shakespeare. Other areas of expertise include literature and ideology, performance and adaptation studies. In the years 2016–19 she managed a state-funded project to establish the digital repository of all Polish nineteenth-century Shakespeare translations (http://polskieszekspir.uw.edu.pl), expanded in 2018 to include the twentieth and twenty-first centuries.

Janet Clare is Emeritus Professor of Renaissance Literature at the University of Hull and is currently Research Professor in English at the University of Bristol and Research Fellow at the Institute of English Studies, University of London. In 2016 she was Visiting Professor at the Università degli Studi di Firenze and has lectured in France, Germany, Italy, Austria, Brazil and Japan. She is the author of *Art Made Tongue-Tied by Authority: Elizabethan and Jacobean Dramatic Censorship* (second edition, 1999); *Drama of the English Republic, 1649–1660* (2002); *Revenge Tragedies of the Renaissance* (2006) and *Shakespeare's Stage Traffic: Imitation, Borrowing and Competition in Renaissance Theatre* (2014, 2017) She has published many articles on Renaissance and Early Modern literature and drama and co-edited the *Journal of Early Modern Studies* 2, Shakespeare and Early Modern Popular Culture. Her most recent book is *From Republic to Restoration: Legacies and Departures* (2017). She is editing *What You Will* for the Oxford *Complete Works of John Marston*.

Maria Luisa De Rinaldis is an Associate Professor of English Literature at the University of Salento. Her research includes work on Anglo-Italian relations and translation in the early modern period, on Shakespearean criticism in the late nineteenth century and on Walter Pater. She is the author of the monographs *Giacomo Castelvetro Renaissance Translator* (2003), *Corpi umani e corpi divini. Il personaggio in Walter Pater* (2010). She has written articles on A. S. Byatt, G. Baretti and Charles Dickens, and has more recently investigated the representation of subjectivity through song in Shakespeare and Fletcher ('Shakespeare, Fletcher e l'imprevedibilità della canzone', *Lingue e Linguaggi*, 2018). She is a member of the current board of Iasems – Italian Association of Shakespearean and Early Modern Studies.

Balz Engler is Professor Emeritus of English Literature at Basel University, Switzerland. He has written books on Shakespeare translation, on poetic texts and their modes of communicating, and on literature as performance and its cultural implications; he also initiated the *HyperHamlet* project. His latest publication, *Constructing Shakespeares* (2019), deals with issues of how Shakespeare has become a great author. He served on the board of the Deutsche Shakespeare-Gesellschaft, and was among the founders of ESRA, the European Shakespeare Research Association. His website is at http://www.BalzEngler.ch

Dominique Goy-Blanquet is Professor Emeritus at the University of Picardie, and a member of the editorial board of *En attendant Nadeau*. Her works include *Shakespeare's Early History Plays* (2003), *Shakespeare et l'invention de l'histoire* (third edition, 2014), *Côté cour, côté justice: Shakespeare et l'invention du droit* (2016), essays for *Shakespeare Survey, Cambridge Companion, Moreana, Law and Humanities*, editions of *Joan of Arc: A Saint for all Reasons* (2003), Richard Marienstras's posthumous *Shakespeare et le désordre du monde* (2012), and with François Laroque *Shakespeare, combien de prétendants?* (2016). Her *Shakespeare in the*

Theatre: Patrice Chéreau was published by The Arden Shakespeare in 2018.

Keith Gregor teaches English and Comparative Literature at the University of Murcia, Spain, and heads a government-funded research project on the reception of Shakespeare's work in Spanish and European culture. General co-editor with Dirk Delabastita of the 'Shakespeare in European Culture' series for John Benjamins, he has written widely on Shakespearean translation and performance in Spain and in the rest of Europe. Editor or co-editor of, amongst other volumes, *Shakespeare and Tyranny: Regimes of Reading in Europe and Beyond* (2014), 'Romeo and Juliet' in *European Culture* (2017) and the first neoclassical Spanish versions of *Hamlet*, *Macbeth* and *Romeo and Juliet*, he is also the author of *Shakespeare in the Spanish Theatre: from 1772 to the Present* (2010).

Marina P. Kizima is Doctor of Letters, Professor in the Department of World Literature and Culture at Moscow State Institute of International Relations (University), Russia. Her field of research is comparative literature, particularly English, American and Russian literatures and their cultural ties, reception and translation. She is the author of two monographs: *Glimpses of the Southern Literary Renascence: The Fugitives – The Agrarians – the New Critics* (1995); *Woman on the Threshold of the 20th Century: The Life and Work of Edith Wharton* (2007), as well as numerous articles, including 'Margaret Fuller's Reception in Russia in the 1850's' in *Nineteenth-Century Prose* (vol. 42, no. 2, 2015).

Wolfgang G. Müller is retired Professor of English Literature at the University of Jena. He taught at the universities of Mainz, Leicester and Jena. His book-length publications include Rilke's *New Poems* (1971), *Shakespeare's Political Speeches* (1979), *Concepts of Style from Classical Antiquity to the Twentieth Century* (1981), *English and Scottish Balladry* (1983), *Dialogue und Conversational Culture in the Renaissance* (2004), *Genre in Shakespeare* (2015), and an edition of Shakespeare's *Hamlet*

(2005). At present he runs a research group on the flâneur in British and American literature at the University of Jena. A long-term project is an edition of Shakespeare's *Henry VIII*, which, amongst other things, debates recent theories of authorship.

Jasmine H. Seymour is the founder of the Armenian Shakespeare Association (ASA) which hosts international conferences in Armenia and Europe. Her master's degree on *The Merchant of Venice at the RSC* at the University Paris-7 was supervised by Richard Marienstras. She is currently a PhD candidate in the Department of English and Drama at Queen Mary University of London. She has published articles for the media and press in Armenia, Europe and the United States, and translations of European and American drama. Her recent publications include *Shakespeare in Armenia* for Stanford Global Shakespeare Encyclopaedia, articles in *Cahiers Élisabéthains* and for the Shakespeare Birthplace Trust as well as ongoing proceedings of ASA conferences.

Per Sivefors is Associate Professor of English at Linnaeus University, Sweden. His latest book is *Representing Masculinity in Early Modern English Satire, 1590–1603* (2020), which will be followed in 2021 by the anthology *Satire and the Multiplicity of Forms: Textual and Graphic Transformations 1600–1803*, co-edited with Cecilia Rosengren and Rikard Wingård. He also works on the early reception of Shakespeare in the Nordic countries and is currently preparing a monograph as well as an anthology, co-edited with Nely Keinänen, on the subject. He is chair of the Nordic Shakespeare Society (NorSS).

Detlef Wagenaar is a lecturer and researcher at Saxion University of Applied Sciences, where his research focuses on narrative ethics, in particular the relation between ethics and technology, economics and globalization. After studying English Linguistics and Literature at Radboud University, Nijmegen, he worked there as a researcher, specializing in the fields of Victorian studies and authorship. In 2012 he published his PhD thesis, *The Rise of the Professional Author: the Life* *and Work of Sir Walter Besant*. Currently he is also working on a biography of Shakespeare's translator, L. A. J. Burgersdijk.

Michèle Willems is Professor Emeritus at the University of Rouen. Her publications, both in French and English, are mostly centred on the representation of Shakespeare's drama through the ages, from her early incursion into reception studies (*La genèse du mythe shakespearien, 1660–1780*, 1979), to recent research on '*Hamlet* in France' (hamletworks.org), Voltaire (*Great Shakespeareans* 3, 2010), Ducis's adaptations of Shakespeare (*Shakespeare Survey* 60, 2007); 'Shakespeare or not Shakespeare?' in *Early Modern Drama in Performance* (2015), and contributions, in various French and English publications, to the study of Shakespeare on screen. She has also translated Ben Jonson's *Volpone* and *The Alchemist* (2009).

Mara Yanni is Professor Emeritus of English Literature and Culture in the Faculty of English Studies at the National and Kapodistrian University of Athens. She has studied in Greece and the USA and her publications include: 'A Midsummer Night's Dream in Modern Athens' (*Shakespeare and Greece*, 2017), *Shakespeare's Travels: Greek Representations of Hamlet in the 19th Century* (2005), 'A Hundred Years of Negotiations' (*Shakespeare Yearbook* 14, 2004), *Sense of a Self: Subjectivity and Language in John Donne's Songs and Sonnets* (1992) and *The Faerie Queene and the Greek Romances* (1992).

Introduction

'Migrating Shakespeare'

Janet Clare and Dominique Goy-Blanquet

Shakespeare's presence is now worldwide. No other writer or dramatist has migrated to such an extent. By 'Shakespeare' we here mean both the reputation of the man and the reception and production of his plays as they traversed across Europe, encountering different political, social and artistic situations. In our twenty-first-century world the migrations of peoples, often in tragic circumstances, has become a challenging global concern and for some, essential to survival. Since time immemorial, migrants have fled poverty, natural catastrophes, war, religious or political persecution in search of a better life, often raising suspicion and hostility among the communities they wished to enter. Migrating texts follow similar patterns in so far as every act involves an origin, a destination, sometimes an intervening set of obstacles, and in Shakespeare's case, can become strongly involved in the sufferings, trials and ideological campaigns of the countries they enter. As modern sociology argues, 'when populations migrate, everything moves': the channels of circulation of goods and services multiply, the family networks extend beyond borders, opening new realms of possibilities, systems and teaching languages for the upcoming generations (Delcroix 8). The impediments which beset the migrant are manifold, and this may also be true of the literary text as it leaves its indigenous culture and negotiates cultural, political and religious differences. Successful migration depends on an ability to come to terms with the economic, historical and cultural conditions at the place of destination. As they shift from their place of origin, literary texts inevitably metamorphose and come to occupy an intermediate space where they challenge or accommodate or augment alien tastes and aesthetics. It is the meeting of origin and destination which this volume seeks to explore.

As the bibliographies of chapters in this volume attest, there are a considerable number of works focusing on Shakespeare's reception in individual countries and cultures. *Shakespeare in Europe* (LeWinter) is a useful collection of writings reflecting the impact of Shakespeare on European writers during the eighteenth and nineteenth centuries, with a particular emphasis on France, Germany and Russia. More recently, scholars have taken a long view of Shakespeare in Europe (Pujante and Hoenselaars) and have surveyed Shakespeare from the perspectives of European politics (Delabastita et al.), translation (Dente and Soncini), the 'new Europe' (Hattaway et al.) and the Cold War (Sheen and Karremann). In such a vibrant area of research it is impossible to provide anything like an exhaustive treatment of Shakespeare in Europe. Our choice of destinations has been determined by evidence of Shakespeare's early influence on and dialogue with national cultures. No study of the beginnings of Shakespeare's movement across the continent does so in the configuration of migratory terms we are proposing here. No work has examined the early routes of Shakespeare's migrations, the literary networks which subsequently developed, the hostilities to his work as well as its culturally invigorating impact. Each chapter in the volume considers the itineraries, the encounters, circumstances, hostile and enabling, the political agendas, which led to Shakespeare's involvement in diverse national cultures. Equally significant are the mediators – translators, printers, actors, poets and dramatists, the literati – who were instrumental in drawing attention to Shakespeare at home and abroad. Travelling players, translations, first undertaken in France and Germany, the literary exchanges of pan-European movements, the Enlightenment, Romanticism, producing a European republic of letters, comprised the main networks connecting and spreading migration.

Waves of migration

It is with travelling players that Shakespeare first moved anonymously along trade routes into Polish and German lands. Records survive of strolling players, substantially foreign branches of the English companies, performing in Germany, France and the Spanish Netherlands in the late sixteenth and early seventeenth centuries (Schrickx). In Germany, as Wolfgang Müller observes, the English players – 'die englischen Komödianten' – who travelled across the continent to perform Shakespeare's plays soon began to present their productions in German. The companies expanded to include native German actors, leading to an early form of culturally integrated Shakespeare. A similar pattern can be discerned in the Netherlands. English actors performed simplified versions of plays by Shakespeare and his contemporaries at fairs and festivals and in time they were assimilated into local companies. Detlef Wagenaar shows that the English companies helped to invigorate the didactic native tradition of theatre advanced by the guilds of the young Dutch Republic, although, as elsewhere, classicist rules remained entrenched. Anna Cetera-Włodarczyk describes how in seventeenth-century Poland the English players follow the trade route of the *Via Baltica*, calling at the prosperous urban settings of Gdańsk, Elbląg (the base of the English Eastland

Company) and Königsberg, the second largest city in the region, then to Warsaw, Wrocław (Breslau) and Kraków and on to Vilnius and Riga. As she comments, the players' network of destinations testifies to the scale of migration, particularly amongst multi-cultural merchant communities. Several chapters in the volume illustrate how trade provides a nexus for Shakespeare's migration. In his study of an early production of *Hamlet* at Gothenburg in 1787, Per Sivefors argues that it was the strong trade and cultural links of this harbour with Britain in the late eighteenth century that led to *Hamlet*'s first performance there rather than in Stockholm. British investors in the Swedish East India Company, with its offices and port in Gothenburg, contributed to the pre-eminence of English culture and to the development of reading habits orientated towards English rather than the culturally dominant French literature. Jasmine Seymour describes how, preceding the British by some sixty years, merchants from Armenia settled in India, establishing schools and colleges where Shakespeare was taught to advance oratory skills.

Early encounters

Across Europe the period of Shakespeare's arrival varied from place to place, with a considerable difference in the time marking the moment when he can be said to enter a national consciousness. After the Shakespeare itinerary of the travelling players in the seventeenth century, the next stream of migration occurs through French interest in the literature and theatre of their cross-channel neighbour. Addison and Steele's periodical *The Spectator*, which appeared daily in England from 1710–14, was translated into French – *Le Spectateur* – and published in Amsterdam in 1714. English periodicals, their translation and imitation, fostered a keen interest in English literary culture and helped to form a network amongst the reading publics of France, Germany, the Netherlands, Switzerland and Sweden. Balz Engler details the influence of the *Spectator*'s essays – in translation – on the Zurichois Johann Jakob Bodmer, who in turn influenced the visionary art of his compatriot, Johann Heinrich Füssli, or Fuseli, as he was called when he had moved to London, and a former student of his, Christoph Martin Wieland, the first German to translate a large edition of Shakespeare's works. Bodmer had learnt to appreciate Shakespeare from the Paduan Antonio Schinella Conti's writings, which were also the source of young Voltaire's early inspiration. While exiled in England, Voltaire spent much time in the London playhouses under the guidance of his friend, the Shakespeare adapter and theatre manager, Colley Cibber. His mixed judgements were to create a space for Shakespeare in the intellectual consciousness of the mid-eighteenth century. In his 'Letter XVIII, On Tragedy', Voltaire credits Shakespeare with the creation of the English theatre, praising him as a fecund and powerful genius, though he deplores the poet's lack of good taste or knowledge of the rules. In the following decades in Germany, Shakespeare raised similar reservations with Wieland, but was being enthusiastically approved for his dramaturgy by Gotthold Ephraim Lessing. Voltaire and Lessing illustrate an early recognition of Shakespeare's power as a dramatist, whether perceived as a threat to native culture or as a stimulus. Such a dichotomy plays out in the respective dramaturgies: in France Shakespeare was adapted to a strong native tradition whereas in the German states Shakespeare provided a powerful stimulus towards creating a new native tradition which entailed rejecting the French classical model.

Poland, Russia and Sweden soon received their Shakespeare through France and Germany. In Greece, on the other hand, Shakespeare had no presence during this century. As Mara Yanni points out, touring Italian opera companies introduced Shakespeare to Greek audiences as late as 1860, still several years before he was performed on the Greek stage. This is a century after Shakespeare had taken root in Germany in literary and theatrical circles and was being accommodated in France through the acclaimed adaptations of Jean-François Ducis, the focus of Michèle Willems's chapter.

No history of migration is without a degree of hostility to migrants and the alien culture they are perceived to embody. The mixture of admiration and criticism expressed in Voltaire's early writings on Shakespeare – he is noble, sublime, monstrous – was to be replaced by profound hostility to the language, dramaturgy and mixture of styles of the 'drunken savage', as he labelled the poet in his *Dissertation sur la tragédie* of 1748. Originally, Voltaire's declared aim was to revitalize contemporary drama with new energies, but he soon reneged on his youthful enthusiasm when he felt the whole edifice of neo-classicism shaking. In his later writings Shakespeare bears all the stigmas of the unwelcome migrant: he represents an alien culture; he is an invader and competitor who threatens to undermine the identity of indigenous culture. His famous 'factum against our enemy, Monsieur Letourneur', who threatened to replace Corneille and Racine by English clowns (Voltaire 1776), set the agenda for decades as the chapters on Shakespeare's migration to the Netherlands, Spain, Russia and Sweden illustrate. In Sweden, as Per Sivefors notes, the poet Carl Gustaf af Leopold, a founding member of the Academy and a staunch defender of French taste, described Shakespeare as 'the altogether raw, singular man of the woods', thus associating him with popular vulgarity. Another Swede, the clergyman and playwright, Jacob Wallenberg, an admirer of Garrick, was inspired by Shakespeare in the creation of his own play on a biblical theme. Nevertheless, Wallenberg remained influenced by Voltaire's strictures on Shakespeare's 'taste' and wrote his own play along neo-classical lines. In Spain, Moratín, who was responsible for the first direct translation from the English of a Shakespeare play, *Hamlet* in 1798, still argued, following Voltaire, that the play was quite unfit for the stage. A decade or so later, the exiled Spanish Jesuit thinker, Juan Andrés, as Keith Gregor observes, was to make the same point about Shakespeare in general, declaring his inability to find the supposed beauties of Shakespeare's work 'amid the much and almost constant tastelessness and foolishness'. In Germany, the neo-classicist Johann Christoph Gottsched was influenced by Voltaire, as appears, for example, from his critique of the artisan scenes in *Julius Caesar*, though Lessing disagreed with Gottsched, while Johann Gottfried Herder roundly rejected the French model and celebrated Shakespeare for his fidelity to nature and his social and aesthetic inclusiveness.

The gains of notoriety

Francois-Auguste-René, vicomte de Chateaubriand, one of the leading exponents of Romanticism, confirms it was Voltaire who made Shakespeare known, though he himself considers it a mixed blessing: 'Voltaire had turned England, a country little known at the time, into a kind of wonderland where he placed the heroes, ideas and opinions he might need', and understood too late he had helped, in his own words, 'raise an altar to the monster' (39). The ensuing controversies over Shakespeare's aesthetics had the effect of promoting their rejuvenating potential. As Samuel Taylor Coleridge was to comment in his second lecture on Shakespeare and Milton, the works of Shakespeare on the continent 'are honoured in a double way; by the admiration of Italy and Germany, and by the contempt of the French' (Coleridge 2005: 56–7).

A decisive moment in Shakespeare's European migration occurs during the Romantic era with its celebration of rule-free art, subjectivity, its emphasis on feeling and passion helping to popularize Shakespeare. An exception is the German states where Shakespeare's enthusiastic acceptance during the *Sturm und Drang* years pre-dates the European-wide wave of Romanticism. The intense preoccupation of Goethe and Schiller paved the way for the Schlegel/Tieck translation of Shakespeare's work, published at the height of Romanticism, which was to make an enduring contribution to German literature and the life of the German theatre. In Russia, as Marina Kizima shows, a talented, young Romantic generation regarded Shakespeare as their great predecessor and appropriated him as a pillar in the construction of Russian national culture, a process which reached its height in Pushkin's romantic vision and his

Shakespeare-inspired tragedy, *Boris Godunov*. Although in Poland the strongly religious dimension of Romanticism found no direct counterpart in Shakespeare's plays, the first decades of the nineteenth century saw the emergence of an entire generation whose ambition, inspired by August Wilhelm von Schlegel, was to become Shakespeare translators and critical authorities. Shakespeare himself became the venerated patron-poet of their movement. As a mediator of cultures, Germaine de Staël diagnosed in 1810 that twenty years of revolution and a regicide had created other needs among the public than those fed by the depictions of love or other emotions in the writings of an earlier more temperate society (*De la littérature*). The Romantic Shakespeare took Paris by storm with the performance of *Hamlet* by Charles Kemble's company of actors at the Odéon in 1827. Victor Hugo, Alfred de Vigny, Eugène Delacroix, Charles Nodier, Hector Berlioz, Alexandre Dumas, Théophile Gautier, all present in the auditorium, made Shakespeare the standard bearer of freedom (*Victor Hugo raconté par Adèle Hugo*, Dumas's *Mes Mémoires*, Berlioz' *Mémoires* ...). Throughout the nineteenth century and well into the twentieth, a host of prominent French writers, dramatists, poets, painters and composers drew on his works. As the chapters on France, Italy, Switzerland, Russia and Poland illustrate, Shakespeare – politically and aesthetically – feeds into the revolutionary spirit of the times.

Admirers of Shakespeare's dramaturgy and the national themes of his plays called for a reform of their national theatres. Marina Kizima quotes Pushkin's declaration that 'the spirit of the age demands major changes on *the dramatic stage*' attentive to 'the folk laws' of Shakespeare's drama. In an essay on Shakespeare's dramatic art, from which Hugo silently borrowed, the statesman François Guizot analysed the role of popular theatre in shaping the political culture of nations. A renewal of the national theatre inspired by Shakespeare's poetics must, he argued, be a step towards the complete renewal of the political and social structure. Dramatic poetry is born from the people, it loses its energy and is impoverished when dedicated to the pleasure of the upper classes. Government and poetry share a common duty: 'they must exist for all, satisfy the needs of both the masses and the highest minds' (Guizot cxlix–cl). Pushkin, influenced by Shakespeare and Guizot, expressed similar views, claiming that 'Drama was born in the square and was a folk entertainment'. In Switzerland popular theatre – *Festspiel* – evolved as an occasion when communities would celebrate and reaffirm themselves, dramatizing heroic events from their own past. Even though the Shakespeare influence is not direct, these heroic, historical dramas connect with his histories on a national theme.

The history of Shakespeare in Europe has been constructed as a conflict between neo-classicism, promoted through Voltaire, on one hand, and German proto-Romanticism associated with *Sturm und Drang* in the theatre, on the other, an interpretation supported by the above outline of classical and Romantic responses. France set the law over diplomacy, good manners and culture for decades. Amongst the countries and communities represented in this volume, the language and culture of the elite in Russia, Sweden and Germany was French, and with this cultural dominance came admiration for French theatre and its dramatists, Corneille, Racine, whose aesthetics were far removed from those of Shakespeare. French cultural hegemony was an obstacle, as De Staël showed, and as we see notably in Spain, to the taking root of Shakespeare's rule-defying and poetically hybrid dramaturgy. However, the grand narrative, according to which the neo-classical exceptions taken to Shakespeare were defeated by the explosion of Romanticism first in Germany and then later in France in the manifestos of Stendhal and Hugo, needs to be qualified. There are many traces of Shakespeare in Europe which do not conform to this pattern of rejection or eulogization.

New perspectives

In its attention to Shakespeare's early dispersal across Europe this volume seeks to offer a less totalizing and more nuanced view of Shakespeare's entry into its cultures. Before Voltaire's judgements had taken hold, Justus van Effen in the Netherlands had dedicated a third of his landmark *Dissertation sur la Poësie Angloise* (1717) to Shakespeare and Milton. While Van Effen was pleased to see English writers beginning to respect French writers, and working to reform themselves, as appears from their magazines, *Spectator* and *Tatler*, he recognized that the boldness of English literature, represented in Shakespeare's and Milton's works, owed much to their disdain for rules, and that the French language may have been impoverished by its excessive refinement. Moreover, Voltaire's highly influential verdicts on Shakespeare were variously and widely contested not only in Germany and well before the counter-critiques of Hugo and Stendhal. In her chapter on Shakespeare's progress in Italy, Maria Luisa De Rinaldis examines the contribution of Paolo Rolli, librettist and poet, who in his 'Life of John Milton', prefacing his Italian translation of the first six books of *Paradise Lost* (1729), dismisses Voltaire's judgements. Shakespeare is praised as a genius, as an interpreter of national history and as a model for other nations. In defending Shakespeare, he offered a translation of Hamlet's 'To be or not to be' soliloquy – notoriously translated by Voltaire into rhyming alexandrines – to illustrate how much Voltaire had deviated from the original to include anti-clerical sentiment. In his highest accolade, Rolli compares Shakespeare with Dante. Exception to Voltaire's translation of Hamlet's soliloquy was also registered in Russia by Mikhail Plesheev, who published his translation of 1775 accompanied by a letter signed 'Angloman'. In a memorable image, he claimed that Voltaire 'wrestled' with Shakespeare rather than translated him. The first Polish essays on Shakespeare appeared in 1765 and 1766 in *Monitor*, a magazine patterned after the English *Spectator*, and used the authority of Shakespeare to undermine the doctrine of the dramatic unities. In Zurich, Wieland in his edition of Shakespeare's plays cautiously moved beyond neo-classical taste and defended Shakespeare against Voltaire's parody of *Hamlet*.

Focus on the European literary debate sparked by Shakespeare's unconventional dramaturgy tends to confine the discussion to the pronouncements of an educated elite who left their views in essays and lectures. This volume seeks to broaden the discussion by examining Shakespeare's integration into popular culture. In Italy, Shakespeare initially appears in the popular form of melodrama, then pantomime and ballet. Apostolo Zeno's *Amleto*, a melodramatic redaction of *Hamlet*, was successful not only in Italy but also in England. It travelled to Florence and Naples and was performed in London in the Haymarket theatre in 1712, an illustration of back-migration. As several chapters demonstrate, Shakespeare became the property not only of the elite but of untaught audiences. Jan Vos, a Dutch glass maker by trade, who became one of the first directors of the city theatre in Amsterdam, produced a version of *Titus Andronicus* in 1638 which was popular into the next century. In Switzerland the self-educated peasant, Ulrich Bräker, read a library copy of Wieland's translation in 1777 and was so struck by the power of the plays that in the following years he felt compelled to write a book about them. Under different auspices, Shakespeare was taken up by the politically marginalized and peoples of diasporas. Translations of Shakespeare in mid-nineteenth-century Poland were the work of the gentry, in exile or in isolated households located in eastern borderlands. In Greece, Shakespearean performances in the revived theatre drew their vitality and vibrancy from the strengths and limitations of a semi-literate popularizing context of performance and reception. Greek actors, unfavourably received in Athens, travelled to places outside the boundaries of the free state in the mid-nineteenth century – mostly Constantinople and Smyrna, where Armenian companies were also active – as well as major cities in Cyprus, Egypt, the Danubian principalities and Russia, in search of more welcoming environments. Following unsuccessful performances of *Hamlet* and *Othello* (1866) in Athens, one company, led by Pantelis Soustas, toured the Eastern Mediterranean with *Macbeth*, more popular in Smyrna than it had been in Athens, while in Constantinople, a flourishing anglophile community welcomed the English dramatist. A similar pattern can be seen in the Armenian diaspora. Armenian actors with their mastery of several languages performed Shakespeare in private and public spaces in Constantinople – in French – alongside the celebrated tragedian Ira Aldridge.

Doctoring Shakespeare

In the process of migration, as the text moves from one environment to another and from one language to another, degrees of adaptation are inevitable. Ironically, perhaps – considering Voltaire's waging of war against the foreign invader – France became the greatest exporter of a doctored Shakespeare. Before any Shakespeare play had ever been performed in France or in most of continental Europe, Jean-François Ducis, a poet and dramatist who could not read English, re-wrote six of his tragedies based on the free translations of Pierre-Antoine de La Place (1746–9). Ducis regarded his adaptations as re-workings of raw material into a finished art form, well-suited to audiences reared on neo-classic precepts and definite notions of dramatic decorum. Major and minor changes to the plays, including the substitution of an urn for the supernatural Old Hamlet, the removal of references to Desdemona's handkerchief (in Ducis's version a diamond tiara), and the displacement of the witches in *Macbeth* to the world of dream, may strike the modern reader as comic or absurd. Yet, as Willems notes, the best part of continental Europe discovered Shakespeare on the stage through translations of French adaptations not based on an original text. The director of the National Theatre in Warsaw, Wojciech Bogusławski, staged *Othello* (1801) and *King Lear* (1805) for the first time in Polish in Ludwik Osiński's translations of Ducis's French adaptation. Ducis's version of *Othello* was popular in Russia: it inspired the statesman and man of letters Ivan Velyaminov to write his own adaptation of the play in Russian (1808), a version which was used in the theatre for several decades. Ducis's *Hamlet* was performed in Madrid's Corral del Príncipe theatre in 1772, in a translation attributed to Ramón de la Cruz. Apart from the attempt to work in certain allusions to contemporary Spanish politics, the translation deviates very little from the original French. Two years later Ducis's *Hamlet* – advertised as a tragedy of Ducis in imitation of Shakespeare – was performed in Venice. The adapter of the adaptation, Francesco Gritti, praises Ducis's merits in re-presenting the monstrous Shakespeare. Nevertheless, some critics felt that Ducis and Gritti had not gone far enough in reforming the Shakespearean supernatural, anathema to rational Enlightenment taste.

The migrant's conquests

As with Ducis's versions and their vernacular translations, texts in transit demand a degree of flexibility as they variously respond to conditions at the place of destination. The obverse of this aspect of migration is true. In crossing national boundaries – often fluctuating ones – the migrant text may modify the character and art of the recipient culture. Further, migration may contribute to the regeneration of a national culture which for various reasons has been suppressed or lost through conquest, national fragmentation and dispersal. In the process of naturalization Shakespeare emerges as an integrating part of German culture, a national author and decisive shaping force of its literature. Notably, Shakespeare was part of the school and university curricula earlier than in Britain. In the troubled history of Poland and its partition at the end of the eighteenth century Shakespeare was enrolled in the endeavour to create a national theatre designed to confirm the strength and vitality of the otherwise collapsing native culture. At the same time, English literature was included in the university curriculum in Vilnius. In Spain, its own Golden Age Drama – the theatre of Calderón and Lope de Vega – was denigrated alongside that of Shakespeare's by neo-classical critics raised on French ideas of taste. With emerging admiration of Shakespeare as Romanticism took hold on arbiters of taste in Spain so, too, did respect revive for its own drama. Bodmer laments the lack of a Shakespeare in the Swiss states to whom the people as a nation might turn. In Russia, at the close of the eighteenth century, the English poet was seen not only as a source of a new art, free from the norms of classicism and true to nature, but a force sharing in the general effort to reform Russian culture and Russian national literature manifest in the writing of Nikolai Karamzin. In Italy, the first major translation of Shakespeare by Michele Leoni was undertaken in the midst of calls for freedom from Napoleon's despotism and from the Austro-Hungarian Empire, when Italian writers were beginning to reject French cultural dogmatism and grew more receptive to different models. Shakespeare's preoccupation with national history served as a stimulus to dramatists in Russia, Germany, France, Poland, Greece and Switzerland, encouraging them to turn to their own past and national heroes. Pushkin's *Boris Godunov*, the tragedies of Juliusz Słowacki in Poland, Goethe's *Götz von Berlichingen*, Schiller's *Die Räuber* and *Wilhelm Tell*, Demetrios Vernardakis's *Maria Doxapatri*, Vigny's *Cinq-Mars* are inspired by Shakespeare's dramaturgy and its national preoccupations. Vernardakis's comment that Shakespeare is not only the poet of England or of the Elizabethans but for the Greeks after Homer 'the poet of all times' encapsulates similar statements by Pushkin, Goethe and Schiller.

Shakespeare and geopolitics

The history of Shakespeare in Europe is bound up with shifting national boundaries and struggles for political and cultural independence. In partitioned Poland, cultivating the language through translation of Shakespeare was a way of counteracting the uprooting cultural policies of the partitioning powers. When Shakespeare first crossed the borders of what was to become the Swiss Confederation in 1848, Switzerland was a loose assemblage of states. With four language communities and confessional divides, Shakespeare's entering this world was a complex international affair with cities conveying their cultural leanings through their response to Shakespeare. Theatre was banned in the major cities of Zurich and Geneva, a useful reminder, as Engler observes, that Shakespeare's migration between cultures need not depend on the institution of the theatre. Again, in the case of Italy, approaching Shakespeare through the idea of the nation state – which did not exist until 1861 – can be anachronistic. Until unification, Shakespeare's presence is more evident in some of the Italian republics and principalities than others. An early interest in theatrical adaptations is apparent in Venice whereas major translation work took place in Padua and Milan. In Greece, for centuries under Ottoman rule before the imposition of a foreign monarchy, the appropriation of Shakespeare was a means towards the legitimation of the rightful return of the country to Europe; Shakespeare, in this case, a visible proof that the modern Greeks were still worthy of their ancestors. The dispersed geography of 'stateless nations' could also delay Shakespeare's entrance into their culture: his plays migrated initially not to the historical Armenia, but with Armenians who were themselves migrants in search of safety and who gradually established economically and culturally prosperous communities in Athens, Smyrna, Constantinople and elsewhere.

Literary *versus* theatrical migration

Several chapters illustrate that the trajectories of performance, critical interest and translation were quite distinct and did not necessarily overlap. Shakespeare's early migration to Greece was more evident in the nascent Greek theatre than in the closed circles of the literati. In the Netherlands, Shakespeare's influence and popularity on the stage was established well before translation and literary evaluation were available: it was not until the nineteenth century and the work of Leendert Alexander Johannes Burgersdijk that the gap between the written and the performed was bridged. In Russia, while Empress Catherine II was reading Shakespeare in German or French translations, the theatre-going public were introduced to Shakespeare through the versions of Louis-Sébastien Mercier and Ducis. In Italy, ballets and melodramas drawn from Shakespeare continued to cite Ducis as their authority while Domenico Valentini, Professor of Ecclesiastical History, working with Lewis Theobald's pioneering 1733 edition and the help of English associates, was translating *Julius Caesar*, the first play translated from English into Italian after various adaptations. Goethe, when preparing stage versions for the court theatre at Weimar, revised the plays to suit the refined expectations of the audience. In 1812, for example, he adapted *Romeo and Juliet* to the classical style of his own plays (Heun). There is, of course, nothing controversial in such divergent patterns of performance and translation or editorial work. The critical history of Shakespeare in the theatre and the history of Shakespeare as a literary artist have followed quite different paths to the present day, sometimes producing degrees of antagonism between the practitioners of the different approaches.

The divergences of literary and theatrical practice in continental Europe reflect what happens to Shakespeare at home. Lewis Theobald altered *Richard II* for production at Lincoln's Inn Field, claiming that the play's 'scattered beauties' would have 'stronger charms, if they were interwoven in a regular Fable' (A2r). Yet, as the first systematic editor of Shakespeare, he sought to replace taste with fact or probability (Seary). Though great friends with the actor David Garrick, in his famous Preface the editor Samuel Johnson approaches the plays as literary works, subject to textual analysis. Garrick was involved in altering – a term more commonly used than adapting – Shakespeare and, when the plays were published, they were unashamedly described on their title pages as altered for performance (Cunningham). Migrating Shakespeare is not a stable, trans-historical figure, an Elizabethan playwright and man of the theatre, but a variable cultural construct. As several essays illustrate, admiration of Garrick's acting of the great Shakespearean roles was widespread amongst European travellers, including actors and editors, who saw him perform at Drury Lane, although what they were seeing was not the Shakespeare of the first Folio nor the Shakespeare of the early modern Globe theatre. Nevertheless, the experience undoubtedly fuelled enthusiasm for Shakespeare when they returned home. The German scientist, philosopher and aphorist, Georg Christoph Lichtenberg, a keen London-theatre goer, in 'Letters from England', articles which appeared in the periodical *Deutsches Museum*, left a detailed and appreciative account of Garrick's *Hamlet* which he saw there in 1775. He championed Shakespeare against Voltaire, while deploring the impact on the production of Voltaire's critique:

> Voltaire has, however, gained one victory at Drury Lane. The gravediggers' scene is omitted. They retain it at Covent Garden. Garrick should not have done this. To represent so ancient and superb a piece in all its characteristic rude vigour in these insipid times, when even in this country the language of nature is beginning to yield to fine phrases and conventional twaddle, might have arrested this decline, even if it could not put a stop to it.
>
> Mare and Quarrell 17

Migration was not in one direction: changes to the migrant Shakespeare demanded in France were repeated at Drury Lane.

Versions of Shakespeare's plays migrate across Europe and these adaptations reflect the practice begun in Restoration England of improving Shakespeare, cutting and rewriting to make the plays acceptable to allegedly more refined audiences. Ducis's reforming zeal in response to Shakespeare's irregularities repeats the first wave of reformed Shakespeare in England with William Davenant and John Dryden followed, for example, by Nahum Tate, John Crowne and John Sheffield, Duke of Buckingham. Dryden deplored what he considered Shakespeare's structural defects, his violations of poetic justice, improper language and bombast and in his several adaptations strove to eliminate them. Nahum Tate famously described *King Lear* as 'a Heap of Jewels, unstrung and unpolisht' ('Dedication to my esteemed friend Thomas Boteler, Esq.', 468) and his version replaced Shakespeare's *King Lear* until it, too, was replaced by Garrick's, which held the stage for another sixty years. Garrick adapted Tate by bringing back some of Shakespeare's lines and cutting Tate's, though he retained the love scenes and the happy ending. The Romantic poets, essayists and Shakespeare commentators, Coleridge, Charles Lamb and William Hazlitt never saw a version of *King Lear* as acted by Shakespeare's company, and generally had a poor opinion of theatre performances anyway, compared with the quality of his poetry. A view which Goethe was to articulate in 1815 when he proposed in 'Shakespeare und kein Ende' ['Shakespeare without end'] that 'Shakespeare's general way of proceeding finds something about the actual stage that conflicts with it'.

The free reciprocal flow of ideas about Shakespeare, the border crossings of editions, companies of actors, critical work, is evident throughout this volume. For example, Johann Joachim Eschenburg, who taught at Brunswick, and was indebted to Johnson and Steevens, published his thirteen-volume German translation of Shakespeare – virtually a revision of Wieland's – in Zurich. His annotations were partly included in the standard French edition of Pierre Le Tourneur, first published in 1776 by subscription, which so infuriated Voltaire. The list of subscribers gives a fair idea of the widespread interest in Shakespeare and, possibly, in his lessons in government: on it, after the French royal family, stood Empress Catherine II, and monarchs, princes, statesmen, ambassadors, senior officers from over twenty European countries, as well as churchmen, lawyers, actors, librarians and booksellers.

The circulation and the promotion of cultural ideas had its strongest advocate in Madame de Staël, Napoleon's most resolute enemy, whose ideal of freedom included both literary and political matters. While she expressed the view that countries more refined than England would be revolted by Shakespeare's faults of taste, she praised him for having freed Germany from French literary hegemony. Framing her views on the role of literature in two pioneering essays, *De la Littérature* and *De l'Allemagne,* and in her 'Lettera' to Italian intellectuals when in post-Napoleonic Milan, De Staël promoted the need for cultural exchange, arguing that if a modern nation were to be intellectually 'reduced to its own treasures' it would remain 'poor' forever. In turn, De Staël was strongly influenced by the *Lectures on Dramatic Art and Literature* of August Schlegel, tutor to her sons, and drew the conclusion that his translation had made Shakespeare a European 'compatriot'. Pushkin, too, had a French translation of the *Lectures* in his library. Coleridge, who had met Schlegel and Tieck in Rome in 1806, expressed a wish while lecturing on Shakespeare in 1811 for the London Philosophical Society to see Schlegel's work and he was presented with a copy of the *Lectures* after he had given his eighth lecture. In lecture nine he claimed that Schlegel's sentiments were coincident with his own, expressing some incredulity 'that so many years had elapsed since the time of Shakespeare and that it should remain for foreigners first to feel truly and to appreciate properly his mighty genius'. The explanation he offered, possibly a condensed one since the lectures exist only as reports, is in the difference between the two nations: the English had derived moral and physical advantage from becoming a commercial people; the German nation, unable to act, had been driven into speculation, incapable of acting outwardly what they had acted internally (Coleridge 1987: 103). In their veneration, as Müller points out, the Germans were inclined to attribute their sense of close cultural affinity with Shakespeare as a homecoming on his part.

In exploring the intricacies of Shakespeare's migratory paths it appears that some Shakespeare plays were more popular than others, generally relating to the appeal of the subject or genre. Tragedies, although restyled with happy endings, dominated. Certain plays bear evidence of a trans-European train of transmission. John Sheffield's rearrangement of *Julius Caesar,* performed in London in 1726, inspired Abbot Conti to write in blank verse a *Giulio Cesare* (sometimes referred to as *Il Cesare*), though in his Preface it was Addison's *Cato* which was granted attention as '*la prima tragedia regolare degl'Inglesi*'. Voltaire quoted both Sheffield's and Conti's plays in the Preface to his own *Mort de César*. The poet-philosopher Francesco Algarotti admired Voltaire's innovations and his tact with Shakespeare's '*errori innumerabili e pensieri inimitabili*', faults innumerable and thoughts inimitable ('Lettera al signor abate Franchini', 169), while William Duncombe adapted *La Mort de César* for the London stage (*Junius Brutus,* 1734), another instance of back-migration. By the turn of the century, twenty-six more translations of Voltaire's play were printed, in Dutch, Italian, English, German, Polish, Portuguese, Swedish, Russian and Spanish.

As productions and critical work attest, the play has an ideological flexibility, lending itself to a celebration of a supreme national leader or to a wishful enactment of tyrannicide. In France, *La Mort de César* had its heyday during the revolutionary period, when Brutus provided the Assemblée with a heroic model for political assassination, while famous actors like François-Joseph Talma and theatre managers aimed to instruct the people with patriotic plays, sometimes refitting Voltaire's with an adequate republican denouement. Its most spectacular performance took place in Weimar, during the Erfurt meeting with Tsar Alexander, where Napoleon promised Talma he would perform before 'un beau parterre de rois', an assembly of kings, and pressed Goethe to translate it, to show how Caesar could have made 'the happiness of humanity, had he been allowed time to accomplish his vast plans' (Müller 240). Plans that history would again frustrate. In Italy, where successive translations of *Julius Caesar* illustrated the Italian fascination with Shakespeare's Rome, Leoni – in the first major translation of Shakespeare's works – began with *Julius Caesar*. Despite his admiration for Shakespeare, Leoni revised the play, amplifying the myth of Caesar and supercharging the language of religious sacrifice. On the other hand, the play was enrolled in the interests of liberty as it spread from West to East. Its first

Armenian translator, Thaliadian, in 1853 published Act Three in the periodical of the Venetian Mekhitarists, justifying the killing of a despot who threatened democracy by men 'burning with the love of freedom', Seymour notes, clearly prompting his readers to stand against foreign oppression. In Russia, *Julius Caesar* was the first play to be fully translated from English, and Nikolai Karamzin's translation marked a defining moment in Russian Shakespeare, although this moment was politically untimely. Translated by a former Freemason and published by a leader of the Russian Freemasons soon after the assassination of Tsar Peter III, the play was banned. In Athens, ruled by an unpopular Bavarian monarch, and in Constantinople, under Ottoman control, the theme of 'killing the king' made the play equally liable to censorship.

Hamlet spoke to and for a generation of Romantic poets and political dissenters, who praised elements – like the vulgar gravediggers' scene – repeatedly condemned by the neo-classicists. In his Preface to *Cromwell,* which becomes the manifesto of the young generation, Hugo turns each piece of criticism levelled at Shakespeare's work into so much evidence of his genius, beginning with *Hamlet*'s mixture of the grotesque and the sublime. Stendhal, who called the hero a 'German character', a silly student enamoured with words, in marginal notes of January 1830 to his copy of the play (Crouzet 57), undertook to endow him with more stamina and resolution but failed to conclude his plan to rewrite it. However, his fellow writers were fascinated, and France was soon submerged by the wave of Hamletism. The Polish *Hamlet* also derived from German sources. Bogusławski's highly successful staged version showed a hero crushed by political difficulties that prevented him from taking action: it came in the wake of the failed 1794 uprising, the final partition of Poland, and the death in exile of King Stanisław Poniatowski. After the defeat of the Cadet Revolution, 'To be or not to be', interpreted as 'to fight or not to fight', became the motto of the national cause. As Cetera-Włodarczyk points out, Polish romanticism adhered to the vision of a Hamlet who put emotions and intuitive thinking above rational judgement. Chameleon-like, *Hamlet* can embody and espouse a large variety of agendas. Rather than an isolated event, the Gothenburg production, performed in the context of political conflicts between Sweden and Denmark, played a significant part in the wider historical arena of the time. Among populations living under oppressive rulers like diasporic Greece or Armenia, or dissenting subjects of the Tsar, the thoughtful powerless hero often seemed a natural mouthpiece for the sufferings of their country. Vissarion Belinsky's 'volcanic' Hamlet, which inspired both Russian and Armenian stagings of the play, made an exception to the general focus on the tragedy of the intellect, by pointing out that Shakespeare stood above the aesthetics of Romanticism, and making Hamlet the centre of a complex network of characters and interests, thus anticipating Grigori Kozintsev's revolutionary view of the play by over a century.

Amongst the comedies almost alone *The Merchant of Venice* exerted fascination and cultural identification. As with *Hamlet* and *Julius Caesar*, it could be used for conflicting purposes, mostly focused on Shylock, greedy murderous usurer or tragic figure of a persecuted people. The performance of Edmund Kean – who first played the part in 1814 – went against the tradition of the comic villain, endowing him with a complex humanity. Three separate translations of Shakespeare's *Merchant* were performed the same year in Paris, weeks before the July Revolution of 1830, two of which, following Kean's lead, cut the last act to concentrate on Shylock. In Du Lac's version, Shylock's plea included Article One of the Déclaration des Droits de l'Homme: all men are born free and equal in rights. Three translations also appeared in Italy in the 1830s. The play was performed as *Shylock* in Milan in Ernesto Rossi's production of 1869 in a controversial version, adapted to focus on Shylock's oppression and desperation. Despite this sympathetic treatment, the production had a limited run because Rossi was anxious not to revive religious conflict by prolonging it. In the Netherlands, Louis Bouwmeester's Shylock in 1880 was described as neither a Jewish caricature nor a victim of antisemitism, managing to draw compassion from the audience, while remaining very much a villain. The role established its interpreter as the most celebrated actor of his age. In Poland which held the largest Jewish population in Eastern Europe, the migrating *dramatis persona* was, of all Shakespeare's characters, the only one whose identity seemed entirely local, and apt to serve different ideological purposes, ethnic slander, expiation or a means of collective therapy. The play was translated from English into Armenian by Aram Karapet Teteyan, one of two brothers who established in 1851 a publishing house in Smyrna. Shylock and the Venetian ghetto seemed familiar to Georgian, Armenian, Polish, Ukrainian, Greek communities who could well identify with the Jew's anger and desire for revenge.

Romeo and Juliet was an early success, mostly in Ducis's version, which ranked in Italy nearly as high as his *Hamlet*, whereas *Othello* only became successful there through Verdi. Ducis's version started a wave of 'Othellomania' in Spain. The play had a personal appeal for Pushkin, whose African ancestor had served Peter the Great, but failed to please in Milan, Tiflis or Athens. Rather far behind in popularity came *Macbeth*, *King Lear* and one history play, *Richard III*. Shakespeare's comedies appeared even more incompatible with the rules of verisimilitude or common sense than his tragedies, though they did inspire authors of fantastic tales like Charles Nodier or Auguste Villiers de l'Isle Adam, and catch the imagination of painters like Füssli. Catherine II had her own adaptation of *The Merry Wives* staged at the court theatre of Saint Petersburg, while *The Winter's Tale* stimulated national interest in Poland, mostly because of its allegedly Slavic sources, and because the matter of the plot could find parallels in a contemporary affair at the Tsarist court. These isolated cases, however, failed to stimulate followers. As Gregor records, enlightened early readers like Juan Andrés had no patience with the 'vulgar pleasantries, indecencies and plebeian buffoonery' of *A Midsummer Night's Dream*. An early adaptation of the *Dream* proved highly popular in Germany, but in Greece, like the other plays with a 'Greek' context, it attracted no interest. Not until a thorough reassessment of the Elizabethan dramaturgy and stage conditions began in the early twentieth century with the researches of Edward Gordon Craig, Adolphe Appia, Vsevolod Meyerhold, Jacques Copeau and other experimentators would the comedies attract serious interest.

By the mid-nineteenth century, across Europe, Shakespeare had been elevated by translators, readers and audiences to a position of high cultural status and was also valued as an exponent of folk art. He had become embedded in the repertoires of travelling players, national theatres, education, philosophical and aesthetic writing, his plays constantly altered and reinvented as they encountered different sets of circumstances at their place of arrival. Collectively, the chapters in this volume help to explain how through chains of transmission, the enthusiastic promotion of critics and essayists, the talents of actors, adverse publicity, trade and travel, Shakespeare's migration was so successful. Pragmatically, we can see how the plays' resilience is connected to their ideological flexibility and narrative adaptability, the narratives themselves sometimes already familiar. But Shakespeare's poetic dramaturgy – not revolutionary in its own time and place – transposed into different milieus confronted and confounded received attitudes and ideas, literary and political. The plays often arrived in sleepy Illyrias, oppressive Romes, little academies like that of Navarre, where they upset rigid traditions, challenged political or cultural authorities, and energized playwrights, actors, poets and novelists. Now, it could be said that Shakespeare has become the property of theatres and universities and the object of unquestioning veneration. Absorbed and naturalized, he has forfeited the quality of the new and different.

References

Algarotti, Francesco [1735] (1736), 'Lettera al signor abate Franchini', 12 October, in *La Mort de César*, *The Complete Works of Voltaire*, vol. 8, ed. D. J. Fletcher, 169–72.

Berlioz, Hector (1870), 'Apparition de Shakespeare', *Mémoires*, Paris: Michel Lévy, vol. XVIII.

Chateaubriand, François-René de [1801] (1838), *'SHAKSPERE, ou SHAKSPEAR, ou SHAKESPEAR'*, Mercure de France, April, repr. in *Mélanges littéraires, Œuvres complètes de M. le Vicomte de Chateaubriand*, Paris: Pourrat, tome VIII, 38–60.

Coleridge, Samuel T. (1987), 'Lectures, 1808–1819 on Literature', *The Collected Works of Samuel Taylor Coleridge*, 5:1, ed. R. A. Foakes, London and New Jersey: Princeton University Press.

Coleridge, Samuel T. (2005), 'Collier's Diary: The transcripts of Lectures 1 and 2', *Coleridge on Shakespeare: The text of the lectures of 1811–12*, ed. R. A. Foakes, London: Routledge, 56–7.

Conti, Antonio Schinella (1726), *Il Cesare*, Faenza.

Crouzet, Michel (1987), 'Stendhal shakespearien', in K. G. McWatters and C. W. Thompson, eds, *Stendhal et l'Angleterre*, Liverpool: Liverpool University Press.

Cunningham, Vanessa (2008), *Shakespeare and Garrick*, Cambridge: Cambridge University Press.

Delabastita, Dirk, Jozef De Vos and Paul Franssen eds, (2008), *Shakespeare and European Politics,* Newark: University of Delaware Press.

Delcroix, Catherine et al. (2016), 'Migrants: entre contraintes et résistances', *Migrations Société*, no. 164.

Dente, Carla and Sara Soncini eds, (2008), *Shakespeare translation in present-day Europe*, Pisa: Pisa University Press.

Du Lac, and J.E. Alboise (1830), *Shylock, drame en trois actes imité de Shakespeare*, Paris: Bezou libraire.

Dumas, Alexandre (1863), *Mes Mémoires*, Paris: Michel Lévy Frères, ch. CIX.

Goethe, Johann Wolfgang [1813–16] (1950), 'Shakespeare und kein Ende', *Gedenkausgabe der Werke, Briefe und Gespräche*, vol. 14, Zurich: Artemis.

Guizot, François [1821] (1872), *Vie de Shakespeare* in *Œuvres de Shakespeare*, Paris: Didier, tome I.

Hattaway, Michael, Boika Sokolova and Derek Roper, eds (2015), *Shakespeare in the New Europe*, London: Bloomsbury Academic.

Heun, Hans Georg (1965), *Shakespeares 'Romeo und Julia' in Goethes Bearbeitung*, Berlin: Erich Schmidt Verlag.

Hugo, Adèle (1985), *Victor Hugo raconté par Adèle Hugo*, ed. Anne Ubersfeld and Guy Rosa, Paris: Plon.

Hugo, Victor [1827] (2001), *Préface de 'Cromwell'*, ed. Evelyne Amon, Paris: Larousse.

Le Tourneur, Pierre (1776), 'Noms de MM. les Souscripteurs', *Shakespeare traduit de l'anglois dédié au Roi*, Paris: Veuve Duchesne, tome premier, n.p.

LeWinter, Oswald ed., (1970), *Shakespeare in Europe*, Harmondsworth: Penguin.

Mare, Margaret L. and W. H. Quarrell eds, (1938), *Lichtenberg's Visits to England as described in his Letters and Diaries*, Oxford: Clarendon Press.

Moreau, Charles F. J-B. (1827), *Mémoires historiques et littéraires sur F.J. Talma*.

Müller, Friedrich von, Chancellor of Saxe-Weimar [1806–13] (1992), *Souvenirs des années de guerre*, trans. Charles-Otto Zieseniss, Fondation Napoléon, Paris: Tallandier.

Pujante, A. Luis and Ton Hoenselaars (2003), *Four Hundred Years of Shakespeare in Europe*, Newark: University of Delaware Press.

Schlegel, August Wilhelm von (1815), *A Course of Lectures on Dramatic Art and Literature*, trans. John Black, 2 vols, London.

Schrickx, Willem (1981), 'English Actors at the Courts of Wolfenbüttel, Brussels and Graz during the Lifetime of Shakespeare', *Shakespeare Survey* 33: 153–68.

Seary, Peter (1990), *Lewis Theobald and the Editing of Shakespeare*, Oxford: Clarendon Press.

Sheen, Erica and Isabel Karreman eds, (2016), *Shakespeare in Cold War Europe: Conflict, commemoration, celebration*, Basingstoke: Palgrave Macmillan.

Staël-Holstein, Germaine de [1800] (1836) *De la littérature considérée dans ses rapports avec les institutions sociales*, Paris: Maradan in *Œuvres complètes*, Paris: Firmin Didot, tome I.

Staël-Holstein, Germaine de [1810] (1814), *De l'Allemagne*, in *Œuvres complètes*, Paris, H. Nicolle, tome II.

Staël-Holstein, Germaine de (1816), 'Sulla maniera e utilità de traduzioni', trans. Pietro Giordani from *De l'esprit des traductions*, *Biblioteca italiana*, Jan.

Stendhal, Henri Beyle [1825] (1926), *Racine et Shakespeare*, Paris: Le Divan.

Tate, Nahum [1681] (1880), 'Dedication to my Esteemed Friend Thomas Boteler, Esq.' *The History of King Lear*, repr. in *A New Variorum Edition of Shakespeare*, ed. H. H. Furness, vol. 5, Philadelphia: Lippincott.

Theobald, L. (1720), 'The Preface', *The Tragedy of Richard the II; As it is Acted at the Theatre in Lincoln's-Inn-Fields. Altered from Shakespear*, London.

Van Effen, Justus (1717), 'Dissertation sur la Poësie Angloise', in *Journal Littéraire de l'Année MDCCXVII*, The Hague, 157–217.

Voltaire, François-Marie Arouet [1733] (1994), 'Letter XVIII, On Tragedy', in *Letters Concerning the English Nation*, ed. Nicholas Cronk, Oxford: Oxford University Press.

Voltaire, François-Marie Arouet (1988), *La Mort de César*, ed. Dennis Fletcher, *The Complete Works of Voltaire*, general editor W. H. Barber, The Voltaire Foundation, vol. 8, 1731–2, Oxford.

Voltaire, François-Marie Arouet [1748] (2003), 'Dissertation sur la tragédie ancienne et moderne', Preface to *Semiramis*, in *Complete Works*, vol. 30 A, 1746–8, Oxford.

Voltaire, François-Marie Arouet [1776] (1827), *Lettre de Monsieur de Voltaire à l'Académie française*, 25 August, repr. in *Lettres de M. de Voltaire à l'Académie française sur Shakespeare et son théâtre*, Paris: Renduel.

Voltaire, François-Marie Arouet (1998), Letters to Jean d'Alembert, 26 July and 13 August 1776, and to Charles-Augustin d'Argental, 19 July and 27 August 1776, in *Voltaire: Correspondance (1775–1777)*, ed. Theodore Besterman, Paris: Gallimard Pléiade, vol. XII.

1

'Michelangelo of tragedy'

Shakespeare's tortuous Italian routes

Maria Luisa De Rinaldis

Approaching Shakespeare's migration to Europe through the idea of the nation state can be anachronistic. Indeed a nation state did not exist in Italy until unification in 1861. In Shakespeare's time Italy was fragmented, a fact capitalized upon by early modern playwrights in their use of diverse city states as locations. When Bonaparte presented himself as a liberator from reigning powers in 1796, the country was still composed of various states: Milan, which was part of the Austrian Empire, the Republic of Genoa, the Kingdom of Piedmont-Sardinia, the Republic of Venice, the Duchy of Modena, the Duchy of Parma, the Grand-Duchy of Tuscany, the Republic of Lucca, the Papal States and the Kingdom of Naples. This chapter aims to reconstruct the early stages of Shakespeare's migration to Italy through critical responses, performance and translations – trajectories which rarely overlapped – before he became firmly established and even hailed by the translator Michele Leoni as a 'Michelangelo of tragedy'.

Early modern Anglo-Italian communications were limited. Observations on English theatrical performances written in 1618 by Orazio Busino, chaplain to the Venetian Embassy in London, and by Gregorio Leti in his Teatro Britannico (1683) reveal an interest in the sophistication of spectacles and in theatrical architecture, but no playwright was mentioned by name (Collison-Morley). In part this was because, with such a highly developed literary culture of their own, Italians were hardly receptive to migrant literatures, especially one from a predominantly Protestant nation. A major exception to this generalization was Venice, where a number of political tracts, including a proclamation by Elizabeth I and works by Robert Cecil and James I, were translated for the Venetian élites when there were hopes Venice could be won to the Protestant cause (De Rinaldis). Moreover, as a centre for trade, Venice was more open and receptive than the rest of Italy to foreign cultural influences.

Critical work

One of the earliest Italian engagements with Shakespeare was in the early eighteenth century when the Paduan Antonio Schinella (1677–1749), better known as abbot Conti, wrote his work *Il Cesare*, which circulated in manuscript form before it was published in 1726.[1] Conti, translator of Racine and Pope, had earlier visited England in order to meet Isaac Newton, and there had read John Sheffield's neo-classical re-writings of *Julius Caesar* in two plays, *Julius Caesar* and *Marcus Brutus*. Inspired by these plays, he wrote *Il Cesare* (1726a), shortly before translating Voltaire's *Mérope*; like Voltaire, he would dedicate another Roman play, *Giunio Bruto* (1743), to the founder of the Republic. In the text which prefaces *Il Cesare,* 'Risposta al Sig. Iacopo Martelli', Conti refers to Sheffield's work as 'Sasper's *Caesar* cut in two' and, although he does not acknowledge Shakespeare as a direct source, he discusses his value: 'Sasper è il

Cornelio degl'Inglesi, ma solo più irregolare del Cornelio, sebbene al pari di lui pregno di grandi idee, e di nobili sentimenti' (1726b: 54, 'Shakespeare is the English Corneille, only more irregular than Corneille, although similarly full of great ideas and noble feelings'). He finds faults in Shakespeare's plot, nevertheless he acknowledges that tragedy had to 'please', and that Shakespeare's plots, as in Spanish tragedies, were a rich combination of events that appealed to seventeenth-century readers. Conti's response neatly exemplifies the pattern of attraction and repulsion through which Shakespeare was approached in the eighteenth century. In his dramatic hierarchy, it was Addison's *Cato* that he valued as 'la prima tragedia regolare degl'Inglesi' (55, 'the first regular English tragedy'). In the 'Risposta' he defends his version against those who were critical of his aesthetic distance from tragic pathos, intimating that Shakespeare has his admirers in Italy who appreciate the emotional power of his texts. Nonetheless, Conti insists on the serious quality of his own material, that is, the story of the greatest Republic, and the death of the most celebrated man the Romans ever had. He wrote his own play according to neo-classical standards, limiting the passing of time to the report of Caesar's assassination and respecting the unity of place in locating action in the courtyard of Caesar's house. The extent to which Conti was directly influenced by Shakespeare has been the subject of critical debate, obviously complicated by the fact that he uses the same sources as Shakespeare. Conti's text echoes moments of Shakespeare's dramatic intensity. In *Julius Caesar* Caesar reports Calpurnia's premonition of his death: 'She dreamt tonight she saw my statue, / Which, like a fountain with an hundred spouts, / Did run pure blood' (2.2.76–8), a reference to the bleeding statue of Pompey which Plutarch does not put in the mouth of Calpurnia. In Conti's text, Caesar's wounds are 'cento' as in Shakespeare's image: 'Squarciata è la tua toga, e da ben cento / Ferite sgorga in larga copia il sangue' (4.1, p. 158, 'Your toga is ripped, and blood gushes in abundance from a hundred wounds'). In re-adapting his sources, Conti appears to have been in some contact with Shakespeare (Sestito).

The abbot was part of a circle of cosmopolitan intellectuals, in England he knew Newton, Sheffield and Lady Mary Wortley Montagu, among other aristocrats and scientists; in France he was in contact with philosophers, mathematicians, with writers like Fontenelle (Conti 1726b; Toaldo; Dorris; Petrone Fresco), and Voltaire who mentions him in his correspondence. He also travelled to Germany and Holland. Notably, it was through Conti's writings that the Swiss critic Johann Jakob Bodmer developed his appreciation of Shakespeare (Orsini). Conti's comparison of Shakespeare and Corneille in his 'Risposta' expresses the ideological framework in which his vision of Shakespeare took shape; it was French classicism as codified by Voltaire that dictated current literary parameters.

Paolo Rolli's (1687–1765) comments on Shakespeare were published a few years after Conti's. In his 'Life of John Milton', prefacing his Italian translation of the first six books of *Paradise Lost* (1729), and in his 'Osservazioni' (remarks), published in the Veronese edition of the translation of Milton (1730), Rolli dismissed Voltaire's approach. While, in his *Essay upon the Epick Poetry of all the European Nations* (1727), Voltaire had admired the genius of Shakespeare he had emphasized his aesthetic 'absurdities', negative judgements which were reiterated in subsequent work. In 'Life of John Milton', Rolli, instead, praised Shakespeare as a genius and an interpreter of national history, who elevated the English theatre to 'insuperable sublimity' (11). In his tragic histories, Rolli writes, 'i fatti ed i caratteri de' Personaggi interlocutori sono così viva [*sic*] e poeticamente e con adattissimo stile espressi; che nulla più' ('the facts and the characters of the protagonists are so vividly and poetically expressed and in a most proper style; as cannot be bettered'). Shakespeare is presented as a model, even of style, for other nations, while inelegancies and passages judged un-Shakespearean are disregarded on the supposition that they were 'added' by contemporary actors (12).

Rolli's highest accolade is to compare Shakespeare with Dante (12): 'di lui dico quel che asserisco del Dante; cioè ch'eglino due soli me fanno altamente meravigliare d'aver i primi tanto sublimamente poetato nella loro lingua' ('I can say of him what I say of Dante: they are the only two who astound me with the sublime poetry they were the first to produce in their languages'). His defence of Shakespeare from Voltairean criticism led him to translate Hamlet's 'To be or not to be' in order to illustrate how much Voltaire had deviated, in his own translation, from the style and sentiment of the original. In place of Voltaire's anti-clerical comments:

On nous menace, on dit que cette courte vie,
De tourments éternels est aussi-tôt suivie.
O mort! moment fatal! affreuse éternité,
Tout cœur à ton seul nom se glace, épouvanté.
Eh qui pourroit sans toi supporter cette vie,
De nos Prêtres menteurs bénir l'hypocrisie . . .

Voltaire 82

(They threaten us, they say this short life / is quickly followed by eternal torments. / Oh death! fatal moment! horrible eternity, / every heart at the mention of your name is frozen, scared. / Who would bear this life without you, / bless the hypocrisy of our false Priests)

Rolli gives a more literal version:

Ah
Qui è l'Intoppo! Chè in quel Sonno di Morte
Quai Sogni possan venir poi che avremo
Scossa alla fin questa mortale Spoglia;
Sospendon l'Alma.
. . . Altrimente, chi mai soffrir le atroci
Del suo tempo vorria Sferzate e Scherni,
Torti d'Oppressione, Onte d'Orgoglio

Rolli 1742A: 98

(Ah, there's the rub! For in that sleep of death / what dreams may come after we / discard our mortal body; / pause our soul . . . Otherwise, who ever will / bear the whips and scorns of time / the wrongs of oppression, the shame of pride).

Rolli's response to Shakespeare marks a significant shift in its dissociation from French critical pronouncements and in its recognition of Shakespeare's preoccupation with national history. Moreover, for the first time, Shakespeare is equated with Italian national literary culture. Later, in the second half of the century, Giuseppe Baretti, a controversial intellectual, who spent many years in England where he became a friend to Samuel Johnson, overtly attacked Voltaire's critical categories and developed a pre-Romantic discourse in praise of Shakespeare's natural style. His *Discours sur Shakespeare et sur monsieur de Voltaire* (1777) was a decisive contribution to the reception of Shakespeare in Italian culture.

Stage

The path by which Shakespeare's plays or – more precisely – his plots migrated to the stage took a different one from that of his critical reception. The latter, notably Conti's commentary, illustrates how what were regarded as Shakespeare's formal irregularities militated against his performance in the theatre. A number of plays appeared initially through the popular genre of melodrama, and then in pantomime and ballet. Apostolo Zeno's melodrama *Ambleto*, written with Pietro Pariati, and set to music by Francesco Gasparini, was first performed in 1705 in Venice. Zeno prefaces the work with an *Argomento* in which he presented the plot derived not from Shakespeare but from Saxo Grammaticus's *Gesta Danorum*, and from the histories of Denmark written by Giovanni Meursio (1630) and Giovanni Isacco Pontano (1631). In form and content, the text responds to contemporary taste. It is divided into three acts which contain respectively nineteen, eighteen and nineteen scenes. Events pile on one another, but still take place on a single day, and the work concludes with Ambleto re-establishing order. Zeno's redaction travelled to Florence and Naples and was performed in London at the Haymarket theatre in 1712 (Vittorini 121–34).

Hamlet was the text which most attracted theatrical interest in eighteenth-century Italy, although the first (musical) performance in which Shakespeare's name is mentioned took place only in 1774, again in Venice. Published in the same year, this version was advertised as a tragedy of Ducis in imitation of Shakespeare, *Amleto. Tragedia di Mr Ducis. Ad imitazione della Inglese di Shakespear*. In a third subsequent edition the adaptor of the adaptation was named as the Venetian writer and translator, Francesco Gritti. In the Preface of *Amleto*'s first edition, Gritti – remaining anonymous – presented Ducis's merits in mediating the 'monstrous' Shakespeare: 'L'*Amleto di Shakespear* è per l'Inghilterra ciò, per esempio, che il *Convitato di Pietra* è tuttavia per l'Italia; una, cioè, delle più mostruose e non di meno una delle più frequentate Rappresentazioni Teatrali' ('Shakespear's *Hamlet* is for England what, for example, the *Convitato di Pietra* is for Italy; that is, one of the most monstrous and yet one of the most popular theatrical performances', Vittorini 138).[2] The translator summarizes the plot so that readers could judge whether 'l'Edifizio Francese ha conservato tutte le bellezze e rettificata punto la costruzione deforme di quell'antico bizzarro modello' (ibid. 128, 'the French edifice has maintained all the beauty and corrected the deformed shape of that ancient bizarre model'). The passage illustrates the tortuosity of Shakespeare's Italian migration. Gritti's source for *Hamlet* is Ducis's version, but in exploring the original plot he relies on Voltaire's own summary of Shakespeare's *Hamlet*.

The Italian translation further modifies and adapts Ducis's text. However, for the author of *Notizie Storico-Critiche sull'Amleto*, an appendix to the 1796 edition, there still seems to be not enough distance from the original. The author praises Ducis for erasing the 'double scandal' of fratricide and of the incestuous marriage between Claudio and Gertrude. He is in compliance with Ducis's strictures, but the representation of the Ghost, so controversial to French neo-classicism, as Michèle Willems points out in this volume, is seen as an impossible element to erase on the grounds that it is the core of dramatic action. Despite improvements by both Ducis and the translator, the text remains grounded on an unnatural fact that 'shocks and disgusts' 'wise' spectators or readers (72–5).

Ducis avoided the direct presence of the Ghost on stage while exploiting its dramatic power through the use of an urn containing old Hamlet's ashes. Gritti has to cope with Ducis's reworked scene: more frequently than in the French text, the urn is a 'sacred' object (25), a 'sacred deposit' (48); Norcesto brings on stage a 'covered' urn (48), and shifts attention onto the moral qualities of the dead King, adding the exhortation that he might be 'sempre / A' migliori sovrani esempio e norma' (48, 'forever an example and a model for the best monarchs').

Moral pathos is, moreover, added to Gertrude's reaction when Hamlet asks her to swear her innocence on the urn; the lines in which she expresses remorse are not in Ducis:

AMLETO *[...] Al nuovo e sacro*
Giuramento ond'io voglio ora legarti,
Pensa tu stessa, e inorridisci.
     [va a prender l'urna]
GELTRUDA *Parla.*
(Che sarà mai! ... lassa! ... Ahi! che veggo! L'urna?
Quell'urna stessa, oh ciel! Ove riposa
Il cenere del mio tradito sposo!
O rimorso! O terror!)

(57–8)

HAM.
Think upon the new and sacred bond
To which I wish to tie you, and be horrified.

    (*he goes and takes the urn*)
GEL. Speak.
(What could it be? Alas! Ah! What do I see? The urn?
The very urn, oh Heaven! Where
The ashes of my betrayed husband rest!
Oh remorse! Oh terror!).

Gritti's didactic tone is encapsulated in the added closing lines, referring to a 'suprema volontà del Cielo' (70, 'Heaven's sovereign will') that is arbiter of men's lives. Two subsequent performances of *Hamlet*, first in Florence in 1791 and, then, in Bologna in 1795, inaugurated the series of stage productions which fixed the presence of the play on Italian stages.

Ducis's rewriting of *Romeo and Juliet* was almost as popular as his *Hamlet*. As Willems has shown, Ducis presents the text as a new tragedy derived both from Shakespeare and Dante, and insists on its moral content. There are two Italian translations: *Giulietta e Romeo Tragedia di Mr Ducis dal verso francese trasportata in verso italiano dall'Ab. Antonio Bonucci*, published in Florence in 1778, and *Romeo e Giulietta. Tragedia di monsieur Ducis* (undated), translated by the Venetian, Francesco Balbi (1735–1806). The popularity of Ducis's *Roméo et Juliette* is hardly surprising in the light of its introduction of narratives familiar to the audience, however un-Shakespearean Ducis's amplifications were. A translation of Ducis's *Othello* was published in Bologna between 1794 and 1800, *Othello o sia il Moro di Venezia tragedia del cittad. [citizen] Doucis tradotta dal cittad. Celestino Massucco professore di poetica nell'Università di Genova*.

Ballets and melodramas continued to present Ducis as their authority. Though Giuseppe Maria Foppa refers directly to the Italian sources of his libretto, *Giulietta e Romeo*, performed in Milan in 1796, claiming that these inspired both the Shakespearean original and Ducis's adaptation, Francesco Clerico acknowledges Shakespeare but names Ducis as the only source for his pantomime, *Amleto*, performed in Milan in 1792. He made it clear, however, that the libretto is derived from Ducis's 'substance' but that he introduced 'episodes more adequate to the characteristics of Dance and to the form of a Ballet' (Clerico 1795 in Vittorini 148; Gatti 1968: 12–24).

Staging Shakespeare, or Shakespeare's scenarios, was, for a long time, independent of Shakespeare's texts and it was not until Giuseppe Verdi's *Macbeth*, performed in Florence in 1847, that a production of Shakespeare was based on a libretto which had its origins in Shakespeare and not in Ducis. Verdi's successive *Macbeths* were followed, decades later, by his *Otello* (1886) and *Falstaff* (1892). *Otello* was already popular through Gioacchino Rossini's opera *Otello o il Moro di Venezia*, first performed in 1816. Francesco Berio, author of the successful libretto based on Ducis, had changed Ducis's opening scene with the inclusion of Othello's triumphant arrival in Venice, a scene that Verdi, unsurprisingly, adopted in his own version. In Verdi's productions Shakespeare was variously reused even in non-Shakespearean operas (Weis; Guandalini). Within the scope of this chapter the influence of Shakespeare on Italian opera cannot be discussed. Suffice to say, and as is well known, the translation of Shakespeare into opera, which began in the mid-nineteenth century, was to be one of the major routes for Shakespeare's migration in Europe.

Translations

Translations of Shakespeare in Italy began in the mid-eighteenth century and, as in France and Germany, *Julius Caesar* (1756) was the first play to be translated. The translator Domenico Valentini (1690–1762), professor of Ecclesiastical History at the University of Siena, discusses in the preface his approach to translation. He cites the Romans who used translation as a means to assimilate Greek culture, thus displaying an awareness of the role translation has in reshaping literary and cultural norms. Four essential qualities are listed: the ability to select the author to translate on the basis of morals; knowledge of the language; knowledge of the subject matter; and lastly an intellectual affinity with the author that will make it possible to achieve a perfect correspondence between original and translation. Despite Valentini's assertion that the author should not be 'irregular', he makes an exception for Shakespeare on the grounds that classical rules may be necessary for 'mediocri' writers, arguing, in poetic language, that these would have limited Shakespeare's imagination:

Tal fu la soprabbondanza del di Lui Spirito, e così fervida, e così fertile la sua straordinaria Immaginazione, che lo trasportò a trascurare le Regole prescritte al Dramma, qual impetuoso Fiume, che sdegnando di star ristretto nell'angusto suo Letto, superate le sponde si stende per ogni parte nelle vicine Campagne (1756: xxx^r).

(Such was the over-abundance of his spirit, and so fervent and so fertile his extraordinary Imagination, that it led him to neglect the Rules of Drama, like an impetuous river, that disdaining to be confined in its narrow bed, breaks its banks and floods into the nearby countryside.)

On historical grounds, Valentini goes on to justify the inclusion of low scenes and the variety of dramatic settings in the play.

Despite his championing of Shakespeare, Valentini had no knowledge of the English language. We learn from his preface that he used an English version established by Lewis Theobald, 'Sig. Teobaldo', and that he was assisted by certain English gentlemen conversant with the 'Lingua Toscana' (xxxii^r), the revered literary language of Dante, Petrarch and Boccaccio, who, in the first half of the fourteenth century, gave birth to an Italian 'national' literature. This is the only reference to his unofficial collaborators. Valentini considers his indirect approach to translation and his identity as a translator as legitimate on the basis that he is transposing the meaning of one literary work into another. In anticipation of any critical response he proposed that his role is that of a 'Semitraduttore, o Contraduttore' (xxxiii^v, 'Semi-translator or Co-translator'). Translation is seen as a collaborative and neutral act consisting in semantic transfer in order to reproduce the source text. But translating is never neutral; it always manipulates the original to a certain degree in order to re-situate it in a different cultural system. Lawrence Venuti has shown that the idea of the natural, faithful translation goes back to the seventeenth century and responded to the need to domesticate the foreignness of the source text. Valentini's prose translation generally follows the

English text but nevertheless it reveals current aesthetic and ideological pressures.

The ghost of Julius Caesar is eliminated. The irony of Antony's address after the assassination of Caesar is completely lost as repetition was considered poor literary style; thus 'honourable' is varied with a range of words and phrases: 'molto onorevole', 'di grand'onore', 'verace', 'persona degna di fede', 'onorevole', 'degni d'onore', 'rispettabili', 'nobili'. Valentini erases the viscereal quality of the language. When, for example, Brutus invites the conspirators to be 'sacrificers but not butchers' (2.1.166), 'butchers' is translated as the more refined 'carnefici' and not 'macellai'. A less-disquieting scenario is offered in the translation of 'Let's carve him [Caesar] as a dish fit for the gods, / Not hew him as a carcass fit for hounds' (2.1.172–3) with 'Immoliamolo come una vittima degna de' Numi, e non lo tagliamo in pezzi, come pascolo di voraci Animali' (45). The Italian text here rephrases so that 'dish' becomes 'victim' and 'carcass' becomes 'pasture'. In Shakespeare's text Antony's speech is highly figurative:

> O, pardon me, thou bleeding piece of earth,
> That I am meek and gentle with these butchers.
> Thou art the ruins of the noblest man
> That ever lived in the tide of times.
> ... mothers shall but smile when they behold
> Their infants quartered with the hands of war:
> ...
> And Caesar's spirit ...
> With Ate by his side come hot from hell,
> Shall in these confines, with a monarch's voice,
> Cry havoc and let slip the dogs of war,
> That this foul deed shall smell above the earth
> With carrion men, groaning for burial.
>
> 3.1.254–75

Valentini omits any direct translation of 'piece of earth', 'butchers', 'smile', 'dogs', 'smell', 'carrion', while one concrete image of ruins is rendered less effective as it becomes the laboured 'le tristi reliquie e le miserabili spoglie' (the sad relics and the humble remains):

> *O Voi esangue cadavere, dove una volta abitava la gran mente di Cesare, perdonate, se io docile, e trattabile mi dimostro con questi inumani carnefici; Voi pur siete le triste reliquie e le miserabili spoglie dell'uomo più nobile. . . . le madri quasi insensibili diverranno in veder i lor diletti figlioli lacerati dalle spietate mani di crudeli guerrieri . . . e lo spirito furibondo di Cesare . . . andrà gridando . . . con voce d'imperioso Monarca, vendetta . . . l'inesorabile Aletto, Megera, e Tesifone lasceranno in libertà i fieri mostri di guerra, che copriranno la faccia della Terra di cadaveri miserabilmente gementi per esser privi di sepoltura* (83–5).[3]

(Bloodless corpse, where once the great mind of Caesar lived, forgive me if I am mild and lenient with these inhuman slaughterers. You are the sad relics and the humble remains of the most noble of men . . . mothers will become almost indifferent in seeing their beloved sons ripped apart by the ruthless hands of cruel warriors . . . and the maddened spirit of Caesar . . . will cry out for revenge with the imperious voice of a Monarch . . . the inexorable Alecto, Megaera and Tisiphone will release the fiery monsters of war, which will cover the face of the earth with corpses pitifully groaning at being deprived of burial.)

Living a 'secluded life' (Petrone Fresco 184) may have helped Valentini in his direct engagement with Shakespeare, at a time in Europe when Shakespeare's foreignness tended to be highly mediated. In asserting the translatability of Shakespeare he contradicts Voltairean critical dogmas, although it has to be said that the immediate impact of the translation was negligible. This was also the case with the two unpublished translations of *Hamlet* and *Othello* by Alessandro Verri (1741–1816).[4] It was not until Michele Leoni began his systematic translations of

Shakespeare's work in the following century, when a national agenda was shaking cultural standards, that translations of Shakespeare began to enter the cultural mainstream.

The role of Michele Leoni (1776–1858) in carrying out the first substantial editorial project of Shakespeare's work is seminal to Shakespeare's migration to Italy. Based in Milan from 1806 to 1812, Leoni was working in a fertile intellectual context with the political shaping intellectual debate. While calling for freedom from both Napoleon's despotism and from the Austro-Hungarian Empire, Italian writers were beginning to react against French cultural dogmatism and to revise cultural standards under the impulse of Romanticism. Leoni's work reflects this shifting dynamic context. The highly influential Madame De Staël, whose work crossed the borders of a warring continent, addressed Italian intellectuals in a letter, 'De l'esprit des traductions', published in Italian in the periodical *La Biblioteca Italiana* (1816a). De Staël promoted the need for cultural exchange arguing that if a modern nation were intellectually 'reduced to its own treasures' it would remain 'poor' forever, and that 'the circulation of ideas is, among all kinds of commerce, the one whose advantages are the most certain'. To know what is 'beyond the Alps' is key to a renewal of current classicist codes, lifeless and artificial in their use of images derived from 'ancient mythology'. If looking at German and English poems may help to shift to a more natural idiom, more important is the influence that translation of theatrical plays may have, since theatre is the 'executive power of literature'. Shakespeare is the author to translate. De Staël refers to Schlegel's translation of Shakespeare into German, which made him a 'compatriot', and suggests this could be achieved in Italy as well (294–7). In a subsequent letter to the compilers of the *Biblioteca Italiana*, in which she responded to accusations of being critical of Italy's cultural isolation, she valued the helpful connections among writers 'of all countries and of all centuries', and Leoni's initiative to translate Shakespeare's works: 'Un letterato a Firenze ha fatto studi profondi sulla letteratura inglese e ha intrapresa una traduzione di tutto Shakespeare, poichè, cosa da non credere! non esiste ancora una traduzione italiana di questo grand'uomo' ('A man of letters in Florence has studied English literature in depth and has undertaken a translation of all Shakespeare, since, unbelievable! an Italian translation of such a great man does not yet exist' (1816b: 419–20). The name of the translator is given in a note, 'Il Sig. Leoni'.

The first text Leoni translated and published was *Julius Caesar* in 1811, again illustrating the Italian fascination with Shakespeare's Rome. Curiously it was in his preface to his translation of *Othello*, 'Intendimento e considerazioni del traduttore', published in Florence in 1814, that Leoni reveals the genesis of the translation of *Julius Caesar*. He states he had first read the play in the French version of Pierre Le Tourneur and it was through the process of comparing Le Tourneur's prose, close to paraphrase, with the poetical style of Shakespeare that he recognizes the imperatives of his own translation: 'Intendo dire unicamente, di essermi studiato di mantenere il più possibile il colorito poetico dell'originale, trasportandolo in poesia, e in poesia di lingua più poetica forse, che nol sia qualunque altra vivente' (1814: xii, 'I only wish to say that I have strived to maintain, as far as possible, the poetic colour of the original, translating it into poetry, and in the poetry, perhaps, of the most poetic language of all').

Leoni produced two different translations of the play, *Giulio Cesare* (1811) and *La morte di Giulio Cesare* (1815), highlighting a process of change and revision. In the 1815 edition Leoni states the reasons behind the second text: he had greater knowledge of the subject matter and he wanted to produce a text more reader orientated (v–vii). It is plain that Leoni does not see the role of the translator as inferior to that of the author; the very title *La morte di Giulio Cesare* highlights his awareness of having re-written Shakespeare.

Despite his admiration for Shakespeare, Leoni continues a tradition of modifying according to neo-classical laws of decorum (Sestito). He cuts, for example, the dialogue between Marullo and the cobbler in the opening scene of the 1815 edition, and tends to normalize the style in order to avoid differences between low and elevated modes. Marullus's question 'what trade art thou?' becomes more indirect and poetical, 'E a te, qual arte / Fa si crespe le man?' (1815, what art makes your hands so rough?). The process of stylistic revision is carried out at the level of lexical choices, thus 'honourable men' in Antony's speeches is translated with 'cittadino dabbene', 'chiari spirti' (92) 'alme dabbene' (95) 'liberi spirti' (96); 'honour', generally translated with 'onore', is also significantly rendered with 'decoro' (1815).

Leoni's language is religiously charged as he builds up ideas of Rome's sacredness and highlights patriotic sentiment. Moreover, the myth of Caesar is amplified by his added associations of Caesar with Jove and God. Flavius fears he would 'soar above the view of men, / And keep us all in servile fearfulness' (1.1.75–6); in Leoni, Caesar would exert his power as a 'novello Giove' (1811: 10, new Jupiter), 'monarca, – e Dio' (1815: 5, monarch and God). His body has the sanctity of a 'reliquia' (relic) and 'the hand that shed this costly blood' (3.1.258) becomes in the translation 'sacrilego acciar' (1815: 80, sacrilegious arms). The religious charge of the language is sustained throughout the translation: the bond between the Romans (2.1.24–5) is 'prometter sacro' (1811: 52, sacred oath), it is compared to 'sacrament' (1815: 40), and the praise of the assassination prefigured by Cassio (3.1.116–18) will be 'sacred' for the 'spirti / Che dalla patria lor toglieano il giogo (1815: 72, spirits, / who free their country from oppression).

Emotional involvement is increased through emphatic repetition of Caesar's name and a shift from the second person to the first when Antony first reacts after the assassination: 'O mighty Caesar! Dost thou lie so low?' (3.1.148) becomes 'Giulio, potente Giulio, in quale stato / Deh, ti riveggo io mai?' (1815: 74, 'Giulio, mighty Giulio, in what state do I see you?'). The translation of Brutus's invitation to immolate Caesar 'as a dish fit for the gods' with 'ostia gioconda' (1811, 'jocund Host') and with 'vittima sacra' (1815, 'sacred victim') clearly shows how Leoni projects and reinforces religious associations. Remarkably, Leoni's language anticipates the language of religious sacrifice which was employed for liberation not least by Giuseppe Mazzini, one of the great Italian intellectuals, as he mobilized feelings in the struggle for Italian unity. The oath to become a member of the *Giovane Italia*, the insurrectional association founded in 1831, was made in the name of God, Italy and all the martyrs of the 'holy Italian cause' fallen under foreign and domestic tyranny. Those who wanted to join it pronounced their faith 'in the mission God assigned to Italy', and, aware that virtue consists in action and sacrifice, 'consecrate' themselves to making Italy a unified and free nation (Montazio 49–50).

After translations of single plays, *Tragedie di Shakespeare* in fourteen volumes was published in Verona from 1819 to 1822, bringing together Leoni's editions or re-editions of the single plays: *La Tempesta, Vita e Morte del Re Giovanni, Sogno di una notte di Mezza Estate, Otello, Macbetto, La morte di Giulio Cesare, Romeo e Giulietta, Vita e Morte di Riccardo III, Cimbelino, Amleto, Re Lear, Vita e Morte di Riccardo II, Il Re Arrigo IV parte I, Il Re Arrigo IV parte II*. Leoni had a broad definition of tragedy, since he included *Richard II, Cymbeline* and *A Midsummer Night's Dream*.

In the midst of enthusiastic responses to Shakespeare the comedies were largely ignored in the nineteenth century. Unsurprisingly – considering the Italianate setting – *The Merchant of Venice* and *The Taming of the Shrew* were exceptions. *The Merchant* had various translations in the 1830s (by Giulio Carcano, Pietro Santi, Carlo Rusconi) and it was first performed in Milan in 1869 as *Shylock, o il Mercante di Venezia* in a production by Ernesto Rossi at Teatro Re (Lombardo 2013). Performances in Italy were, however, limited by Rossi, who valued the play but feared that he might revive religious conflict (Rossi; Orecchia 2016: 96). His theatrical practice was based on the valorization of the principal role, played with emphasis and full expression of feelings, in the tradition of the 'grand'attore'. In the 1870s Rossi performed *Shylock* in Vienna and Russia with a text that appears to have been limited to those parts that projected the character of Shylock (Bellavia 2000; Orecchia 2016). G. C. Molineri reviewed the performance in Turin at Teatro Alfieri in November 1887, which was not well attended. He was critical of the cuts to Shakespeare's text and particularly of the elimination of the last act, highlighting how a play dealing with love, friendship and hate had been reduced to this last element. Among other structural modifications, Molineri noted that Rossi had introduced scenes which he considered 'alien' to Shakespeare's intention such as the episode in which Shylock discovers Jessica's elopement and bursts out on stage 'addolorato, quasi demente' (Molineri, 'distressed, nearly mad') – an emotional reaction that was only reported in Shakespeare. In showing the oppressed angry Jew, Rossi is 'sublime, in hate', but he also showed 'with great art' the 'paternal affection of the old Jew'. The actor Ermete Novelli later continued to perform Shylock as an angry Jew; despite comic exaggeration, tragic aspects of Shylock were conveyed on stage, contributing to a more sympathetic characterization and complicating the general negative stereotype of the Jew.

Showing the versatility of Shakespeare on the Italian stage, the play had been turned into a melodrama at the Teatro Comunale in Bologna in 1873. This version, *Il mercante di Venezia: melodramma in quattro atti da Shakespeare*, had a libretto by G. T. Cimino and was set to music by Ciro Pinsuti. This was a representation of a negative stereotype, with words and music emphasizing Shylock's aggressive behaviour, but the text also showed that Shylock's villainy depended on circumstances (Cohen; Brumana and Pagano). Act Three opens in Shylock's house where his lament is heard about the loss of Rebecca; in the trial scene that follows, Shylock reacts to his legal defeat 'in desperation' (stage direction) still talking about his unnamed, 'kidnapped' daughter (Pinsuti 41). In Bologna the episode possibly evoked the recent case of the young boy, Edgardo Mortara, who was baptized and removed from his Jewish family (Cohen). A significant aspect of this version was the amplification of Shylock's Jewish voice; in the final scene Shylock is exiled and two choruses, one of Israelites and one of Christians, are juxtaposed, an addition which possibly reflected concerns with national identities in Italy just a few years after unification (Cohen 392–6; Brumana and Pagano).

Leoni's first volume of the *Tragedies* (Verona, 1819) contains Shakespeare's portrait, combined with another portrait, of a much larger size, that of Leoni. Also included in the first volume are various paratexts: Leoni's dedication to 'Sua Maestà Ferdinando I re delle due Sicilie' ('His Majesty Ferdinand I, King of the Two Sicilies'), a preface by the commissioning editors, the translator's preface, Leoni's translations of extracts from Shakespeare's life by the editor and biographer, Nicholas Rowe, and Samuel Johnson's *Preface* (1765). In its weighty textual apparatus the edition reveals a European dimension, including comments on the plays by A. W. Schlegel, whose *Vorlesungen* (lectures) had been translated into Italian.

In the dedication Leoni stresses the social disparity between the dedicatee and the translator, whilst claiming that the immortal Shakespeare can compete with kings:

Ma quando si passi a considerare il Poeta, del quale consacro a VOSTRA MAESTA' le Opere, da me voltate nella splendida e sonante lingua dell'Arno, sarà ben diverso il giudicio: poiché, rendutosi esso già insigne tra gli scrittori immortali, è degno di gareggiar colla fama de' più generosi Monarchi

(But when we consider the poet, whose works I consecrate to Your Majesty, translated by me into the beautiful and musical language of Arno, judgement will be very diverse: for, already illustrious among immortal writers, he can compete with the reputation of the most generous Monarchs.)

In their preface the editors rejected earlier critical denouncements of Shakespeare on the grounds that he had offended the genius of Italian poetry; if his plays were banned or only partially approved of, this was caused by a misunderstood nationalistic feeling. Defence was no longer possible against the 'interne gagliardissime scosse' ('internal powerful shocks') provided by Shakespeare's texts (Leoni 1819: xii).

In the translator's preface, Leoni further illustrates the varied reactions to Shakespeare's cultural diversity. He expresses surprise at the readers' 'indulgence' towards Shakespeare, which encouraged his work on further translations into Italian. He was sceptical of the way these could be received, given their aesthetic distance from classical works; the task was in fact considered dangerous and Shakespeare was still found 'barbarous' and even 'delirious'; but, Leoni observes, such negative reactions to Shakespeare were limited, coming for the main part from mediocre writers, and associated with rejection of the foreign. Those who can read Shakespeare's work will be struck by his 'intima . . . conoscenza dell'uman cuore' ('intimate knowledge of the human heart'), and his mastery in the 'maneggio delle passioni' ('management of passions').

Leoni's view is that Italy is ready to accept Shakespeare, since there is no longer anyone who does not find his work apt to teach 'lezioni intorno alle più gravi circostanze della vita, e metafisiche dottrine da innestarsi con onore e con frutto nella patria letteratura' ('lessons on the most serious circumstances of life, and metaphysical doctrines to engraft honourably and fruitfully in national literature'). He echoes and gives substance to De Staël's programme validating the importance of mixing national traditions from a comparative perspective. Shakespeare can become a source of inspiration; his genius can counterbalance the poetical scarcity in Italian literature after the long decline following the Renaissance. Leoni's awareness of the creative potential of intellectual tranfers is clear when he remarks that in his dramatic art Shakespeare surpassed the Greeks and reached the incomparable art of Michelangelo:

> *Il perché troppo angusto gli parve forse il campo percorso da' Tragici Greci. Insigni riusciron questi nel genere loro, per efficacia di sentimento e semplicità di disegno. Inarrivabile si mostrò SHAKESPEARE nel suo, per grandiosità di forme e gagliardezza di affetti. Ei fu il Michelangelo della tragedia.*
>
> XIII–IV

(For the course followed by Greek tragedians seemed perhaps too narrow to him. Illustrious they were in their genre, for the power of sentiment and the simplicity of its design. Shakespeare was insuperable in his, for the grandeur of forms and the power of affects. He was the Michelangelo of tragedy.)

Leoni's translations of Shakespeare remained mostly a literary exercise. His version of *Othello* was used, in a revised and adapted form, in 1842 in Milan by Gustavo Modena (Gatti 2015), one of the first Italian actors to be associated with Shakespearean roles. But the production was a failure, with the audience unable to appreciate Shakespeare's unconventionality, and in subsequent productions such as *King Lear* Modena used a version of Ducis (Bellavia 2004). After the failure of *Otello*, Leoni's texts were rarely used in the theatre. However, his edition stimulated a considerable interest in the translation of Shakespeare and it continued to be cited until it was superseded by Giulio Carcano's more faithful verse translation, *Teatro di Shakespeare*, the publication of which was completed in 1882. Leoni's edition had not resolved the tensions between Italian neo-classicism, European Romanticism and Shakespeare's irregularities, yet, as is signified by the inclusion of the portraits of Italian translator and English playwright and Leoni's equation of Shakespeare and Michelangelo, it marks a crucial moment in Shakespeare's assimilation into Italian cultural life.

Notes

1 Early responses to Shakespeare are discussed in Lombardo 1964, Orsini, Ferrando.
2 The grotesque story of Don Juan, presented in the Spanish drama *El Burlador de Sevilla y convidado de piedra* (1616) attributed to Tirso de Molina, was popular in Italy as well. In 1678 a version, *Il Convitato di pietra*, was published in Naples by the playwright and librettist Andrea Perucci.

3 For a full discussion of the translation see Crinò 1950.
4 Further translations were published between 1797 and 1800 by Giustina Renier Michel (*Opere Drammatiche di Shakespeare volgarizzate da una Dama Veneta*). On Verri see Petrone Fresco.

References

Bassi, S. (2016), 'The Tragedies in Italy', in M. Neill and D. Schalkwyk eds, *The Oxford Handbook of Shakespearean Tragedy*, 691–705, Oxford: Oxford University Press.

Bellavia, S. (2000), *La voce del gesto. Le rappresentazioni shakespeariane di Ernesto Rossi sulla scena tedesca*, Roma: Bulzoni.

Bellavia, S. (2004), *L'ombra di Lear. Il Re Lear di Shakespeare e il Teatro Italiano (1858–1995)*, Roma: Bulzoni.

Brumana, B. and Pagano, G. E. (2006), '*Il mercante di Venezia* di Ciro Pinsuti (Bologna 1873)', *Esercizi. Musica e Spettacolo* 20, n. s. 11, 2006-7, 77–111.

Busi, A. (1973), *Otello in Italia*, Bari: Adriatica.

Campanelli, M. (2014), 'Languages', in M. Wyatt ed., *The Cambridge Companion to the Italian Renaissance*, 139–63, Cambridge: Cambridge University Press.

Castagnoli, M. A. (1984), *Michele Leoni*, Quaderni Fidentini, 31, Parma: Tipolitografia Benedettina Editrice.

Cioni, F. (1995), *Le Maschere di Amleto*, Modena: Comune di Modena.

Coduri, M. (2013), *A Travelling Tale. Shakespeare on the Italian Stage*, M. Phil diss., School of European Languages, Culture and Society, University College London. Available online: https://discovery.ucl.ac.uk/id/eprint/

Cohen, J. M. (2017), 'Shylock in Opera, 1871–2014', in E. Nahashon and M. Shapiro eds, *Wrestling with Shylock. Jewish Responses to* The Merchant of Venice, 381–412, Cambridge: Cambridge University Press.

Collison-Morley, L. (1916), *Shakespeare in Italy*, New York: Benjamin Bloom.

Conti, A. (1726a), *Il Cesare*, Faenza: G. Archi.

Conti. A. (1726b), 'Risposta del Signor Abate Antonio Conti al Signore Iacopo Martelli', in A. Conti, *Il Cesare*, 45–76, Faenza: G. Archi.

Crinò, A. M. (1950), *Le Traduzioni di Shakespeare in Italia nel Settecento*, Roma: Edizioni di Storia e Letteratura.

De Rinaldis, M. L. (2003), *Giacomo Castelvetro Renaissance Translator*, Lecce: Milella.

Del Sapio, M., ed. (2002), *La traduzione di Amleto nella cultura europea*, Venezia: Marsilio.

Dorris, G. E. (1967), *Paolo Rolli and the Italian Circle in London 1715–1744*, Mouton & Co; Paris: The Hague.

Ducis, J.-F. (1770), *Hamlet, Tragédie, Imitée de l'Anglois*, Paris: Gogué.

Ducis, J.-F. (1774), *Amleto. Tragedia di Mr Ducis, ad imitazione della Inglese di Shakespeare, tradotta in versi sciolti*, Venezia.

Duggan, C. [2007] (2008), *The Force of Destiny. A History of Italy since 1796*, London: Penguin Books.

Ferrando, G. (1930), 'Shakespeare in Italy', *The Shakespeare Association Bulletin*, 5, no. 4: 157–68.

Gatti, H. (1968), *Shakespeare nei teatri milanesi dell'Ottocento*, Bari: Adriatica.

Gatti, H. (2015), 'Gustavo Modena's *Othello*: The first performance in an Italian theatre of a Shakespearean drama', *Shakespeare*, 11:1, 82–93.

Golinelli, G. (2003), *La formazione del canone shakespeariano tra identità nazionale ed estetica (Inghilterra e Germania 1700-1770)*, Bologna: Pàtron.

Gritti, F. (1796), *Amleto, Tragedia del Signor Ducis, Tradotta dal N. U. Francesco Gritti*, Venezia.

Guandalini, G. (1979), 'I due Macbeth e i molti Lear di Verdi', in L. Caretti ed., *Il teatro del personaggio. Shakespeare sulla scena italiana dell'800*, 115–46, Roma: Bulzoni.

Hermans, T., ed. (1985), *The Manipulation of Literature*, London, Sydney: Croom Helm.

Kuhiwczak, P., and Littau, K., eds (2007), *A Companion to Translation Studies*, Clevedon: Multilingual Matters.

Lefevere, A. (1992), *Translation, Rewriting, and the Manipulation of Literary Fame*, London and New York: Routledge.

Leoni, M. (1811), *Giulio Cesare. Tragedia di Guglielmo Shakespeare*. Tradotta dall'originale in versi italiani da Michele

Leoni di Parma, Milano: Destefanis, Collection Bodleian Libraries.

Leoni, M. (1814), 'Intendimento e considerazioni del traduttore', in *Otello, o il Moro di Venezia, Tragedia di G. Shakespeare, recata in versi italiani da Michele Leoni di Parma*, v–xv, Firenze: Alauzet.

Leoni, M. (1815), *La Morte di Giulio Cesare. Tragedia di G. Shakespeare*. Recata in versi italiani da Michele Leoni di Parma, Pisa: Capurro, The British Library Historical Collection.

Leoni, M. (1819), 'Il Traduttore', in *Tragedie di Shakespeare* (1819–22), vol. I, xiii–xvi, Verona: Società Tipografica.

Leoni, M. (1819–22), *Tragedie di Shakespeare*, Verona: Società Tipografica.

Lombardo, A. (1964), 'Shakespeare e la critica italiana', *Sipario*, 218, 2–14.

Lombardo, A., ed. (2013), *William Shakespeare. Il Mercante di Venezia*, Milano: Feltrinelli.

Minutella, V. (2013), *Reclaiming Romeo and Juliet: Translations from Page to Stage*, Amsterdam, New York: Rodopi.

Molineri, G.C. (1887), 'Il Mercante di Venezia al Teatro Alfieri', 'Gazzetta Piemontese', 19 November.

Montazio, E. (1862), *Giuseppe Mazzini per Enrico Montazio*, Torino: Unione Tipografico-Editrice.

Notizie storico-critiche sull'Amleto (1796), in J.-F. Ducis, *Amleto, Tragedia del Signor Ducis, Tradotta dal N. U. Francesco Gritti*, 71–5, Venezia.

Orecchia, D. (2012), *Il critico e l'attore. Silvio D'Amico e la scena italiana di inizio Novecento*, Torino: Accademia University Press.

Orecchia, D. (2016), 'Appunti su Shylock e la scena teatrale italiana. Da Ernesto Rossi a Memo Benassi attraverso Max Reinhardt', in V. Pavoncello ed., *Shylock e il suo mercante*, 95–114, Ariccia (RM): Aracne.

Orsini, N. (1951), 'Shakespeare in Italy', *Comparative Literature*, 3(2) Spring 1951, 178–80.

Patriarca, S. (2012), 'A Patriotic Emotion: Shame and the Risorgimento', in S. Patriarca and L. Riall eds, *The Risorgimento Revisited. Nationalism and Culture in Nineteenth-Century Italy*, 134–51, Houndmills, Basingstoke: Palgrave Macmillan.

Pennacchia, M. (2006), 'William Shakespeare, Mme De Staël and the Politics of Translation', *Folio, Shakespeare Genootschap van Nederland en Vlanderen*, 13, 1, 9–20.

Petrone Fresco, G. (1993), *Shakespeare's Reception in 18th Century Italy. The Case of Hamlet*, Bern, Berlin, Frankfurt/M., New York, Paris, Wien: Peter Lang.

Pietrini, S. (2017), 'The Eighteenth-Century Reception of Shakespeare. Translation and Adaptation for Italian Audiences', in E. De Francisci and C. Stamatakis eds, *Shakespeare, Italy and Transnational Exchange*, 113–24, New York: Routledge.

Pinsuti, C. (1873), *Il mercante di Venezia: melodramma in quattro atti da Shakespeare/poesia del cavaliere G.T. Cimino; musica del maestro cavaliere Ciro Pinsuti*, Bologna: Società tipografica dei compositori.

Rolli, P. (1742a), 'Vita di Giovanni Milton', in *Il Paradiso Perduto poema inglese di Giovanni Milton*, Tradotto in verso sciolto dal Sig. Paolo Rolli, 71–96, Parigi.

Rolli, P. (1742b), 'Osservazioni', in *Il Paradiso Perduto poema inglese di Giovanni Milton*, Tradotto in verso sciolto dal Sig. Paolo Rolli, 71–96, Parigi.

Rolli, P. (1749), 'Atto III. Scena II. Hamleto', in *Delle Ode d'Anacreonte Teio*. Traduzione di Paolo Rolli, 96–9, London.

Rossi, E. (1887), *Quarant'anni di vita artistica*, II vol., Firenze: L. Niccolai.

Schlegel, A. W. (1817), *Corso di Letteratura drammatica del signor W. A. Schlegel*, trans. G. Gherardini, Milano.

Sestito, M. (1978), *'Julius Caesar' in Italia [1726–1974]*, Bari: Adriatica Editrice.

Shakespeare, W. (1998), *Julius Caesar*, ed. T. S. Dorsch, The Arden Shakespeare, Third Series, London: Bloomsbury.

Staël-Holstein, Germaine de [1816a] (1844), 'De l'esprit des traductions', in *Œuvres complètes de Madame De Staël-Holstein*, vol. 12, 294–7, Paris: Firmin Didot.

Staël-Holstein, Germaine de (1816b), 'Lettera ai Compilatori della Biblioteca Italiana', *Biblioteca Italiana* 2.1, 417–22.

Tinterri, A. (2012), 'The Italian "Grande Attore" and Nineteenth Century Acting', *Acting Archives Essays*, Review Supplement 18, November.

Toaldo, G. (1756), 'Notizie intorno la vita e gli studi del Sig. Abate Antonio Conti', in A. Conti, *Prose e poesie*, vol. II, Venezia: G. Pasquali.
Valentini, D. (1756), *Il Giulio Cesare. Tragedia Istorica di Guglielmo Shakespeare*. Tradotta dall'Inglese in Lingua Toscana dal Dottor Domenico Valentini, Siena: Bindi.
Venuti, L. (1995), *The Translator's Invisibility: A History of Translation*, London: Routledge.
Verdi, G. and Piave, F. M. (1847/1863), *Macbeth*. Available online: www.librettidopera.it
Vittorini, F. (2000), *Shakespeare e il melodramma romantico*, Milano: La Nuova Italia.
Voltaire [1733] (1917), *Lettres Philosophiques*, XVIII, ed. G. Lanson, 2nd edn, vol. 2, 79–88, Paris: Hachette.
Weis, R. (2017), 'Verdi's Shakespeare. Musical Translations and Authenticity', in E. De Francisci and C. Stamatakis eds, *Shakespeare, Italy and Transnational Exchange*, 137–50, New York: Routledge.
Zeno, A. and Pariati, P. [1705] (2010), *Ambleto*, www.librettidopera.it, n. 199.
Zvereva, Irina (2018), *Il dibattito sulla traduzione di Shakespeare in Italia: 1700–1850*, Ph.D. diss., Università di Bologna, Dottorato di Ricerca in Traduzione, Interpretazione e Interculturalità. Available online: http://amsdottorato.unibo.it/.

2

'No stranger here'

Shakespeare in Germany

Wolfgang G. Müller

For centuries the Germans have had a special relationship with Shakespeare. This is to some extent due to the belated formation of a German state and of a national cultural identity. Shakespeare was, after the rejection by neo-classical critics, a decisive influencing factor in the emergence of German culture in the second half of the eighteenth century. In the following decades there was an increasing tendency to assimilate and even appropriate the English dramatist for the German people, a process which was encouraged by the eagerly awaited translations by Schlegel and Tieck. Moreover, Shakespeare's name is often evoked in the nineteenth century with a remarkable degree of intimacy and gratitude, almost as if he were a living person, a phenomenon perhaps unique to his reception in Germany. Metonymy assumes a kind of personal presence as the English dramatist emerges among the Germans in a situation analogous to that of a foreigner among natives.

In the course of his migration Shakespeare becomes part of, or at least a desired part of, the German national culture, and as such a cultural phenomenon constituted by a number of components: by his works, their German translations, adaptations, by the visual representations of the author and of characters and scenes from his plays in paintings, comments in essays and literary texts, and, earlier than in Britain, as parts of school and university curricula. In the nineteenth century German writers came to believe that no nation understood Shakespeare better than the Germans and some even claimed possession of him as a national author ('our Shakespeare', 'unser Shakespeare'). In this context it is significant that on the occasion of the tercentenary birthday of Shakespeare, 1864, the first scholarly-cultural association devoted to him was founded in Weimar, not in Stratford-upon-Avon or elsewhere. It is also significant that this was twenty years before a society devoted to Goethe, considered to be the greatest German writer, was established in Weimar. Homage in the form of a Gesellschaft was paid to the 'immigrant'.

It is the aim of the present chapter to trace the inaugural steps in a development which led from Lessing's use of Shakespeare as a weapon against the dominant rule-based, neo-classical French concept of drama, to the creation of a 'German Shakespeare' by the famous translations of Schlegel and Tieck in the Age of Romanticism and to attempts to define Shakespeare as a German classic. The latter development culminated in the second half of the nineteenth century with endeavours to claim Shakespeare as a poet for the German people. The English author is seen as a kind of migrant naturalized and integrated into the nation's heritage in a process supported by spurious genetic, linguistic and nationalistic arguments (Dehrmann). The stages in the history of the German reception of Shakespeare are those of rejection (neo-Classicism), enthusiastic acceptance (pre-Romanticism), assimilation and identification (Romanticism) and attempts at conquest (later nineteenth century). If we look at Shakespeare as a kind of development agent who had a catalytic function in the rise of German literature and who by virtue of the Schlegel-Tieck translation gained the status of a German classic, we have to take into account that even before the mid-eighteenth century Shakespeare, or rather his works, or some of his works, had a presence in Germany.[1] In the seventeenth and early eighteenth centuries travelling English players – 'die englischen Komödianten' – toured the continent and performed his plays in a much simplified form. This exchange with the continent had begun during Shakespeare's lifetime, although his name never appeared on early repertory lists, reports and other documents. What happened here we might call a theatrical migration. The English actors, who had left their country for unknown reasons (evasion of competition, obstruction, or hope for a new market) soon came to present the plays in German and admitted natives to their ensembles, so that it is possible to speak of a sort of integration. In time, German actors took over, though the companies still called themselves 'English Comedians'. A kind of canon developed, centring on *Hamlet*, *Romeo and Juliet*, *A Midsummer Night's Dream* and *The Merry Wives of Windsor*.[2] The first Shakespeare performances in Germany can be dated back to 1626 at the court of Dresden. There is evidence that at this place (in the principality of Saxony) the troupe of the well-known actor John Greene performed *Romeo and Juliet*, *The Merchant of Venice*, *Julius Caesar*, *Hamlet* and *King Lear*. Since all beginnings are fascinating, it is worthwhile mentioning three remarkably early instances of German play-texts that can be related to works by Shakespeare. One of the first of Shakespeare's plays to be made known on the continent was the tragedy *Titus Andronicus*, probably because of the appeal of its revenge theme and the lure of its abominations and atrocities. Of this play there exists a German version – *Die Tragoedia von Tito Andronico und der hoffertigen Kayserin* (1620) – which is actually the first printed German translation or rather adaptation of a Shakespeare play (in Menenius; Erken 729) A completely different play to enjoy favour in Germany was *A Midsummer Night's Dream*. The artisans' scenes were extremely popular and were performed separately early in the seventeenth century. The original author of the adaptation was Professor Daniel Schwenter (1585–1636) from Altdorf. A play-text was produced by the eminent Baroque poet and dramatist Andreas Gryphius, printed only in 1658, under the title *Absurda Comica oder Herr Peter Squentz/ Schimpff-Spiel*. It is significant that the names of the characters were Germanized: Peter Quince, for example, becomes Peter Squentz. Another, arguably better-known German adaptation is a version of *Hamlet*, listed in the catalogue of the Library of Gotha under the title *Tragoedia Der bestrafte Brudermord oder Prinz Hamlet aus Dänemark (Tragedy Fratricide Punished. Or Prince Hamlet of Denmark)*, which aroused considerable interest for a time as it was believed to be a possible source for *Hamlet* (due to its affinities with the text of the First Quarto) or even for the dubious *Ur-Hamlet*. On linguistic grounds, scholars have dated the text to the middle of the seventeenth century (Schulze), although the earliest extant edition was published in 1790. The rediscovery of this play had an astonishing effect, characteristic of migratory processes in general. *Der bestrafte Brudermord* triggered considerable interchange between Germany and England. The German version of the play went through three editions, and the incredible number of six English translations as well as performances in both English and German in the twentieth century (Klein 137).

Shakespeare enrolled in the fight against classicism

As stated before, in the early history of the performances by strolling players of Shakespeare's plays in Germany, the name of Shakespeare is never mentioned, a situation which was to change radically in the eighteenth century. The name of Shakespeare had gained unparalleled prominence in England through the great number of performances of his plays featuring outstanding actors and actresses and in a steady flow of published plays, to which German critics and translators were to have access. It is one of the ironies of the German reception of Shakespeare, which coincided with the rejection of French rule-based poetics, that the high estimation of English culture in Germany first occurred under the hegemony of French culture (Willenberg 21). Shakespeare became central to a heated discussion on the relative worth of rule-orientated neo-classical poetics, with imitation as a basic principle, and a poetics advocating individual originality and freedom of the creative spirit. For the latter position Shakespeare served as an outstanding example. This conflict was later also carried out in France, via Schlegel and Madame de Staël, but without such far-reaching consequences for the literature and culture of the whole country as in Germany. As Coleridge had done in England, Germaine de Staël was influential in bringing German culture to the attention of the French. Daughter of the Genevan banker and later finance minister under Louis XVI, Jacques Necker, she was a great admirer of Schlegel who was undoubtedly the source of her interest in Shakespeare. The ideas in *De l'Allemagne* (1813), an extensive and pioneering literary and philosophical essay on the role of literature and national traditions in European societies, were to spread across Europe.

The most influential advocate of Shakespeare in eighteenth-century Germany was Gotthold Ephraim Lessing (1729–81), thinker, critic, dramatist, dramaturg and librarian. As one of the most important representatives of the Age of Reason in Germany, his reputation as an intellectual and moral authority still remains today. His dramatic works, among them *Nathan der Weise*, an impressive plea for religious tolerance, and *Minna von Barnhelm*, a great comedy dealing with honour and love, are hardly affected by Shakespeare, they are bourgeois plays in the best sense of the word, deeply rooted in Lessing's enlightenment frame of mind. Yet his pronouncements on Shakespeare played a major role in the second half of the eighteenth century. Unlike Johann Gottfried Herder, whose seminal essay on Shakespeare in *Von Deutscher Art und Kunst / Of German Character and Art* (1773) creates a theory of Shakespeare as a Northern dramatist and provides impressive original comments on several of Shakespeare's plays, Lessing does not discuss Shakespeare in an innovative way, nevertheless, he had a sense of Shakespeare's greatness as a dramatist and he took up arms against his detractors. With his *Seventeenth Literaturbrief* (1759), he became the most authoritative voice to propagate the English dramatist as a model and to reject neo-classical standards drawn from French rule-based poetics and promoted by the influential writer and theoretician, Johann Christoph Gottsched (1700–66). 'The *Literaturbrief* had told the world nothing about Shakespeare it did not already know, but it had effectively silenced the last authoritative anti-Shakespeare voice' (Paulin 2003: 90). To illustrate the asperity of the critical debate, it is necessary to quote Gottsched's criticism of Shakespeare's alleged disregard of the rules:

Die Unordnung und Unwahrscheinlichkeit, welche aus der Hindansetzung der Regeln entspringen, die sind auch bei dem Schakespear so handgreiflich und ekelhaft, daß wohl niemand, der nur je etwas vernünftigers gelesen, daran Belieben tragen wird. Sein Julius Cäsar der noch dazu von den meisten für sein bestes Stück gehalten wird, hat so viel niederträchtiges an sich, daß ihn kein Mensch ohne Ekel lesen kann. Er wirft darinnen alles unter einander. Bald kommen die läppischen Auftritte von Handwerkern und Pöbel, die wohl gar mit Schurken und Schlügeln um sich schmeißen, und tausend Possen machen; bald kommen wiederum die größten römischen Helden, die von den wichtigsten Staatsgeschäften reden; [...]

Blinn 62

(The disorder and improbability which arise from the disregard of the rules are so obvious and loathsome in Shakespeare that nobody who has read anything more reasonable will take pleasure in them. His *Julius Caesar*, which most people believe to be his best play, has so much that is so low that nobody will read it without disgust. He jumbles everything in it. There are silly scenes with artisans and a rabble who even throw about cudgels and rascals and perform a thousand antics, and then the greatest Roman heroes come on the stage, who speak of the most important state business.)

The acerbity of Gottsched's words may indicate that he knew he was about to lose the battle against the increasing number of Shakespeare's admirers in the German-speaking countries. Lessing dealt the death-blow to Gottsched's neo-classical poetics:

Wenn man die Meisterstücke des Shakespear, mit einigen bescheidenen Veränderungen, unsern Deutschen übersetzt hätte, ich weiß gewiß, es würde von bessern Folgen gewesen sein, als daß man sie mit dem Corneille und Racine so bekannt gemacht hat. [. . .] Denn ein **Genie** *kann nur von einem* **Genie** *entzündet werden* [. . .]

Lessing 500

(If the masterpieces of Shakespeare had been, with some modest changes, translated for our German people, I am certain it would have had better consequences than to make them acquainted so much with Corneille and Racine. [. . .] For a genius can only be ignited by a genius [. . .])

Lessing's arguments may not be new, but, together with Friedrich Nicolai, Moses Mendelssohn and others, he took a decisive standpoint against the principle of imitation, and the S*eventeenth Literaturbrief* gained – unlike the texts of Nicolai and Mendelssohn, who communicated with Lessing – a canonical status in the history of the German reception of Shakespeare. This may be attributed to the decisiveness and stylistic brilliance with which he rejects the imitation of French models and calls into doubt the authority of the last important opponent of Shakespeare: Gottsched. In so doing, he presents Shakespeare as the unsurpassable instance of genius with an outstanding capacity for appealing to the emotions. The opposition against imitation as a poetic principle, which amounted to looking at poetry as a teachable art, and the insistence on genius, as evidenced by Shakespeare, stimulating new geniuses, was widespread around the middle of the eighteenth century, as the following quotation from an anonymous writer's text, *Uebersetzung einiger Stellen aus Shakespears Richard dem III.* (1756), testifies:

Shakespear war zu groß, um sich unter die Sklaverey der Regeln zu demüthigen. Er brachte dasjenige, was andere der Kunst und der Nachahmung zu danken haben, aus dem Ueberflusse seines eigenen Geistes hervor. Man muß ihn unter die Anzahl von den Dichtern rechnen, welche man Erfinder nennt, und deren es vielleicht in allen Weltaltern und Völkern zusammen genommen, nicht viel über ein halbes Dutzend wird gegeben haben.

Quoted from Blinn 67

(Shakespeare was too great to humble himself under the slavery of the rules. He brought forth that which others owe to art and imitation, out of the abundance of his own mind. One has to consider him as one of those poets who are called inventors, and of whom there have been not many more than half a dozen in all ages and peoples.)

Germany here re-enacts or enacts on its own what happens in England at the time, for instance in Edward Young's essay *Conjectures on Original Composition*, which appeared in the same year as the *Seventeenth Literaturbrief* (1759).

In the first major stage of the reception of Shakespeare in Germany the English dramatist played an auspicious part in helping the Germans to find their cultural identity by casting off the yoke of French cultural dominance. As his *Hamburg Dramaturgy* (1767–9) shows, it was Lessing's intention to use Shakespeare to promote German theatre, which was sadly underdeveloped at that time. Lessing's prophecy that Shakespeare would be a catalyst for the German theatre, a genius kindling genius, was fulfilled.

Theatre: *Sturm und Drang*

Shakespeare was to be taken by storm by the members of the group of young writers called *Sturm und Drang* (*Storm and Stress*) of the 1760s and 1770s, German and Swiss authors, among them the young Goethe and Schiller in their first phase, who rebelled against classicist formal rules and the suppression of feelings and who championed freedom, self-expression and individuality. This cultural explosion coincided with the prose translation of Shakespeare's dramas by Christoph Martin Wieland (1762–6), discussed in this volume by Balz Engler, which was followed by other translations, most importantly by Johann Joachim Eschenburg (Zurich,1775–7). Eschenburg, who benefitted from the so-called 'Johnson's and Steevens's Edition' of 1773, was a philologically-minded scholar, whose learned annotations were partly included in the simultaneous French standard edition of Pierre Le Tourneur (1776–83). This is just one example of the enormous internationality of the preoccupation with Shakespeare in the eighteenth century, which was characterized by a free reciprocal flow of information. But to come back to the *Storm and Stress* Movement, although Wieland did not belong to the group of wild young men, his prose translation with its many poetic highlights contributed essentially to shaping the image the members of the movement had of Shakespeare and their own literary productions. Goethe's early historical drama *Götz von Berlichingen* (1773) and Schiller's *Die Räuber* (1782), which broke with practically all traditions and conventions of the theatre, would have been impossible without the discovery of Shakespeare. The first version of Goethe's *Götz* (1771) is so radical in its denial of established theatrical norms that Herder could say after reading this first draft: 'Shakespeare hat Euch ganz verdorben' ('Shakespeare has completely spoilt you') (quoted from Gray 58). The fact that Herder criticized Shakespeare's enthusiastic German followers for artistic lawlessness, does not contradict his profound veneration for the English dramatist and his attachment to Goethe and the other representatives of the

Storm and Stress Movement. In the above-mentioned essay on Shakespeare (1773) he refers to 'the *individuality* of each play, each single cosmos' ('Dies *Individuelle* jedes Stücks, jedes einzelnen Weltalls') and characterizes the poet's work as: 'A world of dramatic history, as immense and deep as nature; moreover the creator lends us eyes and a vantage point to see so immensely and deeply' ('Eine Welt dramatischer Geschichte, so groß und tief wie die Natur; aber der Schöpfer gibt uns Auge und Gesichtspunkt, so groß und tief zu sehen!') (Herder 86, 83). As far as Goethe is concerned, Herder and the young poet were connected by a deep friendship which was reinforced by their shared love for Shakespeare (Herder 93). At the end of his essay on the British dramatist Herder addresses Goethe personally, referring to their embracing more than once before Shakespeare's 'holy image' ('vor seinem heiligen Bild'). His argument is intricate. He speaks of Goethe's 'sweet dream, worthy of his self', of erecting Shakespeare's monument in the form of his *Götz* 'in our language'. It is not possible to exhaust the full potential of this passage, in which veneration of Shakespeare and intimate friendship go together with awareness of Germany's cultural situation. A German historical play (*Götz*) is here paradoxically conceived as a 'monument of Shakespeare from our age of chivalry in our language' ('sein Denkmal aus unsern Ritterzeiten in unserer Sprache'), meant 'for our degenerated fatherland' ('unserm so weit abgearteten Vaterlande') (Herder 93).

The most glowing document, though, recording the enthusiasm Shakespeare created at that time is the euphoric speech the 22-year-old Goethe delivered on the anniversary of Shakespeare's birthday in 1771, in which he said that 'the first page of his I read made me his own for life' and that 'when I was finished with the first play I stood like someone blind to whom a magical hand had suddenly given sight'[3] (Goethe 1963, 12: 224–5). A less exclamatory but equally passionate comment comes from the pen of J. M. R. Lenz in his *Anmerkungen übers Theater/ Annotations on the Theatre* (1774), in which Shakespeare's creation of a theatre for the whole world is praised and his capacity for convincingly representing people from all stages of society, an appreciation which flies in the face of the neo-classical rejection of Shakespeare's mixing low and high styles and characters from all ranks of society. Attached to Lenz's text is a translation of Shakespeare's *Love's Labour's Lost*. These are examples of the incredibly powerful impact Shakespeare was to have on German writers, because, unlike England or France in the eighteenth century, Germany could not rely on a comprehensive and deeply rooted national tradition of literature. With hindsight Lessing's axiomatic prophecy turned out to be true. But the indubitable fact that Shakespeare was and has remained an essential element in the context of the development and continuity of German culture cannot hide the fact that the strong identification of German culture in its formative stage with a dominant foreign force could also cause frictions and problems of identity.

Translation and naturalization

While the national element does not yet manifest itself in the German reception of Shakespeare in the eighteenth century, during which Germany joined the international republic of letters, the concern with the English poet became increasingly nationalized in the nineteenth century. In this process the romantic project of translating Shakespeare into German played a major role. The story of the so-called Schlegel-Tieck translation has frequently been told and its circumstances and peculiarities have been well researched. Only essential aspects will be mentioned here. Including preliminary work, the genesis of the project encompassed the years 1789 to 1833. Translators engaged in the project were August Wilhelm Schlegel, Wolf Heinrich von Baudissin and Dorothea Tieck. An indispensable manager and supervisor was Ludwig Tieck. He ensured the completion of the project by delegating five plays to his daughter, Dorothea, and thirteen plays to Baudissin. The real creative initiator of this first complete German verse translation of Shakespeare was Schlegel, who saw the need for translating Shakespeare in blank verse, after first attempts to use alexandrines. Schlegel had a fine eye for dramatic effects and succeeded in finding poetic equivalents to Shakespeare's specific linguistic creativeness. In particular he superbly used blank verse to render dialogue. The first plays to be translated, after careful methodical considerations and the production of samples, were *A Midsummer Night's Dream* (1795) and *Romeo and Juliet* (1796). The edition was published piece by piece, in the form of single-play editions and collections of groups of plays, before the complete edition appeared between 1830 and 1833.

Despite being a professional translator, Dorothea Tieck did not get much recognition for her work. Indeed, the name Tieck in the Schlegel-Tieck edition does not refer to Dorothea, but to Ludwig, who was important as an initiator of the project and as a reader, corrector and adviser. He did not do any translating, his daughter preferred to remain anonymous. She proposed a gendered view of the work of translation, which ties in with the stereotyped role of females prevalent at that time. In a letter to Friedrich von Üchtritz dated 15 July 1831 (Üchtritz 157), she said: 'Ich glaube, das Übersetzen ist eigentlich mehr ein Geschäft für Frauen als für Männer, gerade weil es uns nicht gestattet ist, etwas eigenes hervorzubringen.' ('I believe translation is really more a job for women than men, precisely because it is not permitted to us to produce something of our own.') In contrast to Schlegel's poetic aspirations she preferred a more literal approach in her rendition of the English original. In order to stress Dorothea's contribution to the project, it may be useful to list the plays she translated: *Macbeth*, *Cymbeline*, *The Two Gentlemen of Verona*, *Timon of Athens*, *The Winter's Tale* and two more plays she translated in collaboration with Baudissin, *Much Ado About Nothing* and *The Taming of the Shrew*. It is also noteworthy that the completion of the whole translation project lay in her hands.

Before going more deeply into the fundamental impact of the Schlegel-Tieck translation on the German reception of

Shakespeare, it is pertinent to ask what English text served as the basis for this translation. There is not much evidence, except for a remark Schlegel made in his 'Vorerinnerung' (a word which means something like 'pre-memory'), added to his translation of *Hamlet*, which was published in 1800: 'In Ansehung des englischen Textes habe ich mich hauptsächlich an eine Ausgabe: London 1786, gehalten, worin er aus der Malone'schen abgedruckt ist, zugleich aber auch die ältere von Johnson und Steevens zu Rathe gezogen' (Shakespeare 343). ('As to the English text, I mainly adhered to an edition of London 1786, which prints the text of Malone, but at the same time I also consulted the older edition of Johnson and Steevens.')[4] The matter seems rather complex, but one thing is clear: as had been the case with Wieland's prose version of 1762–6 and subsequent translations, Schlegel confirms he had free access to English editions. With the Schlegel-Tieck translation, which – in spite of a steady flow of translations that were to follow – continues to be venerated as a cultural asset and is still used in performances, the 'German Shakespeare' was created. The 'national' theme had manifested itself in Schlegel's 1796 article on Shakespeare in 'Etwas über William Shakespeare bei Gelegenheit Wilhelm Meisters' ('Something on William Shakespeare occasioned by Wilhelm Meister'), written before he began the translation. He emphasizes the special importance of Shakespeare for the Germans. The following passage is crucial to our argument:

> [. . .] *und man darf kühnlich behaupten, daß er nächst den Engländern keinem Volke so eigenthümlich angehört, wie den Deutschen, weil er von keinem im Original und in der Kopie so viel gelesen, so tief studirt, so warm geliebt, und so einsichtsvoll bewundert wird. Und dieß ist nicht etwa eine vorübergehende Mode; es ist nicht, daß wir uns auch einmahl zu dieser Form dramatischer Poesie bequemt hätten, wie wir immer vor andern Nazionen geneigt und fertig sind, uns in fremde Denkarten und Sitten zu fügen. Nein, er ist uns nicht fremd: wir brauchen keinen Schritt aus*

> *unserm Charakter herauszugehn, um ihn ganz unser nennen zu dürfen. Die Sonne kann zuweilen durch Nebel, der Genius durch Vorurtheile verdunkelt werden; aber bis etwa aller Sinn für Einhalt und Wahrheit unter uns ausstirbt, werden wir immer mit Liebe zu ihm zurückkehren.*
>
> Schlegel, A. W. 79

If we paraphrase Schlegel in English, he asserts that it would be legitimate to 'maintain that next to the English he [Shakespeare] belongs to no other nation in such a special way as to the Germans, because nobody reads and studies him so much and loves him so warmly and admires him with so much insight'. He continues, 'Shakespeare is no stranger to us. We need not take a step out of our character, to call him entirely our own.' The Germans, for whom Shakespeare had already in the period of *Storm and Stress* become, as Paulin puts it, 'a kind of national preoccupation' (Paulin 2003: 134), now set out to appropriate him. The process of Germanizing the English poet is taken to a point of identification by the German Romantics. Taking up ideas of his brother, Friedrich Schlegel applies the word 'German' ('deutsch') to Shakespeare: 'Among all romantic poets no one is as closely related to us Germans as he, no one is as to outer form as well as to inner spirit so entirely German as he' (Schlegel, F. 99–100). Such quotations prompt the question whether the act of appropriating a foreign author in the search for cultural identity should be called unlawful taking possession of him. In this context it is interesting to see how A. W. Schlegel deals with the 'Aneignung' ('appropriation') of Shakespeare in the twelfth of his *Lectures on Dramatic Art and Literature: Part II*:

> *Shakespeare ist der Stolz seiner Nation. Ein neuerer Dichter hat ihn mit Recht den Genius der britischen Inseln genannt. [. . .] Als eine bedeutende Ausbreitung seines Ruhmes dürfen wir wohl die enthusiastische Aneignung eines obgleich in der Fremde gebohrnen Landsmannes anrechnen, womit er in Deutschland aufgenommen worden ist, seit man ihn kennt.*
>
> Schlegel 1923: 23

This statement is hardly nationalistic. To paraphrase Schlegel's words again, he calls Shakespeare 'pride of his nation' and alludes to a 'recent poet' naming him 'the genius of the British Isles'. Yet he refers to 'appropriation' ('Aneignung') and speaks of the poet as a compatriot ('Landsmann'), who has been, 'though born in a foreign land' ('obgleich in der Fremde geboren'), received in Germany with enthusiasm. This looks almost like the idea of dual citizenship transferred to the realm of letters. Again, Shakespeare appears in the role of a migrant, an alien who has been accepted and integrated. It is significant that Madame de Staël, whose life Schlegel shared for several years as tutor of her sons, expressed the same idea, namely that Shakespeare translated and performed on stage becomes a fellow-countryman to a German dramatist like Schiller:

A. W. Schlegel has done a translation of Shakespeare which, joining exactness with inspiration, is completely national in Germany. English plays transmitted in this way are performed on the German stage, and Shakespeare and Schiller have become fellow-countrymen.

Paulin 2016: 311, De Staël vol. 18: 335

From Schlegel's enthusiasm concerning the appropriation of Shakespeare by the Germans the way may not be far to nationalism and overweening pride. L. Tieck contended that no Englishman, to judge from their printed works, has ever understood Shakespeare – 'kein gedruckter Engländer [hat] ihn je verstanden' (Tieck 159). That an Anglophobe, nationalistic attitude can also surface in Schlegel is shown in a letter to Tieck, referring to the book on Shakespeare Tieck was planning: 'I hope you will prove in your work among other things that Shakespeare was not an Englishman. How could he have arisen among the frosty, stupid souls on this brutal island?' ('Ich hoffe, Sie werden in Ihrer Schrift unter anderem beweisen, Shakespeare sey kein Engländer gewesen. Wie kam er nur unter die frostigen, stupiden Seelen auf dieser brutalen Insel?') (Lohner 23). This statement in a private letter may have been made in a jocular mood, but remains problematic. However, the nowadays abstruse idea of proving that Shakespeare was not English, was not rare at the time and needs to be seen in its immediate context. Tieck's remark on the defective understanding on the part of the English of their great national poet occurs in a letter which appreciates the achievement of A. W. Schlegel's translation, which had, so to speak, created Shakespeare anew, 'gleichsam neu erschaffen' (Tieck 147).

Translation and performance can, of course, follow different trajectories and in this respect Goethe's life-long concern with Shakespeare is illuminating. We have seen that as a young man Goethe in his speech on Shakespeare's anniversary delivered the most euphoric praise of Shakespeare ever to be formulated in a German text, and that his first dramatic efforts, with their total disregard of the established conventions of theatrical production, would have been impossible without the influence of Shakespeare. Much later, when he was engaged in the arrangement of Schlegel's translation of *Romeo and Juliet* for a performance at Weimar in 1812, he provided a version cleared from 'Fremdartigem' ('repugnant') and offensive details, i.e. coarse oaths, bold wordplay, lewd images, etc. (Heun). However, later he pleaded for a kind of translation which eschews adaptation and attempts to make the translation identical with the original, 'dem Original identisch machen' (Goethe, 2, 1965: 256). Goethe's treatment of *Romeo and Juliet* relates to the time and the circumstance of his adaptation: under the auspices of the Weimar court. How much Goethe was personally drawn to Shakespeare is manifest early in his career in *Wilhelm Meisters Lehrjahre* (1795–6), whose protagonist is, in many ways, a projection of the author. Wilhelm, who bears, not by coincidence, Shakespeare's Christian name, finds his identity through an intense involvement with the text and a performance of *Hamlet*. Goethe's most conspicuous personal devotion to Shakespeare is revealed in his poem 'Zwischen beiden Welten' ('Between Both Worlds', 1820), which celebrates the author's relationship to a woman, Frau von Stein, whom he had adored for a long time, and a poet (William Shakespeare), who had been his lodestar through all his life.

Einer Einzigen angehören,
Einen Einzigen verehren,
Wie vereint es Herz und Sinn!
Lida! Glück der nächsten Nähe,
William! Stern der schönsten Höhe,
Euch verdank ich, was ich bin.

Goethe, 1, 1966: 373

(To belong to a single woman, to revere a single man, how does that unite heart and sense! Lida, happiness of the closest nearness, William, star of the fairest height, I owe you what I am.)

Shakespeare does not appear here – in the context of this poem – as a poet of the past, whose works have been read in a book or seen on stage, but as an imagined presence, apotheosized as the metaphor 'star of the fairest height' indicates. Goethe parallels the German woman and the English poet as equally powerful in his life, though in different spheres. Shakespeare is even addressed by his first name, William, suggesting the intimacy of personal encounter. Metonymy as a shift from an author's works to his name here gains a life of its own; it grows into a quasi-personal identity, a phenomenon which also appears in a larger context, when Shakespeare is called 'one of us' by the Germans.

German Shakespeare

At the beginning of this chapter, the foundation of the German Shakespeare Society in 1864 was referred to as being well ahead of any other society devoted to Shakespeare. The pride or gratification that may be occasioned by this event is tempered by the sporadic and increasingly frequent emergence of a Germanized image of Shakespeare, which has recently been identified by Dehrmann both in the form of the tradition of a Proto-Germanic ('urgermanisch') and a naturalized Shakespeare ('eingebürgerter

Shakespeare').[5] Indeed, the speech made by August Koberstein on the occasion of the Shakespeare Festival in Pforta on 23 April 1864, and published in the following year as the first contribution to the first volume of the *Shakespeare-Jahrbuch*, 1865, provides evidence for Dehrmann's thesis: the two topoi identified by Dehrmann stand out conspicuously in this speech. The long and convoluted syntax is cut short in my following translation. Koberstein says, Shakespeare is 'no stranger to us'. He is 'more than any other could have become, a property of the German people, which England has to share with us'. We, the Germans, managed to 'naturalise and appropriate him completely in our literature and on our stage'. On account of his 'proto-Germanic nature' ('seiner urgermanischen Natur nach') and 'kinship with the German mind' he needed only to speak our language to exert an influence on the spiritual nature of the Germans, 'as if he had been born and raised in our country' (Koberstein 2–3). The quoted passage concludes with the statement that Shakespeare has ultimately gained presence in Germany as if he had been born in Germany (Dehrmann 29–30).

For the way Shakespeare was regarded in the mid-nineteenth century, Franz Dingelstedt, translator, man of the theatre and one of the founders of the German Shakespeare Society, who played a pioneering role in the tercentenary celebrations, used the term 'nostrification', 'Nostrifizierung', 'ganz unser machen' (Dingelstedt 58). Such statements, which occur quite frequently in nineteenth-century Germany (more examples in Müller 2007, Dehrmann), continue in the proprietary gestures made in World War I, such as the claim of the dramatist Gerhart Hauptmann that there is 'no nation, not even the English nation, that has, as the German nation has, acquired a right to Shakespeare' (Hauptmann xii). In the case of Hauptmann this is an isolated remark, which is belied by the generally 'pacifist and cosmopolitan tenor' of his speech (Höfele 3, n. 7), which calls Shakespeare the common 'treasure of humanity', almost anticipating Harold Bloom's *Shakespeare. The Invention of the Human* (1998). Hauptmann was soon to set his mind against the war. A great non-nationalistic teleological narrative written by Friedrich

Gundolf in 1911 is *Shakespeare and the German Mind* ('Shakespeare und der deutsche Geist'), portraying Shakespeare's inspirational power peaking in German Classicism and Romanticism. He celebrates Shakespeare as a powerful force contributing to the birth of German culture and assumes a symbiosis of Shakespeare and the German mind. For the rest of the century he diagnoses a decline. Another much-quoted remark comes from the pen of Ludwig Fulda (1916), translator, dramatist and propagandist, who speaks of the right of intellectual conquest and proposes that in the event of Germany's victory in the war Shakespeare would have to be handed over to Germany as part of the peace treaty. In the same year, 1916, the festschrift *A Book of Homage to Shakespeare* (ed. I. Gollancz) was published, to which German scholars were not invited to make contributions as a consequence of the war.[6]

Leading scholars like Roger Paulin (2003) and Christine Roger (2003, 2008) warn against the highly problematic assumption of a teleological, progressive development in the Germanization of Shakespeare, which leads from the late eighteenth to the early twentieth century. Indeed there is a contrary strand in the reception of Shakespeare which is wary of German usurpation. To invoke A. W. Schlegel once again, there is evidence that he should not be located in the philological tradition that tried to turn Shakespeare into a German as can be seen in the following quotation, which sets the two languages side by side as equally beautiful:

Doch zu so herrlichen Schätzen ist die englische Sprache der einzige Schlüssel; zwar nicht ein goldner, wie Gibbon mit Recht die Griechische Sprache nennt, doch wenn schon aus mehr gemischtem, gewiß aus eben so edlem Metall, als die unsrige.

Schlegel, A. W. 1796: 80

(Yet English is the only key to such glorious treasures; however not a golden one, as Gibbons rightly calls Greek, yet made of metal, though more mixed, which is just as noble as ours.)

It is also important to recognize scholars, described by Dehrmann as 'cosmopolitan' (27), who were cautious about monopolizing Shakespeare for Germany. Franz Horn, for instance, feared that the term nostrification could be misunderstood, proposing that the appropriation of Shakespeare ought to be widened to include all nations:

> *Wir wollen streben, daß Shakespeare ganz der unsrige werde; doch weil dieses Wort [Nostrifizierung] gemisdeutet werden könnte, auch gern hinzusetzten: daß wir ihn, wie sich ohnehin von selbst versteht, niemandem rauben wollen, ja daß wir sehr wünschen, alle Nationen möchten streben, ihn den Ihrigen nennen zu dürfen.*
>
> Horn 43

(We will endeavour to make Shakespeare altogether ours; but since this word [nostrification] could easily be misinterpreted, we freely add, which is in any case self-evident, that we do not want to steal him from anyone, indeed, that we wish very much that *all* nations should strive to call him their own.)

To conclude, the Germans' relation to Shakespeare is indeed a unique and remarkable phenomenon in the history of cultural appropriation. At the same time, the problematic nature of Shakespeare's appropriation in Germany, as this chapter has sought to demonstrate, ought to be recognized. So strong was the identification with Shakespeare at times that even a German disposition was accorded to him. Yet, his contribution to German literature and culture is inestimable. The English dramatist was admired and worshipped, and had an inspirational effect, releasing creative energies and helping to bring German literature into its own. Shakespeare was seen as a kind of integrated cultural migrant, a citizen by adoption. If this contribution has emphasized the German reception of Shakespeare, it should not be forgotten – as other chapters in this volume illustrate – that the German Shakespeare is a contribution to a general humanistic or European culture.[7]

Notes

1 For a useful, though uncommented, overview of Shakespeare translations see *Shakespeare in Europe*. University of Basel, Switzerland. English Seminar. 2007, https://shine.unibas.ch/translators.htm

2 Important comprehensive works are Brandt and Hogendoorn, Williams, Brennecke. A very useful brief account of early German Shakespeare adaptations is to be found in Klein (2011). For the English comedians in Germany see Haekel.

3 For part of the translation I am indebted to Höfele (5).

4 My attention was drawn to this quotation by Ina Schabert.

5 For the idea of a German Shakespeare see, among others: Blinn 64–5; Ledebur; Paulin 2003; Roger 2003, 2008; Habicht.

6 There is a rather generous article contained in the volume on German Shakespeare criticism from an English perspective by Herford, 231–5. For the context see Engler.

7 Schabert (2013) points out that it is necessary to look at the reception of Shakespeare from a European perspective. This is what the present volume attempts to accomplish in its entirety. I am indebted to her for reading an earlier version of this chapter and making valuable suggestions. Inestimable gratitude is owed to the editors of this volume.

References

Blinn, H., ed. (1982), *Shakespeare-Rezeption: Die Diskussion um Shakespeare in Deutschland*. Band 2: Ausgewählte Texte von 1741 bis 1788, Berlin: Erich Schmidt Verlag.

Brandt, G. W. and W. Hogendoorn, eds (1993), *Theatre in Europe: A Documentary History: German and Dutch Theatre, 1600–1848*, Cambridge: Cambridge University Press.

Brennecke, E. (1964), *Shakespeare in Germany 1590–1700*, Chicago: Chicago Press.
Dehrmann, M. -G. (2015), 'Urgermanisch oder eingebürgert? Wie Shakespeare im 19. Jahrhundert zum "Deutschen" wird' in C. Jansohn ed., *Shakespeare unter den Deutschen*, 15–31, Stuttgart: Franz Steiner Verlag.
Dingelstedt, F. (1858), *Studien und Copien nach Shakespeare*, Pest, Vienna, Leipzig: Hartleben.
Engler, B. (1992), 'Shakespeare in the Trenches', *Shakespeare Survey*, 44: 105–11.
Erken, G. (2009), 'Das Werk auf der Bühne' in I. Schabert ed., *Shakespeare Handbuch*, 5th edn, 696–752, Stuttgart: Kröner.
Fulda, L. (1916), *Deutsche Kultur und Ausländerei*, Leipzig: Hirzel.
Goethe, J. W. (1963–), *Goethes Werke*. Hamburger Ausgabe. E. Trunz et al. eds, vol. 10, Hamburg: Christian Wegener Verlag.
Gollancz, I., ed. (1916), *A Book of Homage to Shakespeare*, Oxford: Oxford University Press. Reissued by G. McMullan (2016), Oxford: Oxford University Press.
Gray, R. (1967), *Goethe. A Critical Introduction*, Cambridge: Cambridge University Press.
Gundolf, F. (1911), *Shakespeare und der deutsche Geist*, Godesberg: Verlag Bondi.
Habicht, W. (1995), *Shakespeare and the German Imagination*, Hertford: International Shakespeare Association, 1994.
Haekel, R. (2004), *Die Englischen Komödianten in Deutschland im 17. und 18. Jahrhundert. Eine Einführung in die Ursprünge des deutschen Berufsschauspiels*, Heidelberg: Winter.
Hauptmann, G. (1915), 'Deutschland und Shakespeare'. *Jahrbuch der Deutschen Shakespeare-Gesellschaft*, 51: vii–xii.
Herder, J. G. (2014), 'Shakespear' in H. Korte, ed., *Herder. Goethe. Frisi. Möser. Von deutscher Art und Kunst*, 69–94, Stuttgart: Reclam.
Herford. C. H. (1916), 'The German Contribution to Shakespeare Criticism'. In I. Gollancz, ed., *A Book of Homage to Shakespeare*, Oxford: Oxford University Press, 231–5.
Heun, H. G. (1965), *Shakespeares 'Romeo und Julia' in Goethes Bearbeitung. Eine Stiluntersuchung.* Berlin: Erich Schmidt.
Höfele, A. (2016), *No Hamlets. German Shakespeare from Nietzsche to Carl Schmitt*, Oxford: Oxford University Press.
Horn, F. (1823), *Shakespeare's Schauspiele. Erster Theil*, Leipzig: Brockhaus.

Klein, K. (2011), '*Romeo und Julieta*. A Case Study of an Early German Shakespeare Adaptation', *Shakespeare-Jahrbuch*, 147: 135–44.

Koberstein, A. (1865), 'Shakespeare in Deutschland. Rede zur Shakespearefeier in Pforta, Horden 23 April 1864', *Shakespeare-Jahrbuch*, 1: 1–17.

Korte, H. (2014), 'Nachwort', in H. Korte, ed., *Herder. Goethe. Frisi. Möser. Von deutscher Art und Kunst*, 166–213, Stuttgart: Reclam.

Ledebur, R. V. (2002), *Der Mythos vom deutschen Shakespeare. Die Deutsche Shakespeare-Gesellschaft zwischen Politik und Wissenschaft 1918–1945*. Köln: Böhlau.

Lessing, G. E. (1985), *Gotthold Ephraim Lessing: Werke 1758–1760*, G. E. Grimm, ed., Frankfurt a. M.: Deutscher Klassiker Verlag.

Lenz, J. M. R. (1774), *Anmerkungen übers Theater. Nebst angehangten übersetzten Stück Shakespears*, Leipzig: Weygandsche Buchhandlung.

Lohner, E. ed. (1972), *Ludwig Tieck und die Brüder Schlegel, Briefe*, München: Winkler.

Menenius, F. (1620), *Engelische Comedien und Tragedien*, Leipzig.

Müller, W. G. (2007), 'Formen der Aneignung Shakespeares in der deutschen Literatur- und Kulturgeschichte' in B. Engler and I. Klaiber, eds, *Kulturelle Leitfiguren – Figurationen und Refigurationen*, 115–31, Berlin: Duncker und Humblot.

Paulin, R. (2003), *The Critical Reception of Shakespeare in Germany 1682–1914: Native Literature and Foreign Genius*, Hildesheim: Olms.

Paulin, R. (2016), *The Life of August Wilhelm Schlegel. Cosmopolitan Art and Poetry*, Cambridge: Open Book Publishers.

Roger, C. (2003), 'Die Shakespeare-Rezeption in Deutschland (1815–1850): Verbreitung und Einbürgerung eines fremden Paradigmas'. *Recherches germaniques*, 33: 59–80.

Roger, C. (2008), *La réception de Shakespeare en Allemagne de 1815 à 1850. Propagation et assimilation de la référence étrangère,* Bern: Peter Lang.

Schabert, I., ed. (2009), *Shakespeare Handbuch,* 5th edn, Stuttgart: Kröner.

Schabert, I. (2013). *Shakespeares. Die unendliche Vielfalt der Bilder*, Stuttgart: Kröner.

Schlegel, A. W. (1796), 'Etwas über William Shakespeare bey Gelegenheit Wilhelm Meisters', *Die Horen*, 6(4): 57–112.
Schlegel, A. W. (1923), *Vorlesungen über dramatische Kunst und Literatur*, vol. 2. *Zwölfte Vorlesung*, G. V. Amoretti ed., Bonn/Leipzig: Kurt SchroederVerlag.
Schlegel, F. (1962), *Kritische Friedrich-Schlegel-Ausgabe*, Vol.11: *Wissenschaft der europäischen Literatur*, E. Behler ed., München: Schöningh.
Schulze, F. W. (1956), *Hamlet. Geschichtssubstanzen zwischen Rohstoff und Endform des Gedichts*, Halle: Max Niemeyer.
Shakespeare, W. (1891), *Shakespeares dramatische Werke*. Trans. A. W. v. Schlegel and L. Tieck. Ed. Michael Bernays. 2. Abdruck. Vierter Band, Berlin: Reimer.
Staël, Madame de (1820–4), *Œuvres complètes de Madame de Staël*, 19 vols, Brussels : Wahlen.
Tieck, L. (1948), *Kritische Schriften*. vol. 1, Leipzig: Brockhaus.
Üchtritz. F. (1884), *Erinnerungen*. Leipzig. publisher not known.
Wieland, C. M. (1762–6), *Shakespear: Theatralische Werke*. 8 vols, Zürich: Orell, Geßner und Comp.
Willenberg, J. (2008), *Distribution und Übersetzung englischen Schrifttums im Deutschland des 18. Jahrhunderts*. München: Saur.
Williams, S. (1990), *Shakespeare on the German Stage*. vol. 1: 1586–1914, Cambridge: Cambridge University Press.

3

Shakespeare at cultural crossroads

Switzerland

Balz Engler

'Where is my Switzers?' the King demands in *Hamlet* 4.5.97, in the only passage where the Swiss have managed to enter the world of Shakespeare's plays, typically as mercenaries in foreign service. The passage also shows that there was an – admittedly limited – notion of the Swiss even though Switzerland as a nation state only came into existence in the nineteenth century. Shakespeare entering this world was a complex international affair, a world that was hostile to the theatre but open to the kind of imaginative encounter made possible by print. Only later did the man of the theatre contribute, albeit indirectly, to shaping the nation as a cultural space.

Two episodes can be singled out in these first encounters: in the mid-eighteenth and in the early nineteenth century. They took place in two different contexts: as part of a poetological debate and as part of an attempt to forge a common culture, and they concerned two different media: as part of a literary culture and as a theatrical project. They will be discussed here in turn.

A cultural space?

'Swiss culture' is a challenging concept. According to the *OED*. culture may be defined as follows: 'The distinctive ideas, customs, social behaviour, products, or way of life of a particular nation, society, people, or period. Hence: a society or group characterized by such customs, etc' (*OED* 7.a.). The terms *distinctive* and *particular* in this definition draw attention to the fact that culture only becomes visible in comparisons, in difference. The features compared may vary but language and literature have traditionally been important factors. Migration between cultures, in translation, criticism or even the performances of touring companies highlight the differences between cultures and also lead to diminishing them. Taking these considerations into account, Switzerland, as we know it today, presents an interesting case: a small country, in which four languages are used in official life, three of them shared with large countries on which it borders, France, Germany and Italy. Two of these, France and Germany, were instrumental in the migration of Shakespeare to the Continent, receiving him in their own right (as discussed elsewhere in this book) but also serving as gateways to Romance and Eastern European countries.

It has, half-jokingly, been argued that Switzerland has only formed a coherent cultural space to the extent that its various linguistic communities do not want to be absorbed by their powerful neighbours. As we shall see, the diversity of the country has also meant that there is a constant need to re-affirm unity. The small size and the balance between unity and diversity have also meant that the country could serve, in Roger Paulin's apt words, as 'the great trade centre of three cultures' (Paulin 2007: 19), receiving and exporting cultural goods. Contacts with other cultures have always been close. As we shall see, this was also very much the case with Shakespeare.

Early encounters

The contacts between Britain and Switzerland had for long been close (Wraight), partly for religious reasons, especially among Puritans who were looking towards Swiss Protestantism, and, not least, Calvin's Geneva. During the reign of Queen Mary in England Swiss cities offered exile to English refugees. John Foxe, for example, wrote much of his *Acts and Monuments* in Basel and published its first Latin edition there (1559).

The first contact of a Swiss with Shakespeare is recorded in Thomas Platter's (1574–1628) account of his travels in England, where, in a passage well-known to Shakespeareans as the first eye-witness report of a performance, he mentions seeing 'the tragedy of the first Emperor Julius Caesar' 'in the house with the thatched roof' (Williams 166), i.e. the Globe. This encounter did not lead anywhere, and it may be considered significant that Platter does not mention the author's name.

When Shakespeare first crossed the borders of what became the Swiss Confederation in 1848, Switzerland was a loose assemblage of states collaborating in certain areas of shared interests. There was no capital (or even a court) that could have served as a cultural centre. In religion there was dissension: in the Catholic states there was a theatrical tradition often associated with the Church, while in the Protestant states, theatre was generally disapproved of. There were no standing theatre companies (Fehr). In major cities like Zurich and Geneva theatre was even banned.

It may therefore come as a surprise that Shakespeare first played a major role in Protestant Zurich, but it is also a useful reminder that Shakespeare's migration between cultures need not depend on the institution of the theatre. The interest in him grew out of a general interest in English culture which was particularly strong in the Protestant parts of Europe. In Switzerland this is documented, for example, by de Muralt's *Lettres sur les Anglois et les François* (1725) as well as the libraries of Laurenz Zellweger in Trogen and of the Basel theology professors Johann Grynäus and Johann Ludwig Frey (Küry 42). Shakespeare did not play a prominent part in these. Muralt, for example, mentions him once, as *un de leurs meilleurs anciens poètes* (one of their best old poets) (Muralt 31).

In Continental circles Addison's *Spectator* was avidly read in the early eighteenth century, after a substantial selection of its essays was published in French in 1716. As in England, it promoted a middle-class culture of sentiment and familiarized readers with English literature, especially Milton and Shakespeare.

Bodmer and the Marvellous

One of its readers was the Zurichois Johann Jakob Bodmer (1698–1783), who first came across it as a young man on a visit to Lyon in 1720 (Bircher 1968b: 60). He was also the first person in the German-speaking world documented, in his letters to Zellweger, to have read Shakespeare in the original in 1724 (Bircher and Straumann 8). Soon after he wrote a play the title of which suggests that it may have been in the Shakespearean style (*Marc Anton und Cleopatren Verliebung* [The falling in love of Mark Antony and Cleopatra], 1724/25); unfortunately it is lost (Bircher 1968b: 60). Later, in his more than fifty closet dramas, he freely plundered Shakespeare and other authors (Bircher and Straumann 47). Bodmer prepared a prose translation of *Johann Miltons Verlust des Paradieses* (John Milton's *Paradise Lost*) in 1732. Eight years later, in 1740, he published his seminal *Critische Abhandlung von dem Wunderbaren in der Poesie und dessen Verbindung mit dem Wahrscheinlichen* (Critical Treatise on the Marvellous in Poetry and its Relation to the Probable) in which he defended Milton's use of supernatural beings and figures from classical mythology in *Paradise Lost*, against their rejection by Voltaire and critics working in the French classicist tradition, specifically Johann Christoph Gottsched. Significantly, he included a translation of Addison's comments in *The Spectator* on the beauties of *Paradise Lost* in his treatise.

Bodmer did not publish any separate essays on Shakespeare. In his *Critische Abhandlung*, focusing on Milton, Shakespeare is only mentioned among others when he criticizes German readers:

> *Sie sind noch in dem Zustand, in welchem die Engelländer viele Jahre gestanden, eh ihnen geschickte Kunstrichter die Schönheiten in Miltons Gedichte nach und nach wahrzunehmen gegeben, und sie damit bekannt gemacht hatten, ungeachtet diese Nation an ihrem Saspar und andern, den Geschmack zu diesem höhern und feinern Ergetzen zu schärffen, eine Gelegenheit gehabt hatte, der unsere Nation beynahe beraubet ist.*

Bodmer [1740] 1966

(They are still in a state in which the English had lived for many years before astute critics gradually made them perceive and familiarized them with the beauties in Milton's poem even though their nation had had the opportunity to sharpen their sense for this higher and finer kind of enjoyment, in their Saspar and others, a sense of which our nation is almost totally deprived.)

n.p. Translation BE

Strangely, Bodmer uses the spelling 'Saspar' (and 'Sasper' in his 1741 *Critische Betrachtungen über die poetischen Gemälde der Dichter* [Critical Observations on the poetical pictures of the poets]). This is not a sign of his ignorance but rather of his European horizon: he obviously adopted the spellings from the Italian critic Antonio Conti who, introducing Shakespeare in the preface to his tragedy *Il Cesare* (1726), had written *Sasper è il Cornelio degl'Inglesi* ('Shakespeare is the Corneille of the

English', Conti 54–5). According to Paulin (19) it was Conti who introduced Bodmer to a non-rational aesthetic.

In his *Critische Betrachtungen* Bodmer approvingly summarizes Addison's argument for the Marvellous (Bodmer 1741: 593). Quoting Dryden's phrase of the 'fairy way of writing' Addison had written in *Spectator* 419 (1 July 1712):

> There is a kind of Writing, wherein the Poet quite loses sight of Nature, and entertains his Reader's Imagination with the Characters and Actions of such Persons as have many of them no Existence, but what he bestows on them. Such are Fairies, Witches, Magicians, Demons, and departed Spirits.
>
> Addison and Steele III, 570

Among English writers Addison mentions Spenser and Milton, but

> Shakespear has incomparably excelled all others. That noble Extravagance of Fancy, which he had in so great Perfection, thoroughly qualified him to touch this weak superstitious Part of his Reader's Imagination; and made him capable of succeeding, where he had nothing to support him besides the Strength of his own Genius. There is something so wild and yet so solemn in the Speeches of his Ghosts, Fairies, Witches, and the like Imaginary Persons, that we cannot forbear thinking them natural, tho' we have no Rule by which to judge of them, and must confess, if there are such Beings in the World, it looks highly probable they should talk and act as he has represented them.
>
> Addison and Steele III, 572–3

Early translations

Bodmer's promotion of Shakespeare led to important early translations, like Simon Grynäus' *Romeo und Juliet,* the first translation of a Shakespeare play into German blank verse, published in 1758 (Engler), and *Coriolanus* by Johann Jakob Kitt between 1767 and 1773 (Bircher 1968a). Johann Heinrich Füssli – yes, the painter, of whom more later – as a young man translated *Macbeth* and was planning a German version of *Julius Caesar*, both unfortunately lost (Bircher and Straumann 89). But the most important achievement was the first collected edition of Shakespeare's plays in German, prepared and published by Christoph Martin Wieland (1733–1813) in Zurich. He translated twenty-two plays, *A Midsummer Night's Dream* into verse, the others into prose, occasionally censuring passages he considered to be of bad taste.

To give just one example, which illustrates how Wieland cautiously moved beyond classicist taste: In *Romeo and Juliet*, 1.1.116–18, Benvolio tells Romeo's mother that he saw her son 'an hour before the worshipped sun / Peered forth the golden window of the east, [...]'. Wieland renders this, probably as better suitable to the context, simply as 'eine Stunde eh die Sonne aufgieng' ('an hour before the sun rose'), but adds a footnote, which offers a literal translation and the observation: 'Es ist nichts leichters, als durch eine allzuwörtliche Uebersezung den Shakespear lächerlich zu machen' ('Nothing is easier than to ridicule Shakespeare by too literal a translation'). But he goes on to defend Shakespeare against Voltaire's parody, 'eine Schulknaben-mäßige Nachäffung' ('a schoolboy-like aping') of *Hamlet* in his *Appel à toutes les nations de l'Europe des jugements d'un écrivain anglais* (1761).

Wieland chose prose for his translation, obviously not because he would have found verse too difficult but because he felt that 'the essential elements of Shakespeare's plays could be reproduced in prose' (Roger and Paulin 98). His edition was revised and completed by Johann Joachim Eschenburg (1743–1820) between 1775 and 1782, who had the new critical editions by Johnson and Steevens at his disposal. It was the Wieland/Eschenburg edition from which the writers of the *Sturm und Drang* came to know Shakespeare and which was commonly used in the theatre.

Bodmer's influence can be studied in two early Swiss reactions, which could not be more different from each other, the writings of Ulrich Bräker and the art of Johann Heinrich Füssli, better known in the English-speaking world as Henry Fuseli.

Bräker: among my saints

The Wieland/Eschenburg translation made the early encounter between Shakespeare and a rather unusual Swiss self-educated peasant and cotton pedlar possible: Ulrich Bräker (1735–1798), whose colourful autobiography is also available in English (Bräker 1970), began reading Shakespeare in 1777 in a library copy and wrote *Etwas über William Shakespeares Schauspiele* (Something on William Shakespeare's Plays) in 1780, the full text of which was only published in the nineteenth century (Götzinger 1877). In this little book he addresses Shakespeare like a fellow human being, using the familiar 'du', and briefly deals with all the plays he found in his edition, partly summarizing them, focusing on Shakespeare's genius in creating impressive characters and the affective reactions they call up. He says explicitly that his aim is not to write a critique of the plays, 'ich hatte pur allein die Absicht, aus allen Stücken des vortrefflichen Shakespeares etwas in ein Bändchen zu sammeln, was mir aus einem jeden das Schönste, das Angenehmste wär' (Bräker 1942: 145), 'it was purely my intention to collect in a small volume what I considered to be most beautiful, most pleasant in each play by the excellent Shakespeare'. As he puts it in his final, typically exalted remarks: '[I]ch zähle dich unter meine Heiligen und verehre dich in deinen Werken als einen Liebling des Himmels' (Bräker 1942: 143), 'I count you among my saints and revere you in your works as a darling of Heaven.'

He rarely disapproves of Shakespeare but interestingly does not share Addison's and Bodmer's understanding of the non-rational. He writes on the witches in *Macbeth:*

William, warum bringst du da in drei Hexen die halbe Hölle auf die Welt, das Scheußlichste, das ich in meinem Leben gehört habe? Ists dein Ernst, warst du nach der damaligen Moden auch so ein Hexenmacher? Nein, ich kanns nicht glauben, so ein Geist wie der deinige hat sich weit über diese Sphären erhoben, so ein Mann, der die große und kleine Welt uß- und inwendig kennt, bindet sich nicht an die allgemeinen Moden. Aber du wolltest den schrecklichen Aberglauben in einer ungeheuren Gestalt zeigen, der Nachwelt hinterlassen, welche gräßliche Phantaseyen die damaligen Köpfe beherrschten. [. . .] Pfui, fort mit den Hexen und ihrem schmutzigen Geköch. Wegen der Geistererscheinungen will ich ein ander Mal mit dir reden.

Bräker 1942: 73

(William, why are you bringing half hell into the world, in three witches, the most horrible thing I've ever heard in my life? Are you serious, were you also such a witch-maker after the fashion of the times? No, I cannot believe it, such a mind as yours has risen far beyond these spheres, such a man who knows the great and little worlds inside out does not conform to common fashion. But you wanted to show horrible superstition in a monstrous shape, to let posterity know which dreadful fantasies dominated the minds of those days. [. . .] Fie, away with the witches and their dirty cooking. As to the ghosts I want to talk with you another time.)

Fuseli: a Zurichois in London

Bräker seems to be caught in a pre-Bodmerian enlightenment position. Johann Heinrich Füssli (1741–1825), on the other hand, goes far beyond Bodmer, in his fascination with the non-rational. He was born in Zurich and was taught by Bodmer as a student of theology, training to become a Protestant parson. From Bodmer he learned to admire the works of Homer,

Dante, Milton and Shakespeare. Having exposed a case of corruption, he had to leave Zurich for Germany, working as a writer and translator. In 1765 he moved to London where, after a stay in Rome on the advice of Sir Joshua Reynolds from 1770 to 1779, he would eventually settle, becoming Henry Fuseli. It was only in London that his career as an artist took off. He became famous as a painter of mythological motifs and an illustrator of works of literature, largely by the same authors he had come to know through Bodmer.

Fuseli frequently turned to Shakespearean motifs, in particular he seems to have liked the witches in *Macbeth,* the fairies in *A Midsummer Night's Dream*, and Hamlet meeting the Ghost. In his eighty-five Shakespearean paintings, drawings, sketches and engravings (Licht) he abandoned rational reticence in setting the power of the imagination to work. His paintings became visions based on Shakespeare's text. They invoke intense moments, often of fear, with figures emerging from a black background into bright light (Kutha 51–4). Only a few early watercolours depicted theatrical performances. He had been impressed by Garrick's acting, and an early, rather conventional watercolour of 1766, now at the Zurich Kunsthaus, shows 'Garrick and Mrs. Pritchard as Macbeth and Lady Macbeth after the Murder of Duncan', Lady Macbeth taking hold of the daggers in Act Two Scene Two. When he painted the same moment in 1812, in 'Lady Macbeth Seizing the Daggers', now in the Tate Collection, the scene was not theatrical but entirely visionary – in a way that made him one of the great Romantic painters. His presentation of Shakespeare, though benefitting from Garrick's 'excellent imitation of the passions' (Knowles 39), seems to have remained rooted in reading his plays. On his 'Macbeth with the witches at the cauldron' (4.1), a scene he felt was lacking a sense of terror, he commented: 'I have endeavoured to supply what is deficient in the poetry' (Knowles 190).

Creating a cultural space

Shakespeare, the man of the theatre, arrived in Switzerland only later. As indicated earlier there were no standing companies in eighteenth-century Switzerland, and touring companies were not welcome in the cities, except in Catholic Lucerne. However, other forms of the theatre were advocated by enlightened citizens, forms that served the purpose of education and community building.

On the model of classical Greek theatre, the Genevan Jean-Jacques Rousseau developed, most prominently in his *Considérations sur le gouvernement de Pologne* (Reflexions on the Government of Poland, 1771), the idea of public occasions when communities would celebrate and re-affirm themselves, dramatizing heroic events from their own past (Stadler 74–6) – a genre that answered the needs of a nation as diverse as Switzerland. The form of theatre that eventually emerged from this was the *Festspiel* (Engler and Kreis). It has been defined as performances by the people for the people on public occasions recalling historical moments, preferably in the place of the occasion memorialized, using specially written texts and including singing and dance under an open sky (Stadler 74).

Theatre of this kind has not played an important role in the English tradition, the closest equivalent being perhaps the medieval mystery plays. Shakespeare's plays were obviously written for quite a different kind of stage, one that was professional and commercial. In the history plays, however, events from a shared past are presented, often raising political issues but not necessarily celebrating a heroic past. The possible exception is *Henry V,* presenting an ideal king, celebrating the collaboration of the nations on British soil and using epic features like the choruses.

While such ideas of a patriotic theatre were being discussed, invigorated by the French conquest of Switzerland in 1798 and the attempt to establish a centralized state, Friedrich Schiller in faraway Weimar was writing a play that was to suit such a programme, using elements like dialogue in blank verse, rapidly changing scenes, etc., as they had been adopted from Shakespeare's works on the German stage since the *Sturm und Drang* movement. The play, first performed in 1804, was *Wilhelm Tell*, set in central Switzerland. Goethe had become familiar with the story on one of his trips to Switzerland and had drawn Schiller's attention to it. As the Weimar theatre manager at the time, he supported Schiller in writing the play by staging Shakespeare's *Julius Caesar*, another play on the murder of a tyrant, in 1803, while Schiller was at work on his *Tell*. As Goethe wrote in a letter to Schiller on 2 October 1803: 'Ich will gern gestehn, daß ich es auch in dem Sinn unternahm Ihre wichtige Arbeit zu fördern' (Schiller-Goethe Briefwechsel), 'I gladly confess that I undertook it with the view of promoting your important work.'

In Switzerland Schiller's play did not seem to create much enthusiasm at first. As an anonymous critic put it in 1805: 'Es ist zu viel und zu wenig *Shakespearisch*, jenes in der Form, dieses im inneren Gehalt' (in Zeller 106), 'It is both too Shakespearean in form and too little in inner substance.' But already in 1807, which was then considered to be the 500th anniversary of the country, it was proposed that *Wilhelm Tell* should be performed at a national event in its original locations (Stadler 80). By the 1830s *Wilhelm Tell* had established itself as the standard national drama (Zeller 108–9). Performances of the play, in its entirety or in part, became a frequent feature of patriotic occasions, and it served as a model for other plays of a similar kind (von Matt 23), promoting and celebrating social unity on a national scale including all the linguistic communities (Zeller 110).

Shakespeare, as it were, had sneaked into Swiss culture in a circuitous fashion, twice and in different guises. He first entered Switzerland on the printed page, as part of a critical debate, riding on Milton's coat-tails, so to speak. This encounter, guided by the reading of the French translation of *The Spectator*, led to the first translations into German eagerly absorbed by the dramatists of the German *Sturm und Drang*. This happened under the conditions of the diversity and the international orientation of a small country. Exchanges therefore took place on a European scale, also including Italian criticism in the early days and English art later on. Shakespeare, the man of the theatre, only arrived later, indirectly via Germany this time, and answering specific political needs.

References

Addison, J. and R. Steele (1965), *The Spectator*, Oxford: Clarendon Press.

Bircher, M. (1968a), *Die früheste deutsche 'Coriolan'-Übersetzung: Ein Fragment des Zürchers Johann Jakob Kitt <1747–1796>*, Heidelberg: s.n.

Bircher, M. (1968b), 'Shakespeare im Zürich des 18. Jahrhunderts', in M. Bircher, F. Hafner and R. Zürcher, eds, *Geist und Schönheit im Zürich des 18. Jahrhunderts*: 59–104, Zürich: Orell Füssli.

Bircher, M. and H. Straumann (1971), *Shakespeare und die deutsche Schweiz bis zum Beginn des 19. Jahrhunderts: Eine Bibliographie raisonnée*, Bern: Francke.

Bodmer, J. J. ([1740] 1966), *Critische Abhandlung von dem Wunderbaren in der Poesie und dessen Verbindung mit dem Wahrscheinlichen: In einer Vertheidigung des Gedichtes Joh. Miltons von dem verlohrenen Paradiese*, Stuttgart: Metzler.

Bodmer, J. J. (1741), *Critische Betrachtungen uber die Poetischen Gemählde der Dichter*, Zürich: C. Orell und Comp.

Bräker, U. (1942), *Etwas über William Shakespeare's Schauspiele: Von einem armen ungelehrten Weltbürger, der das Glück genoß, ihn zu lesen*, Basel: Schwabe.

Bräker, U. (1970), *The Life Story and Real Adventures of the Poor Man of Toggenburg*. Trans. Derek Bowman, Edinburgh: Edinburgh University Press.

Conti, A. (1726), *Il Cesare*, Faenza: G.A. Archi.

Engler, B. (2007), 'Was bedeutet es, Shakespeare zu übersetzen? Die erste deutsche Fassung von *Romeo and Juliet*', in R. Paulin, ed., *Shakespeare im 18. Jahrhundert*: 39–47, Göttingen: Wallstein-Verlag.

Engler, B. and G. Kreis, eds, (1988), *Das Festspiel: Formen, Funktionen, Perspektiven*, Willisau: Theaterkultur-Verlag.

Eschenburg, J. J., ed., (1775–1782), *William Shakespear's Schauspiele*, Zürich: Orell, Gessner.
Fehr, M. (1949), *Die wandernden Theatertruppen in der Schweiz*, Einsiedeln: Waldstatt-Verlag.
Götzinger, E. (1877), 'Das Shakespeare-Büchlein des Armen Mannes im Toggenburg vom Jahr 1780: Nach der Original-Handschrift mitgetheilt', *Shakespeare-Jahrbuch*, 12: 100–68.
Knowles, J. (1831), *The Life and Writings of Henry Fuseli*, London: Henry Colburn and Richard Bentley.
Küry, H. (1964), 'Eine baslerische "Romeo und Julia" aus dem Jahre 1758', in E. Stadler, ed., *Shakespeare und die Schweiz*: 39–48, Bern: Theaterkultur-Verlag.
Kutha, R. J. (1997), ' "Un'oscura roccia nera e una tetra caverna". La libera interpretazione di Füssli dell'opera di Shakespeare', in F. Licht ed., *Füssli pittore di Shakespeare: Pittura e teatro 1775–1825*: 51–5, Milano: Electa.
Licht, F., ed. (1997) *Füssli pittore di Shakespeare: Pittura e teatro 1775–1825*, Milano: Electa.
Martineau, J., ed. (2003), *Shakespeare in Art,* London: Merrell.
Muralt, B. -L. de (1725), 'Lettres sur les Anglois et les François'. Available online: https://ebooks-bnr.com/muralt-beat-louis-de-lettres-sur-les-anglais-et-les-francais/ (accessed 23 December 2019).
OED, 'Oxford English Dictionary'. Available online: www.oed.com/ (accessed 23 December 2019).
Paulin, R. (2007), 'Ein deutsch-europäischer Shakespeare im 18. Jahrhundert?', in R. Paulin ed., *Shakespeare im 18. Jahrhundert*: 7–35, Göttingen: Wallstein.
Reifert, E. and C. Blank, eds, (2018), *Fuseli: Drama and Theatre*, Munich, London: Prestel.
Roger, C. and R. Paulin (2010), 'August Wilhelm Schlegel', in Paulin, R., ed., *Great Shakespeareans,* III: 92–127, London: Continuum.
Schiller, F. and W. v. Goethe, 'Correspondence between Schiller and Goethe: from 1794 to 1805'. Available online: https://archive.org/details/correspondencebe02schi (accessed 17 March 2019).
Shakespeare, W. (2014), *Hamlet*, Arden 3. London: Bloomsbury.
Stadler, E. (1988), 'Das nationale Festspiel der Schweiz in Idee und Verwirklichung von 1758 bis1914', in B. Engler and G. Kreis, eds, *Das Festspiel: Formen, Funktionen, Perspektiven*: 73–122, Willisau: Theaterkultur-Verlag.

Voltaire (1761), 'Appel à toutes les nations de l'Europe des jugements d'un écrivain anglais'. Available online: https://gallica.bnf.fr/ark:/12148/bpt6k1268592r/f6.image.texteImage (accessed 23 December 2019).
Von Matt, P. (1988), 'Die ästhetische Identität des Festspiels' in B. Engler and G. Kreis, eds, *Das Festspiel: Formen, Funktionen, Perspektiven*: 12–28, Willisau: Theaterkultur-Verlag.
Wieland, C. M. ed. (1762–6), *Shakespeare Theatralische Werke*, Zürich: Orell, Gessner.
Williams, C. (1937), *Thomas Platter's Travels in England*, London: Jonathan Cape.
Wraight, J. (1987), *The Swiss and the British*, Salisbury: Russell.
Zeller, R. (2013), 'Schiller-Rezeption in der Schweiz: Das Beispiel "Wilhelm Tell" oder wie "Wilhelm Tell" zum schweizerischen Nationaldrama wird', in A. Feler, ed., *Friedrich Schiller in Europa: Konstellationen und Erscheinungsformen einer politischen und ideologischen Rezeption im europäischen Raum vom 18. bis zum 20. Jahrhundert*: 103–20, Heidelberg: Winter.

4

Opening the book

The disclosure of Shakespeare in the Netherlands

Detlef Wagenaar

In his authoritative study *Shakespeare in Nederland* Robert H. Leek speculates on the possibility of a young William Shakespeare spending some of his 'lost years' in the Netherlands. After the assassination, in 1584, of Prince William of Orange, leader of the Dutch Revolt against Spanish rule, the young Protestant republic urged Robert Dudley, Earl of Leicester, to accept the title of Governor-General of the United Provinces and come to their aid. In the midst of his rather disastrous military campaign of 1586, on 23 April (St George's Day and presumably Shakespeare's twenty-second birthday), he held a banquet in Utrecht. In an account of the accompanying revels Sir Philip Sidney singled out 'Will, my Lord Leicester's jesting player' for particular praise for his performance in *The Forces of Hercules*. It is generally assumed that this Will was Will Kempe, who would rise to fame as an actor in the ensuing years before joining, along with Burbage and Shakespeare, the Lord Chamberlain's Men in 1594. Given the vicinity of Leicester's castle, Kenilworth, to Stratford-upon-Avon, where Lord Leicester's Men undoubtedly had performed, it is indeed a tantalizing thought that Shakespeare had perhaps joined the company and that he and Kempe had already been colleagues years before his emergence in the London theatres. The performance of Lord Leicester's Men at Utrecht may have been a singular occasion, but further cultural transference to the continent had started to develop during Shakespeare's lifetime. The pattern of theatrical migration in Germany described elsewhere in this volume can also be found in the Netherlands: English actors performed at fairs and festivals, developing a canon of their own which featured simplified versions of plays by Shakespeare as well as his contemporaries, eventually assimilating with local companies. English theatres were founded in Leiden ('Engelsche Schouwburg', 1638) and Utrecht (William Roe's company, 1645). The spectacular style of the 'Engelschen Komedianten' and their Jacobean treatment of text found instant favour with the Dutch public in many towns.

The literary establishment in Amsterdam, however, regarded this foreign competition with some suspicion, and succeeded for a long time in keeping them beyond the city walls. Literary life in the Low Countries, particularly regarding the theatre, was strongly determined by the 'Rederijkerskamers' (Chambers of Rhetoric), literary societies whose often dogmatic approach to drama was decidedly classicist. Good drama obeyed the rules and, in these revolutionary times, expressed the ideals of the young republic. Because most of its members were amateurs, the Chambers eventually fell into disrepute, but it should be noted that, at this point Holland was entering its Golden Age and was witnessing a flowering of high-quality drama and poetry, with Constantijn Huygens, Pieter Corneliszoon Hooft, Samuel Coster, Gerbrand Bredero and Joost van den Vondel as its major proponents – most of whom at some time had been members of a Chamber of Rhetoric. In most towns the Chambers were closely connected to the local authorities, often acting as a public relations office. This was certainly true of the main Chamber in Amsterdam, 'de Eglantier' (the Eglantine, the emblem of this Chamber). One of its members, the dramatist Gerbrand Bredero (1585–1618) had referred to the English actors quite favourably in his 1615 play *Het Moortje*, commenting on their singing, dancing and acrobatic skills whilst still acting out their parts – 'Sy spreeckent uyt haar geest'('they speak from the soul') – with great virtuosity (Leek 1988: 18). Two years later he followed his friend Samuel Coster when the latter left the Eglantier over artistic differences. Together with the great P. C. Hooft, they founded the 'Eerste Nederduytsche Academie' (the First Dutch Academy), which focused on offering better theatre than the dogmatic Chambers of Rhetoric as well as widening their scope to include the natural sciences and provide higher education for the general public. Ironically, the chairmanship of the Eglantier after the exit of these luminaries fell into the hands of the diplomat and playwright Theodore 'Dirk' Rodenburgh (1574–1644), whose dramatic convictions were certainly not strictly classicist. A former diplomat, stationed in London on behalf of the Hanseatic League, as well as a former envoy to the court of Philip III of Spain, Rodenburgh brought back outlandish tastes. He translated Sidney's *Defense of Poetry* and Thomas Middleton's *The Revenger's Tragedy* into Dutch – the latter work suggesting that he had visited Jacobean playhouses and had perhaps seen Shakespeare's plays – whilst in his own plays trying to emulate Lope de Vega's non-classicist approach. Whether Bredero's admiration of the English theatre tradition fuelled his disenchantment with the Chamber is another matter, but historians such as A. J. Worp have argued that the English companies provided an invigorating effect on the formalized, rather wooden theatre traditions propagated by the Chambers.

As Leek rightly points out, even at this early stage, 'the Netherlands were already plagued by an unfortunate distinction Shakespeare and his contemporaries were spared: that between highbrow and lowbrow culture. Highbrow was the classicist vein, which appealed to the young republic's craving for order and harmony and its Calvinistic sense of propriety' (Leek 1990). Generations of scholars have tried to detect Shakespearean influences in the works of highbrow dramatists such as Vondel, Bredero and Hooft – yet any similarities found usually go back to earlier sources which had been the inspiration of Shakespeare himself. Bredero's *Griane* (1612), for instance, bears some similarities to *The Winter's Tale* but derived its plot from the courtly romance of *Palmerijn van Olijve*. A play by Matthus Gramsbergen, *De Kluchtige Tragedie of den Hartoog van Pierlepon* (The Farcical Tragedy of the Duke of Pierlepon), published in 1650, is often noted as being an adaptation of the Pyramus and Thisbe episode from *A Midsummer Night's Dream*. The Pyramus and Thisbe story, however, appears in many different forms in Dutch literature of the age; direct influence by Shakespeare's play is therefore debatable. Likewise the story of 'Amleth, namaels Coningh van Denemarcken' in Belleforest's *Histoires Tragiques*, which had been translated as early as 1570, is more likely to have inspired *De Veinzende Torquatus* (The Feigning Torquatus, 1645) by Geeraert Brandt than *Hamlet* (Leek 1988: 21). Despite the close Anglo-Dutch relations in this period and the clear cultural influence that seventeenth-century Holland had in science, economics, politics, law, philosophy and the visual arts in Europe, drama seems to be exempted from this cultural exchange. The formidable poet, composer and statesman, Sir Constantijn Huygens the Elder (1596–1687) spent much time in London, was knighted by James I, befriended John Donne and even translated some of his poems, yet the name Shakespeare does not appear in his archives. His eldest son, Constantijn Jr (elder brother of the famous scientist Christiaan), however, was known to own a copy of Shakespeare's first folio during his time in England as secretary to King William III.

It is safe to assume that any influence Shakespeare might have had on Dutch drama came from below, without naming the author, via those strolling English players who contributed to a more lively theatre culture in the Netherlands. Following this line of influence there are two instances in which a Dutch play can be linked to Shakespeare and in both cases the name of actor and playwright Ariaen (Adriaen) van den Bergh (1595?–1652?) is relevant. Van den Bergh was a member of the Chamber of Rhetoric in Utrecht, who had worked closely with the English companies and whose daughter Ariane would become the first professional actress in the Netherlands. In 1654 she would play the lead role in *De Dolle Bruyloft* (The Madcap Wedding), written by travelling actor Abraham Sybant, who had toured Europe with William Roe. His play is a faithful, although slightly abridged, translation of *The Taming of the Shrew*, conventionally written in stately alexandrines.[1] The title page does not acknowledge the source, the play was staged at the Amsterdam Civic Theatre, but was not a great success. It folded in 1656; in the intervening year Sybant had died at the age of twenty-eight. Several decades earlier, in 1621, Ariaen van den Bergh had written an adaptation of *Titus Andronicus* of which, unfortunately, no copies have survived – as opposed to his play *Don Jeronimo*, published in the same year, an adaptation of Thomas Kyd's *The Spanish Tragedy* (which had been performed in Utrecht by John Greene the year before). Given his network, it is likely that he was inspired by performances by English actors to adapt this popular revenge tragedy – alternatively he could have obtained an early copy of the German adaptation of Robert Browne and John Greene's performance, *Die Tragoedia von Tito Andronico und der hoffertigen Kayserin*, which was published in 1620. Either this German adaptation, or more likely Van den Bergh's play, would in turn, inspire one of the most commercially successful plays of the seventeenth century: *Aran en Titus* by Jan Vos.

The poet and playwright Jan Vos (1610–67) was a glass maker by trade and, through his close connections to the rich and powerful in Amsterdam, an influential figure in public life. He wrote *Aran en Titus of Wraak en Weerwraak* (Aran and Titus, or Revenge and Retaliation) in 1638 and staged the play for the first time in 1641. The play was an instant success, and in 1647 Vos became one of the directors of the Theatre of Van Campen, the first city theatre in Amsterdam, a function he held for nearly twenty years. Vos knew what the public wanted and he experimented with special effects, spectacular stage sets and *tableaux vivants*. Apart from producing his own plays Vos directed many of Vondel's tragedies and designed floats for public festivities, the most notorious of which took place in 1660. It was performed in honour of the widow of stadtholder William II of Orange, Mary Stuart, the eldest daughter of Charles I, and featured an all too lively *tableau vivant* of her father's execution. According to contemporary reports the princess fell into a swoon; Vos, who led the parade himself on horseback, endured severe public condemnation for this performance. In 1665 the Amsterdam Theatre underwent a drastic renovation under his directorship for the enormous sum of 36,000 guilders, to accommodate these spectacular and lavish performances. *Aran en Titus* was an immediate success and remained popular for over eighty years; the publication went through more than thirty editions and the play was one of the most successful of the century. In terms of cruelty, Vos's play 'out-horrors' Shakespeare – the grand finale, for instance, focuses on Aran (Aaron) being roasted over a fire on stage, after first witnessing the brutal murder of his infant child, instead of being sentenced to death. The form in which he poured these atrocities was consistent: although he defied decorum, Vos obeyed the classicist rules of unity of time, place and action and the entire play is written in alexandrines, the preferred metre of his great contemporaries. It is his poetic prowess which earned him the immediate endorsement from a prominent figure in Dutch intellectual life, the humanist, theologian, historian and poet Caspar Barlaeus (van Baerle) (1584–1648). Barlaeus was immediately struck by the power of *Aran en Titus*, watched the play seven times in a row and urged his friends, among whom were Huygens, Hooft and Vondel, to see it. Vos was accepted into the most famous literary coterie of its day, the Muiderkring, and is one of the few dramatists to bridge the gap between high and low culture.

The backlash set in shortly after Vos's death in 1667. Following the example of the Académie française, an intellectual society, *Nil Volentibus Arduum* ('nothing is arduous for those who are willing'), was founded in Amsterdam in 1669. This short-lived society organized frequent lectures on scientific and artistic topics, and their series of lectures on dramatic poetry often focused their criticism on the Amsterdam Theatre. Their criticism was fuelled by a sense of Calvinist propriety. They disapproved of violent spectacles in the theatres, the questionable moral standards of the plays – singling out Vos in particular – and of the use of biblical themes and the discussion of political controversies in drama – specifically targeting Joost van den Vondel (who had already been regarded with suspicion since his conversion to Catholicism). In literary terms these critiques were supported by neo-classicist ideas. The society incorporated the modern interpretation of Aristotle's *Poetica* by Pierre Corneille, as exposed in his famous 'Discours sur le poème dramatique' which accompanied his collected works, directly in their lectures and referred to his sharp distinction between the dramatic genres, the strict observance of the unities of time, place and action and the notions of *vraisemblance* (credibility) and *bienséance* (propriety). It is true that the society's influence was limited to a small section of the theatrical world, but this adaptation of French neo-classicism became the most dominant influence on Dutch literature until well into the nineteenth century. However, as Stijn Bussels points out, these ideas were not new to the Republic. The Dutch humanists, Daniel Heinsius and Gerardus Vossius, had written extensively on the poetics of Aristotle and Horace; in his preface to *Le Menteur* (1644) Corneille himself acknowledges 'the celebrated Heinsius who not only translated Aristotle's *Poetica* but also wrote a treatise on the constitution of tragedy' (Bussels 322).

By the beginning of the next century the above-mentioned doctrines had become dogma. The Senecan revenge tragedies of Vos were dismissed on these grounds by the Dutch critic, Justus van Effen (1684–1735) in the *Journal Littéraire de la Haye*, the same periodical which featured the first critical essay on

Shakespeare on the continent – by the same author, in 1717. Van Effen has earned his place in the annals of Dutch literary history as the main exponent of eighteenth-century journalistic prose, published in his highly influential and often imitated journal, *De Hollandsche Spectator* (1731–5). From 1711 onwards Van Effen had worked on five different francophone journals, trying to emulate the works of Addison and Steele, yet it was his final effort, *De Hollandsche Spectator*, which would become his greatest success. As editor and major contributor he filled this periodical with social commentaries (in particular satirizing Dutch bourgeois mores), moral and cultural teachings and didactic literature. The tone in *De Hollandsche Spectator* is more didactic; Van Effen was convinced that in matters cultural the Dutch reading public was in dire need of education. His previous forays in French had a more cosmopolitan focus, particularly in terms of literary criticism; in his discussions of English literature he acted as an intermediary between the two literatures, arguing that as a neutral critic, not hindered by nationalist partiality, he would be able to bring the best of both worlds together. This focus on the international literary field had not come completely by choice. Literary ambition had been sparked off at an early age, but as an officer's son of limited means without connections in the Dutch literary field Van Effen's options were limited. Forced to quit university after his father's death he started working in The Hague as a tutor for various diplomatic families. Within these circles the language of choice was French; moreover, Van Effen moved easily within the network of French Huguenot refugees and expatriate journalists who had come to the Netherlands after the repeal of the Edict of Nantes. In 1715, during his employment as a tutor in the family of the Dutch envoy to King George I, he met Alexander Pope and Isaac Newton, became a member of the Royal Society and translated Defoe's *Robinson Crusoe* and Swift's *A Tale of a Tub* into French. His 'Critique de Shakespear' is part of an extensive essay on English letters, his 'Dissertation sur la Poësie Angloise', judged 'of paramount importance for the spread of English Literature' since it was 'virtually the only source of detailed information' until Voltaire's *Lettres* (Pienaar 213). Van Effen spends as many pages (ten) on Shakespeare as he does on Milton, whose *Paradise Lost* is dealt with in detail and receives high praise. With Shakespeare, however, Van Effen clearly has difficulties.

He opens his review by describing how Shakespeare is still held in the highest regard by his countrymen, despite his many faults. 'We agree that he did not observe the rules, but we forgive him, like a genius above the rules', adding that 'as he wrote, so to speak, at random, he caught inimitable traits from time to time, but often they were accompanied by things so ignoble, that one can doubt if in his writings baseness raises the sublime, or if it is the sublime which makes the baseness felt more strongly' (translation my own). Van Effen visibly struggles with how to frame his criticism: without adhering to the rules that define a tragedy one cannot describe a work as a tragedy – yet these tragic histories, as they are often termed, were meant for the stage. Van Effen states that Shakespeare has not imitated anyone, drawing from his own imagination, yet fails to structure these original and profound ideas. The blatant disregard for the unity of time (there are plays that encompass 'almost an entire lifetime of his heroes'), the unity of place ('his characters flutter from East to West, the audience is forced to follow characters in different parts of the world') but most of all disregard ... for unity of action (the wilful insertion of comic scenes at the high point of tragedy, 'sometimes so ridiculous that they would hardly be serious enough for the Italian theatre'), leave him astonished. *Hamlet* in particular is singled out for violating these rules. Van Effen is scornful of the gravediggers' scene – in particular the bawdy songs and 'nonsense' conversation between Hamlet and the gravedigger, deploring the fact that Shakespeare gave in to the perverse impulse to load bland jokes on an audience ready to 'breathe sighs and shed tears' with the hero on finding out that his mistress was dead. The appearance of the ghost of Hamlet's father is likewise ridiculed as a childish scene which tradition wrongfully tells us to admire: 'Either Shakespear (*sic*) was superstitious, or he had to appear to please the people of his time apparently imbued with these foolish notions'. According to Van Effen, what is good or even excellent in his work is drowned in infinite nonsense: 'le tout paroît plutôt la production d'un cerveau déréglé que d'un génie de premier ordre' ('the whole thing appears to be the product of a deranged brain rather than of a genius of the first order').

Two other plays are discussed by Van Effen: *Richard III* and *Othello*. The history play is rated even less than *Hamlet* – Van Effen seems to be at a loss when confronted with Act Five, Scene Three, where the ghosts of Richard's victims address both the king and Richmond in different locations. He does acknowledge the feat of a single writer in dramatizing the entire history of England – although he mistakenly believes that Shakespeare had dealt with the entire history since the reign of William the Conqueror until his own time – and applauds his diligence, but then it 'is true that when one writes without rules, and by giving free rein to one's imagination, one can write a lot'. His discussion of *Othello* is slightly puzzling; after giving an extensive and not very economical account of the plot, Van Effen argues that further criticism is not necessary as the sins speak for themselves. Presumably his sense of decency is strongly offended, which leads to a discussion of the inherent sense of cruelty, blood-thirstiness and melancholia which appears to be so ingrained in English drama. On the whole Van Effen prefers the contemporary English dramatists, who at least try to rein in their 'bubbling imaginations' with a stricter sense of decorum. It could be argued that devoting ten pages to Shakespeare is some form of recognition, and Van Effen does acknowledge the boldness of the playwright's poetic vision. At the same time the critique makes awkward reading; it is clear that Van Effen is bewildered by the fact that this flawed genius is idolized by the contemporary authors he himself admires – in particular Joseph Addison. Pienaar rightly states that 'Wherever Addison and his work are mentioned, Van Effen prostrates himself', and the *Dissertation* is no exception (Pienaar 223). Van Effen did not mention Shakespeare in *De Hollandsche Spectator*, but he did mention Addison. In

1725 the entire run of *The Spectator* was translated into Dutch by Pieter Leclerq, who dutifully also translated the various passages quoted from Shakespeare in these journals, Hamlet's famous soliloquy being one of them. It is in this indirect way that Shakespeare's works enter Dutch literary culture in the eighteenth century. As important as Van Effen's 'Critique de Shakespear' is for the international field, its role in the migration of Shakespeare in the Netherlands is debatable, as it was clearly not written for a Dutch audience.

It is worth noting that Van Effen's major competitor in the Dutch periodical field, Jacob Campo Weyerman (1677–1747), is the first to reflect on Shakespeare in Dutch. As opposed to the serious moralist Van Effen, Weyerman adopted a lighter satirist's tone in his writings; his appraisal of Shakespeare is also quite positive. He was thought to be the son of one of William III's officers and had presumably seen some of Shakespeare's work on stage in England. He stated in one of his rambling contributions to his journal *Den Rotterdamschen Hermes* in 1721:

De Engelsen hebben een Shakespeer gehad, die wonderlijke treurspelen heeft voortgebragt: Macbeth, Othello en diergelijke, welke zonder de feil bloed op het tooneel te storten, onweêrgadelijk zijn en nog hedendaagsch door verdienstige acteurs in d'uyterste volmaaktheid uitgevoerd worden.

Leek 1988: 27

(The English have had a certain Shakespeare in their midst, who produced wonderous tragedies: such as *Macbeth, Othello* and more, which, without spilling swabs of blood on the stage, are incomparable and are to this day still performed by accomplished actors to the utmost perfection.)

André Hanou has pointed out that this is not the only reference to Shakespeare in Weyerman's writings, but all of them are anecdotal, not critical. Weyerman's small endorsement is not much of a counterpoint to the various descriptions that invariably followed Van Effen's line. In terms of philosophy and culture Dutch intellectuals looked towards France, so when the great Voltaire denounced Shakespeare in his famous 'Lettre à l'Académie Française' (Paris, 1776) the matter was settled. In his 'Over de smaak van de poezij' (1780) (about poetic taste), J. D. Macquet, doctor, mayor of Zierikzee and literary critic, contrasted the fine sensibility of classicist French drama favourably with the low, cruel plays of the English, in which he saw similarities with the by now old-fashioned Vos:

Jan Vos komt zeer veel overeen met den Engelschen Dichter Shakespeare. Daer zijn zeer goede sentimenten in hunne stukken, daer is veel en sterk Pathetiek in, doch alles ligt begraven ondereen' mesthoop van lage, laffe, onbetaemlijke straettael.

Pennink 130

(Jan Vos is very much like the English poet Shakespeare. There are very good sentiments in their plays, with strong pathos, yet everything is buried under a dunghill of low, craven, unseemly street-jargon.)

Macquet continues by comparing both poets to incompetent cooks: their dishes have good ingredients, but the food is burned, tastes of smoke and has a bad sauce; no one of refined taste would want to eat it. This quotation is a good example of the notion of unseemliness and impropriety which colours descriptions of Shakespeare's work. As late as 1833, the Dutch playwright, Samuel Wiselius, astounded by the German veneration for Shakespeare, which was by that time inspiring Dutch authors to translate Shakespeare's plays, argued that the treasure house containing the precious poetic gems of this 'beggarly figure in rags, not fit to sit at your dinner-table' could only be reached by wading through 'pigsties, middens and muck-filled gutters' (Pennink 185).

It is explicitly against this attitude that Laurent van den Bergh (1805–87) reacted when he published an anthology of Shakespearean verse in 1835. Van den Bergh had selected and translated, in verse, famous scenes from sixteen of Shakespeare's plays, focusing on the highlights, for which he provided the necessary context. He referred in his introduction to the insights of Goethe, Herder and Schlegel to convince the Dutch reading public of Shakespeare's great moral, dramatic and philosophical genius. Taking note of the changing attitude to French classicism in Germany, Van den Bergh is the first Dutch critic to emphatically break with French tradition. This process was slow because the Netherlands lacked the type of Romantic movement which turned out to be so essential for the appreciation of Shakespeare across Europe. For years, Romanticism in the Netherlands remained a rather tepid affair – despite the popularity of foreign poets such as Byron, Goethe and Schiller. Dutch poets of the period remained reserved, rational, preferring the pastoral over the sublime; even the most Byronic figure in Holland, Willem Bilderdijk, remained a classicist at heart: extolling Shakespeare's poetic genius, yet bewailing his violations of the rules. Decades later a private teacher from Amsterdam, inspired by the ideas of Goethe, Hazlitt and Coleridge, would express his creed that in order to achieve a greater truth the classicist rules could and should be broken. His name was Abraham Seyne Kok (1831–1915), and he would produce the first complete prose translation of Shakespeare's plays in 1880. Kok was a self-taught literary scholar who had already translated Dante's *Divina Commedia* and had witnessed performances of the legendary Shakespeareans Samuel Phelps and Edmund Kean in London (Leek 1988: 78). In 1860 he wrote a verse translation of *As You Like It*, titled *Orlando en Rosalinde* in Dutch, quickly followed by verse translations of *Hamlet* (1860) and *Richard III* (1861) – the latter was staged twice in Amsterdam in 1864 and all three plays were published in annotated editions by A. C. Kruseman. When the Amsterdam-based publisher Funke took over this project he asked Kok to write prose translations

of all the works (as well as urging him to bowdlerize some of
the passages which were likely to offend). Kok still preferred to
use iambic verse whenever he could, and his prose translations
have a directness which, compared to his competitors, made
them very accessible. Funke's rather shoddy editions, the first of
which appeared in 1873, were cheaply printed, with only the
minimum of annotations, and did not succeed in winning the
public's favour (Leek 1988: 18). Within a few years the public's
attitude would have changed completely.

If one had to pick a date when William Shakespeare is finally
accepted, assimilated and appropriated into the Dutch cultural
consciousness, it would have to be 1888. It was in that year that
the Leiden publisher E. J. Brill published, in twelve lavish
volumes, Dr L. A. J. Burgersdijk's translation of the complete
works – plays, narrative poems and sonnets – in verse. Leendert
Alexander Johannes Burgersdijk (1828–1900) was born in
Alphen aan de Rijn and studied medicine and later biology at
Leiden University, where he received his PhD. He set out for an
academic career, produced scientific publications and textbooks,
but, despite his many efforts, never succeeded in obtaining a
professorship at one of the Dutch universities. He was employed
as a professor of Natural History at the Royal Military Academy
(KMA) in Breda until 1864, when he moved to Deventer to
teach at the new Hogere Beroeps School (HBS) where he
fulfilled the function of director between 1866 and 1876. The
HBS was a new type of vocational secondary school which had
been founded in 1863 by the Dutch government as part of their
educational reform. As a preparation for college it provided an
alternative to the more elitist Latin schools which prepared for
a classical university education and was instrumental in
increasing the percentage of higher educated, middle-class
readers who, incidentally, would make up a large part of
Burgersdijk's future audience. In January 1877 Burgersdijk
witnessed a performance at the Deventer theatre of *Othello* by
the famous Italian actor Ernesto Rossi, at that time on tour in
Europe. When he returned home late at night after Rossi's
performance, he took his volume of the collected works of

Shakespeare – in all likelihood the English text edition with German annotations by the great Shakespeare scholar, Nicolaus Delius – and started leafing through it. On reading the opening scene of *Twelfth Night* he was struck by the fact that he immediately saw a way of translating it into Dutch, whilst retaining its poetic properties. He started translating this play on 9 February; by 1885 he had translated all the plays; the sonnets and the narrative poems were ready by 1887. Johan Herman Rössing, secretary of the 'Vereeniging Het Nederlandsch Tooneel' (The Dutch Theatre Company), commented on his monomania and recalled how 'Time and place no longer mattered to Burgersdijk: many a night passed without any rest. Shakespeare compensated his sleep' (Rössing 1900: 111). His daughter remembered how a guest in their house had heard him recite verses late at night when she was going to sleep, only to find, when waking up the next morning, that she still heard those same noises, realizing that 'father had spent the entire night reading out verses'.

As this last anecdote illustrates, Burgersdijk paid great attention to how the Dutch verses would sound. When the meaning was clear he started to adapt the drafted text by ear before consigning the final version to the right-hand pages of his meticulously neat clothbound notebooks – leaving the left-hand page for future comments, alternatives and, eventually, drafts of stage notes for theatre companies. In his translations he shows a keen awareness of the psychological and dramatic implications of Shakespeare's use of metre – as well as a determination to preserve this aspect of the original. In this respect alone his translations are unprecedented and unparalleled. Burgersdijk approached the project with scientific discipline: throughout his lifetime he never stopped collecting books about Shakespeare, corresponding with other experts, also from England and Germany, and comparing texts, building on his encyclopaedic knowledge, which, according to one of his former students, he could draw from at the slightest hint. Initially he set out to glean the meanings of puns, references, metaphors, idioms etc. as completely as possible and find the best fitting option or alternative, always providing notes to explain the choices he made. As a classically schooled academic Burgersdijk would probably not have had any formal education in English, which was not part of the school curriculum in his youth – his command of the language is generally thought to be self-taught. Astounding as this sounds, it could also have been an advantage. Modern Dutch differs significantly from English as it undergoes spelling reforms every few decades; compared to Shakespeare the classic Dutch dramatists of the seventeenth century have the disadvantage that the orthography of their works seems almost alien to us now. Although he did use modern spelling, Burgersdijk's use of words and syntax seemed archaic even in his own time. Studying the classics, he would draw on a wealth of forgotten words to find the right nuance in his translations, whilst opting in his syntax for ancient contractions as well as case and gender inflections, which, at that time, were actually disappearing in modern Dutch. Burgersdijk created a Dutch Shakespearean tongue, not only in order to create particular moods, but also to solve some metric challenges. Any translator knows that the translation of an English text into Dutch results in a longer text, morphologically Dutch has more unstressed syllables in its sentences as well as different accent patterns. Classicist rules were the main reason that the great Dutch dramatists and poets preferred the alexandrine, but the extra syllables were also more accommodating to the language than the iambic pentameter. Burgersdijk firmly believed that Shakespeare's genius could only be truly transmitted in verse; whenever a translation was finished he would give test-readings for an ever-widening group of friends and fellow-Shakespeareans – as well as for actors, as the stage was on his mind from the beginning.

However, in entering the literary field and the world of the theatre he needed help. In 1877 he struck up a correspondence with Anton Cornelis Loffelt (1841–1906), a theatre critic and Shakespeare expert who would prove to be a staunch ally. Unlike Burgersdijk, Loffelt did not have an academic background; after attending a private secondary school he studied for a teaching certificate in English, for which he spent a year in London. Fascinated by Shakespeare, Loffelt was one of the earliest authors who researched possible relations between Shakespearean and Dutch drama, on which he wrote in various publications (Loffelt 1889). From 1876 onwards he wrote an annual review on Dutch literature for *The Athenaeum*, whilst achieving some notoriety in the Netherlands as a fierce and polemical theatre critic, writing weekly reviews in the popular periodical *Het Vaderland*, whilst also frequently contributing to the influential journals *De Gids* and *De Nederlandsche Spectator*. He became known for his expertise on Shakespeare and his translators in a time when intellectual interest in the playwright was growing. In their early correspondence Burgersdijk and Loffelt exchanged notes on interpretations of Shakespeare's work. Although several years his junior, Loffelt became the mentor Burgersdijk needed to enter the literary field. Likewise Loffelt realized that Burgersdijk could deliver the high quality translations needed to finally establish Shakespeare in Dutch literary culture.

In his writings Loffelt paid extensive attention to Burgersdijk's work from the moment the latter had published *Cymbeline* in 1878, and often included excerpts of forthcoming publications to wet the public's appetite. Burgersdijk published *Cymbeline* in order to establish himself as a legitimate Shakespeare translator; when an excerpt of this translation was published in the German Shakespeare Society's *Jahrbuch* this wish had evidently come true. The choice, incidentally, for this relatively unknown play as a first publication was motivated by the fact that once the play was in print Burgersdijk, as a translator, could not lay any claim on royalties if the play were to be performed – let alone exercise any artistic control over these performances. In a letter of 19 April 1878 Loffelt warns Burgersdijk that the publication of a more popular play might spawn mediocre stage adaptations. Burgersdijk postponed the idea of further publications – but took it up again when a new copyright law in 1881 safeguarded his interest – and devoted himself first and foremost to providing faithful translations. Whenever there was interest in the play he would write a stage adaptation about which he then negotiated with the theatre company in question. Loffelt effectively acted as Burgersdijk's literary agent at this point, and the business side of their relationship is illustrated in the same letter, which deals with securing a first performance, when Loffelt suggests a 6 per cent royalty ('four for you and two for me') for the submission of a stage text (Loffelt 1878).

Throughout the 1870s Loffelt had been critical of the state of Dutch theatre and entertained close ties with like-minded members of the newly established *Nederlandsch Toneelverbond* (Dutch Theatre Union), a group of dramatists and critics who were also concerned about the steady decline of Dutch theatre. They discerned a schism in the theatres: classicist drama was programmed for the cultural elite, whilst the lower middle classes were treated to popular melodrama. At the same time the connection between drama and the literature it sprang from was fading. Their aim of investing in the quality of Dutch theatre as well as elevating the middle classes through exposure to 'high culture' resulted in the establishment, in 1874, of 'De Amsterdamse Toneelschool' (Academy for Dramatic Arts Amsterdam) as well as the periodical *Het Nederlandsch Tooneel* (*The Dutch Stage*) (Koster and Smyth 31). Eventually the idea of a model theatre company, which embodied a modern vision of drama, materialized in the aforementioned 'Vereeniging Het Nederlandsch Toneel' (VHNT). Their early years were fraught with difficulties, however, and it proved to be difficult to realize their ideals. When, after disappointing performances, the VHNT lost their lease of Amsterdam's main theatre in 1879, they were willing to take a risk. Burgersdijk's translations came at the right moment.

Loffelt had lobbied with Johan Rössing, secretary and later stage director at the VHNT to try out one of these new translations, and after extensive deliberations, the choice fell on *Romeo and Juliet*. Barring a few exceptions, most theatre companies up until that point had used poor translations of Jean-François Ducis's mutilated classicist adaptations of Shakespeare's tragedies. The step to Burgersdijk's well-wrought but difficult translations was a great one for directors and actors, most of whom had neither any literary training to speak of nor were versed enough in foreign languages to acquaint themselves with the original texts. Rössing remembered how initially the actors 'were unable to learn Burgersdijk's language, and broke their teeth on it' (Rössing 1900: 110). In their correspondence Loffelt and Burgersdijk were often highly critical of the actors' skills, but Burgersdijk also realized that 'actors were no scholars'. Acknowledging that the gap had to be bridged, both he and Loffelt invested much time in clarifying the text and advising the theatre companies. That their tutoring had an effect is illustrated by Rössing's next remark that the actors admitted that 'the language was so succinct, that once they knew their parts it stood engraved in their memories'. C. W. Schoneveld emphasizes that with 'hardly any Dutch Shakespeare tradition to fall back upon, [...] Burgersdijk's advice, based on his artistic insights as well as his scholarly work, must have been an essential ingredient in the new productions of his translations' (Schoneveld 1990: 263). After a rocky start, Burgersdijk's *Romeo en Julia* became a resounding success. The following year *De Koopman van Venetië* (*The Merchant of Venice*) took to the stage, with Louis Bouwmeester in the role of Shylock. The contemporary reviews describe how Bouwmeester's Shylock is neither a Jewish caricature nor a victim of antisemitism but a character of flesh and blood – at times deserving of the audience's compassion, yet still very much a villain. This interpretation would define Bouwmeester as the most celebrated actor of his age; he would play the role over two thousand times in the forty-four years to come, including performances in the Dutch Indies, Cologne, Berlin, Vienna, Stratford-upon-Avon and, at the age of eighty, in London in 1922 (Leek 1988: 102). Burgersdijk's translation of *Hamlet* was staged in 1882; during his lifetime he would further witness the performances of his translations of *Macbeth*, *Richard III*, *The Winter's Tale*, *Much Ado About Nothing*, *A Midsummer Night's Dream*, *Twelfth Night*, *The Taming of the Shrew*, *Julius Caesar*, *Coriolanus* and *Measure for Measure*.

Burgersdijk's involvement with the staging of his translations became more intense as he became more successful. The left-hand side of his notebooks of *Macbeth* and *A Midsummer Night's Dream* contain extensive stage notes, written for the theatre companies, about clothes, background scenery and drawings for stage sets and even the use of music. These notes betray the influence of the modern approach to staging that was advocated by the Meininger Court Theatre, whose visually spectacular adaptations of *Julius Caesar, Twelfth Night* and *The Winter's Tale* had overwhelmed the Amsterdam theatre audiences in May and June 1880. As directors sometimes had to omit scenes from the original text, Burgersdijk also took great care to explain to them the function of certain scenes in the context of the play, arguing for or against exclusions. His stage notes therefore effectively bridge the gap between the written and the performed word. In the prospectus for the collected works Burgersdijk remarks 'how the great poet has touched upon all questions which have occupied the human mind for centuries [...] the mind which studies Shakespeare acquires a wider perspective and is fortified for the battle of life', adding further on that 'no civilized Dutchman can any longer afford to let the works of Shakespeare remain a closed book' (Burgersdijk 1887). It is Dr Burgersdijk who opened this book, ensuring through his efforts that it remained open.

Notes

1 Dr J. A. Worp first identified this play as a translation of Shakespeare's play in 1880 in an article written for *De Nederlandsche Spectator*. In 1891 the German Shakespeare scholar J. Bolte complimented Worp on his work in an article for the *Shakespeare Jahrbuch,* identifying *De Dolle Bruyloft* as the first direct translation of a Shakespeare play (Bolte).

References

Backer, De, F. and Dudok, G. A., eds (1941), *De Complete Werken van William Shakespeare in de Vertaling van Dr. L.A.J.*

Burgersdijk, (3 vols.), Leiden: A. W. Sijthoff's Uitgeversmaatschappij N.V.

Bergh, L. Ph. C. van den (1835), *Bloemlezing uit de dramatische werken van William Shakespeare*, Amsterdam: Immerzeel Jr.

Bolte, J. (1891) 'Eine holländische Uebersetzung von Shakespeare's *Taming of the Shrew* vom Jahre 1654', *Jahrbuch Deutsche Shakespeare-Gesellschaft*, band 26, 78–86, Bochum: Deutsche Shakespeare-Gesellschaft-West: Available online: www. digizeitschriften.de/dms/resolveppn/?PID=GDZPPN000781886 (accessed 20 December 2019).

Brandt, G. W. and Hogendoorn, W., eds (2009), *German and Dutch Theatre 1600–1848*, Cambridge: Cambridge University Press.

Burgersdijk, L. A. J. (1881), *William Shakespeare, Macbeth, een Treurspel*, MS, Burgersdijk Archive, Atheneum Library Deventer.

Burgersdijk, L. A. J. (1887), *Prospectus: Shakespeare's Werken, in het Nederlandsch vertaald door Dr. L. A. J. Burgersdijk*, Leiden: E. J. Brill.

Bussels, S. (2018), 'Dutch Classicism in Europe' in H. Helmers and G. H. Janssen, eds, *The Cambridge Companion to the Dutch Golden Age*, 308–30, Cambridge: Cambridge University Press.

Buitendijk, W. J. C. ed. (1975), *Jan Vos, Toneelwerken*, Assen: Van Gorcum.

Gram. J. (1907), 'Levensbericht van Anton Cornelis Loffelt. 15 April 1841–24 September 1906', *Jaarboek van de Maatschappij der Nederlansche Letterkunde, 1907*, 56–72, Leiden: E.J. Brill.

Hanou, A. J. (1988), 'Shakespeariana', *Mededelingen van de Stichting Jacob Campo Weyerman*, jaargang11. Available online: https://www.dbnl.org/tekst/_med009198801_01/_ med009198801_01_0017.php (accessed 12 November 2019).

Helmers, H. J. (2015), *The Royalist Republic: Literature, Politics, and Religion in the Anglo-Dutch Public Sphere, 1639–1660*, Cambridge: Cambridge University Press.

Helmers, H. J. and Janssen, G. H., eds (2018), *The Cambridge Companion to the Dutch Golden Age*, Cambridge: Cambridge University Press.

Koster, C. and Smyth, N. (2007), 'Netwerken op z'n negentiende-eeuws: A. C. Loffelt en L. A. J. Burgersdijk als pleitbezorgers van hun Shakespeare', *Filter: Tijdschrift over Vertalen*, Jaargang 14: 3, 23–38.

Leek, R. H. (1988), *Shakespeare in Nederland*, Zutphen: De Walburg Pers.
Leek, R. H. (1990), '"Bless Thee, Bottom, Bless Thee! Thou Art Translated!" The Bard and his Dutch Interpreters', in T. Westerweel and T. D'Haen, eds, *Something Understood: Studies in Anglo-Dutch Literary Translation*, 139–71, Amsterdam-Atlanta: Rodopi.
Loffelt, A. C. (1878), Letter to L.A.J. Burgersdijk, 19 April, MS, Burgersdijk Archive, Atheneum Library Deventer.
Loffelt, A. C. (1885), 'Letterkundige kroniek: *De Werken van William Shakespeare*, vertaald door Dr. L.A.J. Burgersdijk. Derde Deel', review, *De Gids*, 49: part II, 568–74.
Loffelt, A. C. (1889), *Uren met Shakespeare*, Leiden: E.J. Brill.
Pennink, R. (1936), *Nederland en Shakespeare: Achttiende Eeuw en Romantiek*, The Hague: Martinus Nijhoff Uitgevers.
Pienaar, W. B. J. (1929), *English Influences in Dutch Literature and Justus van Effen as Intermediary; An Aspect of Eighteenth-century Achievement*, Cambridge: Cambridge University Press.
Rössing, J. H. (1900), 'Dr. L.A.J. Burgersdijk, Geboren 11 Maart 1828 – Overleden 15 Januari 1900', *Eigen Haard*, jaargang 17: 2, 110–12.
Rössing, J. H. (1904), 'Shakespeare in Nederland, het Shakespeare-gezelschap en de Shakespeare-jaarboeken', *Den Gulden Winkel*, jaargang 3: 1, 1. Available online: www.dbnl. org/tekst/_gul001190401_01/_gul001190401_01_0002.php#2 (accessed 15 December 2019).
Rössing, J. H. (1916), *De Koninklijke Vereeniging Het Neederlandsch Tooneel. Bijdrage tot de geschiedschrijving van het tooneel in Nederland, gedurende meer dan een halve eeuw.*, Amsterdam: N.V. D erven H. van Munster & Zoon.
Schenkeveld-Van der Dussen, M. A. et al, eds, (1993), *Nederlandse Literatuur, een Geschiedenis*, Groningen: Martinus Nijhoff Uitgevers.
Schoneveld, C. W. (1988), 'Het ontstaan en de verspreiding van Burgersdijk vertaling van Shakespeare', in *Deventer Jaarboek 1988*, Deventer: Arko, 61–72.
Schoneveld, C. W. (1990), 'Transmitting the Bard into Dutch: Dr L.A.J. Burgersdijk's Principles of Translation and his Role in the Reception of Shakespeare in The Netherlands to 1900', in B. Westerweel and T. D'Haen, eds, *Something Understood:*

Studies in Anglo-Dutch Literary Translation, 249–70, Amsterdam-Atlanta: Rodopi.

Schorr, J. L. (2014), 'Van Effen, Spectators, and The Republic of Letters in 1723', *Études Épistémè*, 26. Available online: https://journals.openedition.org/episteme/308 (accessed 12 November 2019).

Van Effen, Justus (1717), 'Dissertation sur la Poësie Angloise', in *Journal Littéraire de l'Année MDCCXVII*, vol. 9, 202–12, The Hague : Jean van Duren.

Worp, J. A. (1903, 1907), *Geschiedenis van het Drama en van het Tooneel in Nederland*, 2 vols, Rotterdam: Langerveld.

5

Jean-François Ducis, global *passeur*

Shakespeare's migration in Continental Europe[1]

Michèle Willems

Between 1769 and 1792, before any Shakespeare play had ever been performed in France or in Continental Europe, Jean-François Ducis, a poet and dramatist who could not read English, re-wrote six of his tragedies. This was in a context when Voltaire, after introducing 'l'auteur d'*Hamlet*' into France and most of Europe in 1734 through his 'Letter 18 on Tragedy',[2] stated in his 1776 *Letter to the Academy* that the tragedies of the now undesirable dramatist could never be performed elsewhere than in England:

> *Lisez ces pièces, messieurs, et la raison pour laquelle on ne peut les jouer ailleurs se découvrira bientôt à votre discernement.*
>
> Besterman 206

(Read these plays, Gentlemen, and the reason why they cannot be played elsewhere will soon become clear to your understanding.)

And yet, by 1776, Ducis's *Hamlet* had been performed not only at the Comédie française in 1769, but also as *Hamleto* in Madrid in 1772 and as *Amleto* in Venice in 1774. Over the years, Portugal, Holland, Sweden, Romania, Poland and Russia would follow suit. In effect, the best part of continental Europe discovered Shakespeare on the stage through translations of adaptations which were themselves second-hand, since the adaptor had to rely on previous translations, however approximate. While Voltaire was doing his best to ostracize the foreign dramatist he had first welcomed, Ducis was integrating him into French culture and, probably unwittingly, opening the way to his migration across Europe. Even in Latin America, countries like Brazil discovered Shakespeare through Portuguese translations of Ducis's adaptations which eclipsed Shakespeare until the nineteenth century (O'Shea 25–36).

Voltaire's role in the reception of Shakespeare in France and Europe has been well documented, but Ducis's part in the transmission of his plays over the continent has been mostly ignored or bypassed. Monaco's (1974) and Golder's (1992) monographs merely mention the migration of his adaptations. Now that, with the development of reception studies and the demise of the canonical text, contextualization prevails over lamentation in the study of adaptation, it may be time to explore and explain Ducis's imitations and their migration in connection with the critical, cultural and even political scenes of the late eighteenth century.

The classicists' reception of Shakespeare

C'est moi qui le premier montrai aux Français quelques perles que j'avais trouvées dans son énorme fumier

Voltaire, 1776 [Besterman 175]

The main pearl which Voltaire prided himself on having discovered in Shakespeare's dunghill was Hamlet's 'To be or not to be' soliloquy which he had translated early on into rhyming alexandrines, a domestication of Shakespeare's blank verse which familiarized the readers with a speech soon to become iconic (1734). But by 1776, he was busy enriching his collection of Shakespearean 'turpitudes' for the benefit of the 'gentlemen' of the Academy. His object was to demonstrate the dramatist's lack of taste (a mortal sin in a classical age) with examples ranging from the porter scene in *Macbeth* to Hamlet's mother's shoes or Francisco's mouse, with a special mention for Iago's obscenities. Calling attention to such defects was part of what he called his patriotic war against the foreign invader whom he identified as a dangerous rival to the French masters now that Shakespeare's plays were attracting the attention of readers and critics. This was due to the publication, from 1746, of Pierre-Antoine de La Place's anthology, *Le Théâtre anglois,* which included ten Shakespeare plays, then, from 1776, of Pierre Le Tourneur's twenty-volume *Shakespeare traduit de l'Anglois* preceded by a long Preface. La Place who, as he wrote in his own Preface, was eager to spare Shakespeare 'our compatriots' criticism' for passages they might consider as 'weak, ridiculous or improper' (1746, 'Discours', I: cx1), had chosen to translate into alexandrines some carefully selected scenes which he alternated with paraphrase or synopses of the rest. Le Tourneur's comparatively faithful prose translation also resorted to omission and glossing over to avoid shocking the refined taste of his noble subscribers. Voltaire, already irked by La Place's positive selectiveness, was incensed by the success of 'Pierrot-Letourneur, a companion to Gilles-Shakespeare' (1776 [Besterman 182]). In July 1776, he wrote in fury to his friend the Comte d'Argental:

Ce misérable ... veut nous faire regarder Shakespeare comme le seul modèle de la véritable tragédie ... Il ne daigne pas même nommer Corneille et Racine.

1734 [Besterman 174]

(The wretch ... wants to make us consider Shakespeare as the only model for tragedy ... he does not condescend to name Corneille and Racine.)

The irate *Lettre à l'Académie française* which followed was directed not so much at Shakespeare as at his 'translators' who had chosen to highlight the pearls and bypass the dunghill.

Voltaire's quip certainly reflects the contradictions of the discoverer-turned-deprecator, but it also epitomizes the classicists' ambiguous response to Shakespeare: they agree with Ben Jonson that 'he wanted art' but they cannot help wondering at his achievements. This ambivalence was already perceptible in England from 1660, after the return of the Royalist exiles who had imbibed the classical traditions in France. When Voltaire writes in his 'Letter 18' that '*Shakespear* ... was natural and sublime, but had not so much as a Single Spark of good Taste, or knew one rule of the Drama (1729 [Besterman 44]), he expresses the same dismay as Dryden who had translated more metaphorically the critics' ambivalent reception of the dramatist in his own country: 'He is the very Janus of poets. He wears everywhere two faces and you have scarce begun to admire the one ere you despise the other' (170). And the same Dryden seems to anticipate Voltaire's much reviled description of Shakespeare's drama as pearls in a dunghill when he sums up his own work as an adaptor in the 1675 Preface to his re-writing of *Troilus and Cressida*: 'I undertook to remove that heap of rubbish under which many excellent thoughts lay wholly bury'd.' (ibid.) In parallel to the critics' selectiveness, dramatists sift out the pearls from the dunghill, like Tate who, finding in *King Lear* 'a heap of jewels, unstrung and unpolisht' decides to re-model the story (Epistle Dedicatory, 2–3).

The same causes will produce the same effects on the other side of the Channel: almost a century later, when Jean-François Ducis undertakes to put a Shakespeare play on the French stage for the first time, on 14 April 1769, he lists for Garrick 'des irrégularités sauvages et des ressorts dramatiques absolument inacceptables sur notre scène', the wild irregularities and the dramatic devices of the original have compelled him to write a new play (Ducis 1879: 20). This 'pièce nouvelle' was *Hamlet*, 'imité de l'anglais', which, as we can infer from the *Avertissement*, was in fact imitated from La Place's own imitation. The play was performed at the Comédie française in September 1769 in front of an audience of almost 1,000 people. This success with spectators, then with readers (the 1770 edition was reprinted seven times) encouraged the adaptor to persist in his Shakespearean venture: his *Roméo et Juliette* was performed in 1772, *Le roi Léar* in 1783, *Macbeth* in 1784, *Jean Sans-Terre ou la mort d'Arthur* in 1791 (his only historical play, which turned out to be a failure), and finally *Othello* in 1792.

Ducis's re-writings have often been defined as 'frenchified'. But when Francesco Gritti, the Italian translator of his *Hamlet*, congratulates the adaptor in his Preface for doing away with the deformities of Shakespeare's 'ancient and bizarre model', 'quell'antico bizzarro modello' (in Vittorini 2000: 138) what he praises is its adaptation to a new model, with which he and the subsequent translators were familiar: the classical one. This had indeed been codified in France during the reign of Louis XIV, but it had been disseminated into the rest of Europe as a result of French cultural imperialism, amply relayed, in the eighteenth century, by Voltaire and his strictures on Shakespeare: it is revealing that Gritti's only contact with *Hamlet* appears, throughout his Preface, to have been Voltaire's parodic summaries of its plot. Ducis's compliance with the model advocated by Voltaire explains that, though La Place's anthology included *Les Femmes de bonne humeur, ou les Commères de Windsor* as well as *Cymbeline*, he did not venture into comedy. This was considered a low genre, just good enough, in Voltaire's opinion, to be performed on the Pont Neuf and certainly not at Versailles where Ducis's plays were first performed once they had been accepted by the readers of the conservative Comédie française. The critics' crusade for taste, regularity and rationality signals the incompatibility between Shakespeare's drama and the ideal of tragedy represented by the French masters. In this context, an adaptor had no choice but to find an idiom and a dramatic strategy that would respect the classical tenets and avoid the critical bogeys. Yet in 1993 an Italian critic could still write that Ducis's 'naïve good faith prevented him from realizing the mess he was making of *Hamlet*' (Gaby 121). I shall rather endeavour to show, through a synthetic analysis of his adaptations, that there was method in this 'mess'.

Shakespeare normalized

In play after play, Ducis resorts basically to the same devices since his classical book of rules does not change. His source may be La Place or Le Tourneur's more faithful prose translation, his characters always speak in rhymed alexandrines and respect the obligatory linguistic propriety: a prince speaks like a prince and words pertaining to everyday life are banned; hence the uproar when the word *mouchoir* was spoken for the first time on the stage in Alfred de Vigny's more authentic version of *Othello, Le More de Venise* which, in 1829, did not survive its first season, although it attracted some favourable reviews. In Ducis's play, Othello's present is a much more decorous diamond tiara. Similarly, in *Macbeth,* the heroine's marker of femininity is not the 'nipple' but the spinning-wheel:

> *Tu vois ce faible bras au fuseau destiné . . .*
> *Mais le projet conçu, je l'aurais achevé.* (3.5)

(Do you see this weak arm made for the spinning-wheel . . . Yet, once I had hatched my plot, I would have carried it through.)[3]

Ducis's elevated style was praised by contemporary critics and it certainly appealed to theatre-goers bred on the rhythms of the alexandrines and on the coded vocabulary of classical plays where lovers declare their *feux* and criminals are *perfides* and errors *funestes*, as when Gertrude tells Claudius whom she refuses to marry: 'Périsse de nos feux la mémoire funeste' (1.2). A modern reader may often feel that all the characters speak the same stereotyped language, especially when the constraints of rhyme and metre bring the alexandrines to the verge of parody, as when Hamlet reports the ghost's revelation of his mother's culpability:

Ta mère, qui l'eût dit ? Oui, ta mère perfide
Osa me présenter un poison parricide. (2.5)

(Your mother, who would have thought it? Your perfidious mother/Durst present me with a parricide poison.)

Parricide here, as in many classical plays, means the murder of one's sovereign as well as of one's father.

The normalization which affects the language also applies to the plot. The basic situation of the original play is retained, but the number of characters is drastically reduced: there are eight speaking parts in *Hamlet* and in *Macbeth*, twelve in *Le roi Léar*, and only seven in *Roméo et Juliette* and in *Othello*. The subplots are eliminated, which avoids the risk of mixing genres, social classes and languages. Lear's fool and Macbeth's porter are logical casualties, as are Hamlet's conversation with the gravediggers, his punning and quibbling, and, consequently, his antic disposition. The remaining plots are compressed, a paring down anticipated by La Place. Ducis's dramatic equivalent for his synopses is narration which replaces on-stage action; to this end, some characters, rescued from the original plays, are transformed into confidants to whom past events are related and future plans revealed. The plays thus start in *medias res*, generally with some revelation that will determine the course of the plot: 'Oui, cher Polonius' is followed by Claudius's evocation of Old Hamlet's death and of young Hamlet's *langueur,* then by the revelation of his plans to usurp his throne. Duncan reveals to Glamis that his son Malcolme, who is supposed to have died at birth, has in fact been entrusted to the care and instruction of

Sévar, a wise old man living in the mountains. In order to achieve this compression, Ducis tightens the family relationships: Ophelia is not the daughter of Polonius, but of Claudius who is not the old king's brother, which eliminates the incest. The original subplot can thus be recycled into a fleshed-out love story between Hamlet and Ophelia; this soon comes into conflict with the original revenge plot since Hamlet's mission, imposed by the ghost, is to kill Claudius, here the father of his lover: hence a neat Corneillean conflict between love and duty. And since the ghost has demanded vengeance on both Claudius and Gertrude (who have been lovers but are not married), Hamlet is also caught between his duty to his father and his love for his mother, which justifies his procrastination.

The presence of a speaking ghost on stage ('le spectre tout avoué qui parle longtemps' as he wrote to Garrick) was one of the hurdles that Ducis had to negotiate in his very first play. At the same time, he regretted having to part with this speaking ghost, 'l'ombre terrible qui expose le crime et demande vengeance' ('the awesome shade which narrates the murder and demands revenge'). The perception of the ghost as both an unnatural ingredient in a tragedy and a powerful stage effect is typical of the ambivalent reactions to Shakespeare's drama. Voltaire himself was so conscious of the character's potential theatrical impact that he introduced a ghost in *Eriphyle* (1732), and another one in *Semiramis* (1748), but both spectres were greeted with laughter by the spectators on the stage. Ducis prefers to keep his ghost in the wings. The prince's very first words at Act Two Scene Five are spoken off-stage:

> ... *Fuis, spectre épouvantable,*
> *Porte au fond des tombeaux ton aspect redoutable.*

(Away, horrid ghost, / Go hide in some dark tomb your awful aspect.)

Then he makes his stage entrance as if pursued by a ghost invisible to all, and he relates to Norceste, a recycled Horatio, its off-stage call for revenge on both Claudius and Gertrude. His friend later suggests using the urn which contains his father's ashes to check whether the ghost's accusations against his mother are true. The urn, also presented as the only way of appeasing the father, replaces both the ghost and the play-within-the-play as a test of Gertrude's culpability: this astute device works both as a metonymy for the dead father, and as a metaphor for the son's mission. When Hamlet confronts his mother, the ghost's voice was heard in some versions, but his stage presence seems to be attested only in the 1807 version. In *Macbeth,* the witches are also kept off stage, their apparition being related by Macbeth in the form of a dream. Iphyctone, 'interprète et ministre des dieux' (1.1) who is said to relay the message of the witches, is never seen either, but is reported to haunt the battlefield and then the palace. In the first performance (18 January 1784), the ghost of Duncan was given three separate appearances during the original crowning scene. Precise stage directions ensured that the actor would be seen only by Macbeth and by the audience. 'Le parterre a tout applaudi avec transport' ('The audience applauded it all warmly'), the *Journal de Paris* reported on the same date. Not so the critics. Less than one month later, the ghost had disappeared: 'On ne voit plus cette ombre qui faisait un jeu de théâtre assez voisin du ridicule' (ibid.) ('That ghost, with its rather ridiculous pantomime, is no longer seen'.)

Rationalism being a prerequisite, it follows that the motivation is plausible and intelligible: Gertrude is explicitly guilty and Hamlet clearly in love. Such a concern for rational motives may explain that, when he adapted *Roméo et Juliette,* Ducis chose to flesh out the original love story with Count Ugolino's gruesome tale in the eighth circle of Dante's *Inferno.* Golder (75) justifies the adaptor's resort to a second source by the fact that La Place's *Théâtre anglois* only provided him with a synopsis of the play. But since even this summary was closer to the original than the resulting adaptation, I find it more enlightening to turn to the precedent of the English dramatist Thomas Otway, who, in the same neo-classical context, had adapted *Romeo and Juliet* one century earlier, claiming in his Prologue that he had only 'rifled [Shakespeare] of half a play' (1680). Both adaptors seem to have been at pains to find plausible reasons for the feud which causes the tragedy. In Shakespeare's play, this is a given, a hereditary hatred between two families, a fatality which crushes the 'star-crossed lovers'. Conversely, Otway explains the enmity between Marius Senior/ Montague and Sylla/Capulet by rooting it in a political rivalry for the ruling of Rome. The adaptation is entitled *The History and Fall of Caius Marius*, and the political strife for the ruling of Rome occupies a good half of the play, which justifies the Prologue's statement. Similarly, Ducis justifies Montaigu's thirst for revenge on the Capulets by borrowing from Dante the ordeals and torments of Ugolino, imprisoned in the Tower of Hunger with his sons who starved to death before his very eyes. In deference to decorum, Ducis's character only hints at the full horror of Ugolino's ordeal as told by Dante, in two lines evoking his dying sons' offer of their blood to nourish him (4.5). It thus appears that whatever the language, whatever the country, the same classical tenets produce the same adapting effects, which also explains the success of Ducis's plays in translation.

In Ducis's *Roméo et Juliette*, the figure of Ugolino/Montaigu looms as an impending doom even before he returns to Verona after twenty years of exile and imprisonment. Doveldo, Juliette's secret lover, is actually Roméo, his only surviving son, kidnapped at an early age and adopted by Capulet. He is no sooner reunited with his real father than he is drawn into a fight to defend him. It then appears that he has killed Theobaldo, who is not Juliette's cousin but her brother, and thus Capulet's son. Paradoxically, Ducis does not hesitate to stretch probability in order to engineer a variety of conflicts between love and duty. Roméo's filial duty is here divided between two fathers. From Act Three on, the plot revolves upon his unsolvable dilemmas. First, he is urged by Montaigu to restore the family honour by killing Capulet, a mission which comes into conflict with his love for Juliette, then Capulet, who has yet to hear of the recent developments, demands that he kill Montaigu in lines reminiscent of Don Diègue's famous injunction to Rodrigue in Corneille's *Le Cid*, 'Va, cours, vole et me venge':

*Va, pars, combats, triomphe, et revolant vers moi
Si mon fils est vengé je le retrouve en toi* (3, 5).

Roméo, then revealing both his filiation and his love for Juliette, sums up his dilemma in his reply to Capulet: 'Tu dois venger ton fils, j'ai dû sauver mon père.' ('You must revenge your son. I had to save my father') (ibid). Ducis even goes one better than Corneille when Montaigu orders his son to avenge his brothers by killing Juliette, whose death, he hopes, will kill Capulet, a morbid refinement in revenge which multiplies Roméo's inner conflicts.

Ducis's last play *Othello*, appears even more clearly centred on a conflict between love and family honour. In spite of its Shakespearean title, the play actually focuses on the heroine's dilemma. Hédelmone/Desdemona, who is present in twenty-six scenes out of thirty-six, is a motherless daughter who appears burdened by guilt and a sense of doom as soon as Odalbert, her father, condemns her love for Othello in words reminiscent of Brabantio's: 'Une épouse si chère/ Peut tromper son époux, ayant trompé son père' (1.6).[4] From then on, she is torn between her love for Othello and her duty to her father. Contrary to what Odalbert first believes, the lovers are not married at the beginning of the play. Hédelmone keeps postponing the marriage until, unable to resist her father's emotional blackmail, she signs a letter in which she promises to marry Lorédan (a conflation of Cassio and Roderigo) who is then revealed to be the Doge's son. Ducis likes to create conflicts based on 'filial piety', of which he explains that his Hamlet is a model. Daughters prepared to sacrifice their love to their filial duty are a variation upon the theme: Ophelia hurries to protect her father, even though he may be a criminal. 'Je n'examine point si mon père est coupable' (5.2). ('I do not ask myself whether my father is guilty.') Juliette accepts marriage to Pâris in spite of her love for Roméo: 'Je m'immole à l'état, j'obéis à mon père' (1.4) ('I sacrifice myself to the state; I obey my father'); as for Hédelmone, she does not survive her sense of duty to her father.

It appears from Ducis's correspondence with his friend Thomas (1830, IV, 31, 50) that *Othello* was ten years in the making. In fact, imitating Shakespeare's play posed him a number of problems: not so much that of Othello's colour, which he solved by opting for a 'copper colour as befits an African', as that of copying the character of Iago. He confided to Garrick that, though the English could calmly watch the manoeuvres of such a monster on their stages, the French would never put up with his presence. So, Iago is a victim not so much of his indecent language as of his devilish duplicity. He is replaced by Pézare, who appears to be nothing more than Othello's confidant until, after the murder of Hédelmone, the Doge reveals that the schemes which this unsuspected villain exercised off stage have just been exposed, confessed and justified by his love for Hédelmone, all this in the wings. One line is then sufficient to announce the deserved punishment of such a vapid character: 'Et son trépas s'achève au milieu des tortures' (5.6) ('And he goes to his death in the throes of torture'). Desdemona's death was not so easily accepted. As reported in the Foreword (III, 12), when Talma raised his dagger to stab Hédelmone (smothering her under a pillow was out of the question), all the spectators rose and shrieked, and several women fainted. Four months later, Ducis supplied a happy ending which reunited the lovers after some improbable last-minute reversals and revelations. On 22 March 1792, *Othello* was announced 'avec un nouveau dénouement'.

Dénouements were another hurdle for an adaptor, since poetic justice had to be respected without any death being performed on stage. One possibility was to engineer a happy ending, however acrobatic. Ducis, like Tate, closes his *Léar* on Helmonde/Cordelia's reunion with her father who then gives his blessing to her marriage with Edgard. The first stage version of *Hamlet*, which only lasted a few months, ended with the off-stage suicides of Claudius, then of Gertrude who blessed the union of Ophelia and Hamlet as she died, a just and happy ending. The 1770 edition opts for two murders, that of Gertrude stabbed off-stage by Claudius (the body was vaguely seen at the back of the stage), which gives Hamlet a good reason for killing him, but means he has to sacrifice his love for Ophelia. In that version, he is tempted by suicide. But the 'dagger' which, he says, is all he has left, is later replaced by his 'virtue', which prompts the legitimate heir to respond, as in every subsequent version, to the call of duty:

Mais je suis homme et roi. Réservé pour souffrir
Je saurai vivre encore et fais plus que mourir. (5.9)

(But I am man and king. I was born to suffer/
And will go on living, which is worse than dying.)

At the end of *Roméo et Juliette,* the impossibility of reconciliation between the families drives both lovers to successive and separate deaths. Juliette, another dutiful daughter, has taken poison to save both her country and her father ('ma patrie et mon père'). A desperate Roméo stabs himself after her death. Ducis leaves a space for one last scene between the lovers before Montaigu's last-minute speech of contrition. This ending, initiated by Otway, was followed by Theophilus Cibber in 1744 and improved upon by Garrick in 1748. Operas later exploited this brief reunion between the lovers as an opportunity for one last love-duet.

Remorse is a means of satisfying the classical demand for moralism which Ducis often achieves at the cost of inconsistencies in his characters' motives: Gertrude who has murdered her husband because she loved Claudius, becomes suddenly concerned for her son's future:

Quand par un crime affreux je l'ai privé d'un père
Il est bien juste au moins qu'il retrouve une mère. (1.2)

(Since my foul crime deprived him of a father
'Tis only fair he should retrieve a mother.)

Macbeth who has killed Duncan and Glamis to usurp the throne, suddenly decides to return it to Malcolme, the legitimate heir. He will nevertheless commit suicide, like Gertrude, to atone for his crimes. Frédegonde, on the contrary, persists in crime to the end, without qualms or questions. The change of name from Lady Macbeth is for once an index to the character's motivations: her historical namesake was a sixth-century queen who murdered the king, her husband, in order to reign with her son. Ducis provides his character with a son, but though maternal love may explain her ambition to usurp the throne, it is not treated as an extenuating circumstance. On the contrary, Frédegonde is made to bear the whole responsibility for the murders: she is a dominant wife who convinces her husband that Glamis is planning his death, then shames him into killing him as well as Duncan, before she eventually organizes the murders herself. As she pretended early on that Iphyctone validated the witches' predictions, she appears as their relay, if not as a witch herself. In her sleep-walking scene which shows her briefly trying to rub off a blood stain, she is actually on her way to murdering Malcolme, but she mistakenly kills her own son instead, a stroke of morbid irony which reconciles poetic justice and morality; she is then denied death and condemned to live on. In a classical perspective, which Ducis, a devout Catholic, readily adopted, it is important to show that crime does not pay but that remorse rehabilitates, 'Seul bien des criminels le repentir nous reste' (1.2) ('Yet have we repentance, the criminal's only good'), Gertrude tells Claudius when she refuses to marry him. The primacy of contrition explains why Hamlet rejects the ghost's off-stage injunction to kill her once she has silently confessed her guilt by fainting over the urn: 'Rien n'est perdu pour vous, si le remords vous reste' (5.4) ('All is not lost provided you repent'), the son assures his mother.

From normalization to appropriation

Such didacticism draws Ducis's adaptations towards moral sentimental drama, a popular genre which attracted a new bourgeois public at the end of the century. Interestingly, his normalization of Shakespeare's plays generates all the ingredients of melodrama, from contrived plots to artificial dénouements through sudden revelations and recognition scenes: even as Ducis regularizes Shakespeare's plays, he transposes them into the new contemporary theatrical tradition. It is symptomatic that Molé, the first actor to interpret his Hamlet, was acting at the same time in Diderot's very successful *Le père de famille*. When tragic heroes are seen as family persons, their Corneillean dilemmas are not much different from the divided loyalties characteristic of Diderot's domestic dramas which favour edifying family reunions, like that of Lear with his daughter or Hamlet with his mother.

By focusing on individual concerns rather than on metaphysical problems, Ducis also redirects and updates Shakespeare's reflection on evil. Rousseau's theory that man is naturally virtuous but corrupted by civilization is a widely recognized influence. In almost every play, we find young characters who have been brought up, like his Émile, in natural surroundings which Ducis fills with wise old men: Duncan has chosen to protect Malcolme from the dangers and the noxious influence of the court by entrusting him, from his birth, to the care and instruction of Sévar. Lorédan, later revealed to be the Doge's son, has been, for the same reasons, educated away from Venice by 'un vieillard vertueux' and he describes, for Hédelmone's benefit, his idyllic childhood in contact with nature (*Oth*. 3.3). As for Helmonde who is believed to be dead, she has been saved from fatal exile by Edgard and taken refuge in a cave under the protection of Norclète, an old hermit. Most of these characters are known under another name until the revelation of their noble or royal identity changes or clarifies the course of the plot. Concealed identity is a theatrical device more frequently used by Shakespeare than by Rousseau.

Guiderius and Arviragus, the two young sons of Cymbeline, brought up from infancy in the mountains under a different identity, come readily to mind. They were kidnapped at an early age by Belarius, a wrongly banished courtier, who raises them in the Welsh mountains under the names of Polydore and Cadwal. Now *Cymbeline* was the only Shakespeare tragicomedy anthologized in *Le théâtre anglois*, with which we know Ducis was familiar. Act Three, Scene Three, which introduces our characters, is translated by La Place into rhymed alexandrines which are very close to Shakespeare's original. Ducis, as we saw, imagines very similar situations for many of his young characters, apart from the fact that Guiderius and Arviragus resent their rustic life, unlike Malcolme who regrets its loss. Besides, the description of the setting for this scene in *Cymbeline*, the obscure cave in the woods from which the three characters emerge, seems to find an echo in *Léar*, in the description of Norclète's underground grotto, Helmonde and Edgard's hiding place, whose entrance Kent, Edgard's father, discovers in the midst of a forest bristling with rocks. This is where Léar, who is losing his wits, will take refuge from the raging storm and be reunited with his daughter (3.6, 7). My feeling is that La Place's *Cymbeline* may well have inspired Ducis to transpose the Rousseauistic climate of the 1770s into a type of dramatic character to which Doveldo/Roméo is the first approximation. Le Tourneur's closer translation of *Cymbeline*, published in 1778, may then have induced him to integrate more polished characters into the rest of his plays.

From 1782, the adaptor turned to Le Tourneur all the more readily where La Place had dismissed a play with a synopsis, as was the case for *Léar*. As a result, scenes featuring Léar's curse, his madness in the storm, or his reunion with Helmonde, are so close to Le Tourneur's translation that Ducis seems to have transposed his prose to alexandrines (Golder 121–4). And yet the play was hardly a success. The scandal of *Othello*'s dénouement shows that Ducis's Shakespearean venture was not devoid of obstacles, as can be inferred from his prefaces to the published plays. The Foreword to *Macbeth* reveals his alertness to his public's demand for less Shakespeare: 'J'ai fait des retranchements considérables, d'après les avertissements du plus éclairé des juges, le public' (vol. 2, 116). ('I have cut out a considerable number of things, following the admonishments of the audience, that most judicious judge'.) Also aware that he owes the success of some of his Shakespearean audacities to his actors, he pays tribute to the talent of Madame Vestris who made the public accept the infernal ambition of Frédegonde and the novelty of the sleep-walking scene, and in the Foreword to *Othello*, he commends Louise Desgarcins for her interpretation of *La romance du saule* in a bed scene which was in itself a revolution on the stage.

The influence of Talma

The successive versions of the plays, some of which exist only as manuscripts, and the alternative endings or scenes with which *Hamlet*, *Macbeth* and *Othello* were published in the 1813 edition, indicate that Ducis's imitations were in a constant state of elaboration. This was particularly true once François-Joseph Talma had appeared on the scene in 1790. He soon became, at twenty-five, the adaptor's cult actor, then his collaborator, instigating many revisions and the introduction of more Shakespeare. He had lived in London for eight years as a child and knew English perfectly; he had read Shakespeare in the original and seen some of his plays performed on the London stages by Kemble and Mrs Siddons, so that he was very critical of Ducis's adaptations when he discovered them. His abundant correspondence with the adaptor indicates that he gradually acquired the right to correct and even to censure Ducis's adaptations, since he considered that a text for the stage was never fixed but could be changed after each performance. *Macbeth*, after a slow and difficult start when it was presented in 1784, was the first play to benefit from the collaboration between the adaptor and the actor, who then starred in the title role until his death. *Hamlet*, too, had suffered a long eclipse after 1770; it only became a regular success after 1803, when Talma took up the part which he was to play for twenty-three years, with a revised text influenced by his personal knowledge of the original. Like Garrick before him, he increased the centrality of the prince through successive alterations; in 1804, he convinced Ducis to include Hamlet's famous soliloquy, and from 1803 to 1809 he induced him to revise the last act of the play at least six times before the 1813 publication. But the actor's greatest success was *Othello* which he interpreted for thirty-two years, including in the provinces where the play was performed a hundred times between 1792 and 1796, as well as in Belgium and the Netherlands. An index of the play's popularity was the immediate success of its parodies, *Le Maurico de Venise* and *Arlequin Cruello* which were also popular in Spain.

Othello was first performed in 1792 in the midst of the French Revolution, in the actor's own political Théâtre de la République, Talma being then a republican himself. Ducis, on the contrary, had started his writing career as a monarchist and until the 1780s his plays basically convey the ideology of the *ancien régime*, with its quest for order and its fear of illegitimacy. A long scene (5.2) of the 1770 edition of *Hamlet*, which disappears in subsequent ones, has a legitimist Ophélie lecturing her father against rebellion and warning him: 'Tremblez, Seigneur .../ Un Roi, quoi qu'il ordonne, est sûr d'être obéi' (Vanderhoof 126–7). ('Beware, my Lord, ... A King, whatever he orders, is sure to be obeyed'.) In both *Hamlet* and *Léar*, the rebels eventually turn against their leaders to rally round the legitimate king. In *Hamlet*, as in *Macbeth*, usurpation is diverted into the promotion of the legitimate heir through the remorse of the regicide: by refusing to marry Claudius, her former lover, Gertrude bans him from the throne and atones for her crime by devoting herself to the crowning of her son. Macbeth who is haunted in the crowning scene by the ghost of Duncan, decides to return his usurped throne to Malcolme, the legitimate heir. Frédegonde, on the contrary, plans a new regicide to promote her son. Motherly love, which induces Gertrude to fight for her son's legitimate rights, is here subverted into Frédegonde's decision to kill the son after the father ('le fils à son tour'), in order to allow her own son to reign. The transposition of the original plays into moral classical dramas merges with the appropriation of the ideology of the period. The Shakespeare who migrates across the continent is definitely classical but, as Keith Gregor shows with reference to the Spanish translations of *Hamlet* and *Macbeth*, the translators accommodate Ducis's plays to their own political climate.

Under the influence of the Revolution and of Talma's political views, Ducis redirected a number of ideological markers. On 22 April 1798, some months after the Fructidor coup d'état of September 1797, *Macbeth* was performed in the presence of Bonaparte and Joséphine. For this revival, the emblem of power in the crowning scene became 'le livre de la loi' (the Book of the Law), presented by Loclin, a warrior in the list of characters, then transformed into a sort of supercitizen who also pronounced Frédegonde's sentence. In the last published text, he first presents Macbeth with the crown, and later makes him swear

> *sur ce livre terrible,*
> *Qu'au seul bien de l'état ton cœur sera sensible ;*
> *Que tu n'es rien ici qu'un premier citoyen,*
> *Qui peut tout par la loi, qui sans la loi n'est rien.* (4.4)

(on this awesome book,
That thy heart shall be dedicated to the good of the state,
That you are nothing more than the first citizen,
Almighty through the law, powerless without the law.)

Unlike *Macbeth*, *Othello*, first performed in 1792, was directly influenced by the 1789 *Déclaration des droits de l'homme* and by the ongoing debate about slavery, first denounced in 1788, in *L'Esclavage des noirs*, a play written by

Olympe de Gouges, who was also the first French feminist. (Slavery was abolished in 1794 by the *Convention*, then restored by Napoleon, and finally abolished in 1848.) The play is set in Venice, a republic which has just been saved by a stranger and republican, a coloured man whom Ducis refers to as 'mon sans-culotte Africain'. His Othello is an alien who conquered Hédelmone through the narration of his early life as a slave, and gained his place in Venetian society through his merit and not through his birthright: 'la couleur de mon front nuit-elle à mon courage?' (1.5) ('Is my valour impaired by the colour of my brow?'); he is a militant for liberty and equality, coded revolutionary terms which are repeatedly made to rhyme at the end of alexandrine couplets. The play made theatrical history in a context when the public was prepared to accept a coloured hero, a bed scene, the heroine singing with a guitar, but not her murder on stage. Yet, judging from his sarcastic report in his *Mémoires* (III, 231–2), Talma, like some other revolutionaries, disapproved of Ducis's decision to change the ending to pander to the public, and notes sarcastically that he could end the play happily or tragically depending on the audience.

For thirty-two years, Talma interpreted Othello, Hamlet, Macbeth and sometimes Edgard. He was acclaimed not only in Paris, but also in the provinces and abroad, at a time when the French language was understood outside France. (Molé had interpreted Ducis's Hamlet at the court of Sweden at the invitation of King Gustav III.) In October 1811, during the reception organized by Holland in honour of Napoleon, he performed Hamlet in Amsterdam. He was so famous in the scene in which the prince confronts his mother that Louis-Jean-François Lagrenée painted his portrait, clutching the urn, for the 1810 *Salon*. Ducis recreates his performance of Othello in his Foreword to the play:

> *On a vu dans M. Talma, Othello vivant, avec toute son énergie africaine . . . On a entendu le silence affreux de son désespoir et le rugissement de sa jalousie* (vol. 3, 14).

(In M. Talma we have seen Othello alive, with all his African energy ... We have heard the awful silence of his despair and the wild roar of his jealousy.)

Other contemporary testimonies suggest that his acting, which did away with the customary monotonous declamation, managed to bridge the gap between the adaptations and the originals. Judging from Madame de Staël's admiring comments in *De l'Allemagne* he could transform narration into action and make absent characters, present, as in the urn scene or in Macbeth's narration of the witches' predictions.

Il faut voir Talma s'essayer à rendre quelque chose de vulgaire et de bizarre dans l'accent des sorcières et conserver cependant dans cette imitation toute la dignité que notre théâtre exige.

De Staël III, 237

(It is prodigious to see Talma endeavouring to render something of the vulgarity and strangeness of the witches' diction, without losing in this impersonation any of the dignity which our theatre demands.)

Talma, who was fascinated by the great Shakespearean roles somehow preserved by the adaptors, inspired the star actors of continental Europe and beyond: Isidoro Máiquez, who popularized Ducis's adaptations in Spain, went to Paris to learn from him. Even in Brazil, João Caetano was known as the Brazilian Talma. His Otelo, in Ducis's text translated by the dramatist Magalhães, was black-faced, but he imitated Talma's famous *rugissement* (O'Shea 25–36).

Conclusion

Ducis died in 1816 and Talma in 1826. In 1827, Charles Kemble's company roused the enthusiasm of the public with their performances of *Hamlet, Romeo and Juliet* and *Othello* at the Théâtre de l'Odéon. Yet Ducis's *Othello* still drove the original play off the stage. In his chronicles of the contemporary theatre, Théophile Gautier, a romantic novelist and critic who, along with Hugo, Delacroix, Vigny, Berlioz and others, had discovered Shakespeare's *Othello* on the stage, berated the *Comédiens français* for preferring Ducis's *risible* (ludicrous) adaptation to Vigny's 'faithful dramatic version' (Gautier 285). This was written in 1844. Between 1831 and 1840, at the peak of the Romantic movement, Ducis's naturalized *Hamlet* still ran for sixty-five nights. Though the wiser sort of public like Diderot, professed to prefer 'le monstre de Shakespeare à l'épouvantail de Ducis' (Ducis's scarecrow), this was the only *Hamlet* performed at the Comédie française until 1851, with a total of 203 performances over eighty-two years and of thirteen reprints between 1770 and 1880. And in a number of European theatres, Ducis's most popular plays continued to be performed in translation, or re-adapted from his adaptations as in Spain, or 'resurfacing as the subjects of ballets or operas' as in Italy (Tempera 170). In Brazil, Italian or Spanish companies performed Shakespeare in Ducis's imitations until the end of the nineteenth century.

Was Voltaire's 1776 claim that Shakespeare's plays could not be performed outside England, belied or confirmed by the success of Ducis's imitations in France? Was this Shakespeare or not Shakespeare? It was at any rate the only Shakespeare that most European audiences were prepared to accept at that time and in those places. Ducis's adaptations and their migration across continental Europe invite us to reflect on the complex modalities of the transmission of Shakespeare's drama. Their abiding presence on many continental stages signals the resilience of the classical model at the end of the eighteenth century and much later. And yet, from the 1770s, the European consensus on the aesthetics of drama breaks down under the pressure of the Shakespeare model. England, which had claimed Shakespeare as its national poet with the 1769 Shakespeare Jubilee, gradually reinstates his original plays in its theatres. At a time when French was the language of culture, Germany, which had developed an early taste for Shakespeare via French sources, is also the first continental country to shake off the fetters of the classical model advocated by Voltaire.[5] Ducis's quasi-absence from German stages may be the index of their newly gained independence from the norms established in France. The European migration of Shakespeare takes different paths. The paradox is that the most popular one across the continent had been opened by a man who could not read his plays in the original.

Notes

1 I wish to dedicate this essay to Mariangela Tempera whose wide-ranging interests in the transformation of Shakespeare's texts in other cultures included detailed study of the influence of Ducis's plays in Italy.

2 This was first published in English in *Letters concerning the English nation* (1729) at the end of his three-year exile in London, then in French in the *Lettres philosophiques* (1734), in Rouen to escape censure. For a more detailed analysis of Voltaire's reception of Shakespeare, see Willems (2010).

3 Unless otherwise indicated, all the quotations refer to the posthumous 1830 reprint of the final edition of the plays, published in 1813 without any lineation. The translations are my own.

4 Compare with Brabantio's warning to Othello: 'She has betrayed her father, may do thee.' *Othello*, 1.3.293: Ducis's source here is clearly Le Tourneur.

5 E.g. Lessing's strong opposition to Voltaire in his 1767–9 *Hamburgische Dramaturgie*.

References

Besterman, Thomas, ed. (1967), *Voltaire on Shakespeare*, Geneva: Droz.

Dryden, John (1672) *A Defence of the Epilogue of the Second Part of the Conquest of Granada, or an Essay on the Dramatique poetry of the last age.*
Ducis, Jean-François (1830), *Œuvres*, 5 vols, Paris: Bureau des Éditeurs.
Ducis, Jean-François (1879), *Lettres de Jean-François Ducis,* Paul Albert ed., Paris: G. Jousset.
Gaby, Petrone Fresco (1993), *Shakespeare's Reception in Eighteenth Century Italy: The Case of* Hamlet, Verlag: Peter Lang.
Gautier, Théophile (1859), *Histoire de l'art dramatique en France depuis 25 ans*, Paris : Hetzel.
Golder, John (1992), *Shakespeare for the Age of Reason*, Oxford: The Voltaire Foundation.
Gregor, Keith (2014), 'When the Tyrant is a Despot: Jean-François Ducis's Adaptations of Shakespeare', in Keith Gregor ed., *Shakespeare and Tyranny: Regimes of Reading in Europe and Beyond*, 57–76, Newcastle: Cambridge Scholars Publishing.
Gregor, Keith, and Pujante, Ángel-Luis (2005), 'The Four Neoclassical Spanish *Hamlets*: Assimilation and revision', *Sederi* 15, 129–41.
La Place, Pierre-Antoine de (1746–9), 'Discours sur le théâtre anglois', in *Le Théâtre anglois*, 8 vols, I, i–cxi, London : n.d.
Le Tourneur, Pierre (1776–82), *Shakespeare traduit de l'anglois*, 20 vols, Paris: Duchesne.
Monaco, Marion (1974), *Shakespeare on the French Stage in the Eighteenth Century,* Paris: Didier.
O'Shea, José Roberto (2005), 'Early Shakespearean Stars Performing in Brazilian Skies: João Caetano and National Theater' in Bernice W. Kliman and Rick J. Santos eds, *Latin American Shakespeares*, 25–36, Madison: Farleigh Dickinson University Press.
Otway, Thomas [1680] (1959), *The History and Fall of Caius Marius acted at Dorset Gardens*, Cornmarket Press.
Rousseau, Jean-Jacques (1762), *Émile ou De l'éducation*, La Haye.
Staël, Germaine, de [1817] (1969), *De l'Allemagne.* 5 vols, Paris: Hachette.
Tate, Nahum [1681] (1959), *The History of King Lear. First Performed at Dorset Gardens*, Cornmarket Press.
Tempera, Mariangela (2001), 'Staging *King Lear* in Nineteenth-Century Italy', in Boika Sokolova and Evgenia Pancheva eds,

Renaissance Refractions: Essays in Honour of Alexander Shurbanov, 170–8, Sofia: St Kliment Ohridski University Press.

Vanderhoof, Mary B. (1953), '*Hamlet:* A Tragedy Adapted from Shakespeare (1770) by Jean-François Ducis, A Critical Edition', *Proceedings of the American Philosophical Society*, 97(1), 88–142.

Vittorini, Fabio (2000), *Shakespeare e il melodramma romantico*, Firenze, La Nuova Italia.

Voltaire [1729] (1974), 'Letter 18, On Tragedy', in *Letters concerning the English Nation*, London, New York: Burt Franklin Reprints.

Voltaire (1734), 'Lettre sur la tragédie' in *Lettres Philosophiques*, Rouen.

Willems, Michèle (2007), 'The Mouse and the Urn: Re-visions of Shakespeare from Voltaire to Ducis', in R. Paulin ed., *Shakespeare im 18. Jahrhundert*: 231–42, Göttingen: Wallstein-Verlag.

Willems, Michèle (2010), 'Voltaire', in R. Paulin ed., *Great Shakespeareans,* vol. 3, 5–43, London: Continuum.

Willems, Michèle (2015), 'Shakespeare or not Shakespeare? The Propagation of the Plays in Europe through J. F. Ducis's "Imitations"', in D. Farabee, M. Netzloff, and B. D. Ryner eds, *Early Modern Drama in Performance,* 121–36, Newark: University of Delaware Press.

6

'No profit but the name'

The Polish reception of Shakespeare's plays[1]

Anna Cetera-Włodarczyk

Shakespeare's geographical knowledge appears lacking, with the notorious example of Slavic lands stretching as far as the coastline of Bohemia, one of the two major settings in *The Winter's Tale*. In the case of Poles the general sense of location seems correct though Hamlet sees us garrisoned against the invasion of Norwegians, a nation against whom we have never fought any war. And yet as the Prince eventually discerns, we are ready to defend 'a little patch of ground / That hath in it no profit but the name' (4.4.17–18). Appropriately enough, it is precisely such determination which underlines Polish efforts to embrace Shakespeare's dramatic output. The turn of the nineteenth century, as in various parts of Europe, marks the Bard's entry into the heart of Polish national culture, an entry which earned its many heralds no extraordinary profit, but the name.

There were several distinctive routes of Shakespeare's early migration into Polish lands, irrespective of the shape and strength of our shifting borders.[2] Some of these routes appear fairly typical, such as the tours of foreign players (English, German and Austrian in particular) from the early seventeenth to the mid-nineteenth century, the eighteenth- and early nineteenth-century appropriations of French and German theatrical abridgements, and the patronage of aristocrats succumbing to bardolatry on their grand tours. None of these, however, could secure for Shakespeare lasting recognition, since their impact was short-lived, local or societal. It was the emulative zeal of the leading Romantic poets, and the persistence of translators' endeavours which brought genuine change by disseminating the texts of Shakespeare's plays. Soon afterwards they were brought onto the stage.

At first, Elizabethan and Jacobean players had followed the footsteps of merchants, seeking profit in the territories of the Hanseatic League which at the end of the sixteenth century was already in crisis and therefore easily gave way to new trading networks. With a population of about forty thousand people, Gdańsk (Danzig) was the biggest seaport in the Baltic region in the sixteenth and seventeenth centuries, exporting grain, timber, potash and tar, all conveniently carried northwards on the Vistula river, the major waterway of the then Poland. The thriving city was a necessary stop on the Baltic Route (Limon 2009) and is likely to have hosted English players some time before Robert Greene sneeringly acknowledged Shakespeare's presence in London. From 1586 five English players – George Bryan, William Kempe and Thomas Pope among them – performed in Elsinore, and then in Dresden, and it is very tempting to see them arriving in Gdańsk at St Dominic's Fair in August 1587, though no evidence can be advanced to support the claim except for the logic of their itinerary. The conjectural evidence (derived mainly from the interpretation of the sources documenting their activities elsewhere) points also to the presence of English players in Polish lands at the turn of the seventeenth century but again no immediate proof exists of the dissemination of specifically

Shakespeare's plays (Limon 2009, Żurowski 2007). The likelihood increases in the case of the company led by John Greene who in the years 1607–19 would regularly perform in Elbląg, Gdańsk and Warsaw, including a few months' employment (1616–17) at the royal court of Sigismund III Vasa. Assuming that the repertoire in Poland mirrored that known from German sources, Polish audiences could have seen at least two adaptations: *The Two Gentlemen of Verona* and *Titus Andronicus* (Komorowski 2003).

Whoever came first and whatever plays they brought with them, *via Baltica* facilitated the mobility of the English players who in the seventeenth century would regularly call at three prosperous urban settings: Gdańsk, Elbląg (the seat of the English Eastland Company) and Königsberg (the second largest city in the region), and from there further southwards to Warsaw, Wrocław (Breslau) and Kraków, as well as eastwards, to Vilnius and Riga. The dense network of confirmed destinations testifies to the scale of the phenomenon and the intensity of cultural exposure, but it hardly denotes a true absorption of a foreign repertoire into native culture. The respective large merchant communities were typically multicultural and polyglot, and visiting players only augmented the impression of heterogeneity rather than triggered changes in the inherently cosmopolitan costal area. It has been assumed that English players would initially perform in English, whereas in the seventeenth century they would have performed in German, though the local presence of English communities, such as those in Gdańsk and Elbląg, makes English still a viable option (Żurowski 2007: 29). The extant documents record intriguing and diverse reactions. In 1605 some English players were expelled from Elbląg after just two 'outrageous' performances, but the city paid them decent compensation, a token of a sharp difference of opinion among their council members (Limon 2009: 63, Żurowski 2007: 21). In Gdańsk, the year 1611 saw the construction of the Fencing School, the first public playhouse built outside England and modelled after London's Fortune, today a site of the thriving Gdańsk Shakespeare Theatre (Limon 1989).

Fixing the certain date of the documented arrival of Shakespeare in Poland is problematic: in 1664 in Königsberg (at that time a Polish contentious seigniory) Polish Prince Bogusław Radziwiłł watched a German abridgement of *The Taming of the Shrew*, while in 1701 a German company of players staged a revised version of *King Lear* in Toruń (East Prussia, presently Poland). Because the productions were in German, whereas audiences were typically multinational, the shifting state borders only augment the difficulty of designating a relevant date (Żurowski 2007: 43–4). On the whole the assumed presence of English players in the region intensifies during the Thirty Years' War as Poland and the Duchy of Prussia remain relatively safe and friendly at that time (Limon 2016: 84), and then diminishes around 1670 due to the changed historical circumstances both in England and in Poland, where the Polish Commonwealth was destroyed by the war with Sweden, and then increasingly preoccupied with the military threats of the Ottoman Empire.

In the eighteenth century, a Shakespearean repertoire, highly derivative and yet already bearing an authorial stamp, re-emerged in a different migrant context. Polish urban audiences were frequently entertained by visiting players, at this point travelling by land (the so-called Continental Route), usually from Vienna, Prague, Dresden or Berlin as well as from France or Italy (Limon 2009). The paths of visiting companies as well as those of foreign companies based in Poland would often criss-cross, producing intense clashes of dramatic and theatrical conventions. For example, in 1774 and in 1775, the German company of Felix Kurz staged *Romeo and Juliet* in Warsaw, adapted by Felix Christian Weisse. Soon afterwards, in 1778, again in Warsaw, the French company led by Louis Montbrun performed *Roméo et Juliette – Romeusz i Julisia* – an adaptation by Jean-François Ducis. In the spring of 1781, Bartolomeo Constantini, an Italian dancer, became a manager of the German theatre in Warsaw and instantly reached for the play which had recently enjoyed a great success at the Burgtheater in Vienna: *Hamlet, Prinz von Dänemark*, an adaptation by Friedrich Ludwig Schröder based on the translation by Johann Joachim

Eschenburg (Żurowski 2007: 51). Performed in August 1781, the production generated much interest and received the first 'Polish' review of Shakespeare's play. The anonymous review was written in French and appeared in *Journal littéraire de Varsovie*, a literary journal edited by the French staying at the court of King Stanisław Poniatowski. The king himself was known for his well-founded interest in Shakespeare: in 1754, at that time a very unlikely candidate for the crown, Poniatowski would watch Shakespeare's plays staged in London and practise English (in Paris) by translating Shakespeare's *Julius Caesar* into French. The next year Poniatowski travelled to Saint Petersburg in the capacity of the private secretary to the British Ambassador, Sir Charles Hanbury Williams, an assignment hardly likely to have diminished his enthusiasm for Shakespeare.[3]

Setting aside royal patronage, the surge of foreign productions found powerful support in literary circles where Polish men of letters exhibited increasing interest in drama and theatre. In fact, in the second half of the eighteenth century Polish intellectual elites found themselves in continuous dialogue with French and German literature as well as with other authors, Shakespeare included, whose oeuvre these cultures mediated (Gibińska, Schulte). The first Polish essays on Shakespeare appeared in 1765 and 1766, in *Monitor*, a bi-weekly magazine patterned after the English *Spectator*. Both essays offered a favourable opinion on Shakespeare, however, it was the second one (published under a playful nickname Theatralski) which featured extensive translations – possibly via French – of Samuel Johnson's preface to Shakespeare's works of 1765 and used the authority of Shakespeare to discredit the neo-classicist doctrine of three dramatic unities.[4] Thus the highbrow critical debate both mirrored and theorized the daily struggle of French and German acting companies, competing for the privilege of performing in Warsaw and beyond.

The elites would also embark on European tours, thereby getting a first-hand experience of the rise of Shakespeare mania across the continent. The results of these trips varied. In 1794 Polish Princess Izabela Czartoryska paid an exorbitant price to purchase the faked Shakespeare chair in Stratford which she proudly brought home and exhibited in her palace to the amusement of both her contemporaries and posterity. However her son, Prince Adam Czartoryski, pressed for the inclusion of English literature in the university curriculum in Vilnius (which he supervised) and looked for talented students to offer them scholarships in England and Scotland. Two of them, Krystyn Lach-Szyrma and Karol Sienkiewicz, who both visited Stratford, returned home with the first passages of Shakespeare translated into Polish from the original language. Aristocratic libraries soon filled with French, German and English complete editions of Shakespeare's plays, reflecting the linguistic multiplicity of this elitist but immensely significant trend. The royal library of King Stanisław Poniatowski held a particularly rich collection of Shakespeare's works. In 1776 the Polish king also became a subscriber to the twenty-volume French edition of Pierre Le Tourneur's translations, purchased also by Ignacy Massalski (the Bishop of Vilnius), Ignacy Krasicki and many other members of the nobility (Komorowski 2002: 13). A similar collection of the newest editions of Shakespeare could be found in Puławy, the residence of the Czartoryski family. In fact, the circulation of books could have been much wider than the aristocratic houses: from the 1760s on, the booksellers in Warsaw would offer a decent selection of Shakespeare's works in English, French and German, in various editions, and at affordable prices (Komorowski 2002: 13).

However, the end of the eighteenth century brought disastrous changes in the condition of the Polish monarchy which fell into decline after belated social reforms. In 1772, 1793 and 1795 the country was partitioned amongst Russia, Prussia and Austria and gradually lost its sovereignty, with King Stanisław Poniatowski abdicating in 1795. The attempted uprising (1794) brought momentary hopes followed by human losses and further devastation of the land. These calamities, however, only fuelled the dream of a national theatre similar to that established in other countries which would confirm the strength and vitality of the otherwise collapsing native culture.

With Shakespeare's name already representing a recognized high value, his plays appeared to be an obvious choice for the new repertoire, irrespective of their 'sweet irregularity', emphatically eulogized in 1790 by Ignacy Bykowski, a novelist and translator of Voltaire and Alexander Pope (Bykowski 162). However, the ultimate confirmation of Shakespeare's elevated status came again from the monarchy: while embellishing his favourite residence in Warsaw in 1788, the king had had Shakespeare's portrait placed among the world's four greatest playwrights, next to Sophocles, Molière and Racine. When in 1793 another larger pantheon was erected, Shakespeare's figure stood proudly amongst sixteen geniuses of drama, filling the vast abyss of time between Seneca and Calderón (Żurowski 2007: 67–8).

It was, though, Wojciech Bogusławski who truly paved the way for a Polish Shakespeare: in 1796 he staged in Polish *The Tombs of Verona* (*Romeo and Juliet*, an adaptation of Louis-Sébastien Mercier's play of 1783, *Les Tombeaux de Vérone* translated by Józef Kossakowski) and, in 1798, *Hamlet*, both productions in Lvov. While the first Polish *Romeo and Juliet* had a distinctly French provenance, the first *Hamlet* was derived from German sources via an intricate network. Bogusławski is likely to have relied on a playscript borrowed from the theatrical library of Franz Heinrich Bulla, the Czech stage director and manager of the German theatre in Lvov and, for some time, also in Budapest and Warsaw, who in turn got hold of the Vienna version of the play. This version was a compilation of anonymous interpolations with several different rewritings of Schröder's adaptation of the play based on the German prose translation of the original play by Christoph Martin Wieland, revised by Eschenburg. Significantly enough, at the same time, Bogusławski directed the German theatre in Lvov (following the partition of the Polish Commonwealth, Lvov was formally part of Austrian Galicia) where he produced, in German, *King Lear* (1796), *Hamlet* (1796) and *Macbeth* (1797), all based on rewritings of Shakespeare. Similar synergies contributed to the strengthening of Shakespeare's repertoire in

Warsaw where, in 1793, the German theatre managed by Bulla in turn staged *Macbeth* (in the Vienna rewriting of Gottlieb Stephanie) and *King Lear*, both successfully. German and Polish productions were likely to have been watched by the same audience, whereas stage artists would often move between the companies.

Bogusławski soon became the director of the National Theatre in Warsaw, housed since 1779 in a new and imposing building, where he staged *Othello* (1801) and *King Lear* (1805) for the first time in Polish, both plays in Ludwik Osiński's translation of the French adaptation by Ducis. He also brought his *Hamlet* to Warsaw (1805), an exceptionally successful production staged repeatedly for the next twenty-five years. To complete his repertoire, Bogusławski commissioned Stanisław Regulski to translate and re-write Friedrich Schiller's adaptation of *Macbeth*, staged in 1812. The productions, abridged and provided with a happy ending, represented a plausible mixture of tradition and novelty and were positively received, largely due to the fashionable histrionic acting style. The origin of the playscripts and the revisions they were subjected to testify to the complex and heterogeneous nature of aesthetic influences that shaped the Polish stage of the time.

Parallel to the proliferation of productions on the Warsaw stage, Shakespeare's plays were also regularly performed in other cities, particularly in Lvov (where in the years 1809–42 the Polish theatre was masterfully managed by Jan Nepomucen Kamiński, an actor and translator, clearly favouring German appropriations of Shakespeare), in Vilnius (until the closure of the university in 1832 a vibrant cultural centre and a cradle of Polish Romanticism), as well as in Gdańsk, Poznań and Wrocław, all three frequented by German companies. Irrespective of the nature and language of these appropriations, their performance boosted the appetite of local audiences and initiated the prolonged period of waiting for truly Polish Shakespearean works based on the original plays. The first decades of the nineteenth century saw the emergence of an entire generation whose ambition, inspired by Schlegel, was to become Shakespeare translators and critical authorities. Though the ground was already prepared, historical circumstances again intervened. The turning points were the ineffective investment in support of Napoleon and the failed uprising against Russia in 1830 which caused harsh political repression, the closure of universities and the dispersal of elites into the partitioned regions of the former monarchy. Additionally, the post-uprising censorship strove to prevent the proliferation of images of regicide and tyranny, a policy resulting in the complete disappearance of Shakespeare's plays from the repertoires of theatres in the territory controlled by Russia until the late 1860s. The preventive policies also affected translation: in 1840 Ignacy Hołowiński, the translator of *Macbeth*, was forced by the censor to replace all occurrences of *ojczyzna* (homeland) with 'Scotland', or less specific, 'country' (*kraj*) to eliminate any associations between Macduff's condemnation of Macbeth's tyranny with the current situation of the Poles (Cetera 192–3).

In the stifling atmosphere of the occupied country writers withdrew into the safety of their country estates with significant consequences for Shakespeare's migration through print. At last, translations of the plays began to appear in the late 1830s, disclosing a divided aesthetic, caught between past and present literary conventions such as the neo-classicist preference for rhyme and measure and the Romantic elevation of folklore. Other difficulties were the inevitable clash with the bawdy, ribald and obscene elements of Shakespeare's plays and the prosodic problem of polysyllabic, soft and murmuring Polish, burdened with fricatives and considered unfit to render the energies of the English iambic pentameter. Characteristically enough, Ignacy Hołowiński, the first Polish translator of Shakespeare's plays from English, in six translations published in the years 1839–41, used four different types of metre, each time struggling to discover the rhyme pattern which he found indispensable for aesthetic reasons. He meticulously searched for local equivalents of customs, proverbs and accents, often compromising on the side of decency, a rather self-exposing strategy for the future archbishop of the Catholic Church in the East.

With time the stylistic and referential flexibility of some of the pioneering translations of Shakespeare made them acquire extra value deriving from their historicity. This is particularly true of early translators in the eastern borderlands (today no longer Polish), such as Placyd Jankowski, Apollo Korzeniowski (Joseph Conrad's father) or Adam Pług, who inadvertently managed to produce amber-like images of their multi-ethnic communities whose integrity was soon to be destroyed by the brutal geopolitics of the following century (Cetera-Włodarczyk and Kosim). Notwithstanding their cultural resourcefulness, these translations failed to find a permanent place in the canon reserved for texts more cautious in their choice of register and style. From the point of view of critical discourse, the ultimate prosodic and stylistic norms for translating Shakespeare were, to a large extent, set by Józef Korzeniowski, a translator with a very limited output but high literary authority. His translation of *King John* (1844) and the first act of *Richard II* (1860) became models for Polish Shakespeare, a choice reflecting on the one hand the growing interest in historical drama and, on the other hand, the safe investment in chivalric conventions. Incidentally, these preferences exemplified also the deeper attitudes of the social group who became the vehicles of Shakespeare's migration in translation.

The translations of Shakespeare in the nineteenth century were almost exclusively the work of the Polish gentry, completed in exile (usually in France) or in isolated households, many of which were located in eastern borderlands. Characteristically enough, these endeavours were often completely independent of any theatre practice and were perceived by their authors, among other things, as a simulacrum of patriotic service to the country whose sovereignty could not be reclaimed by political or military means. Translators with a significant measure of success, such as Leon Ulrich, Stanisław Egbert Koźmian, Jan Komierowski and Krystyn Ostrowski, had all participated in the failed uprising of 1830, and were living in exile or had withdrawn to country estates. Others, such as Józef Paszkowski, a leading translator of the age, stayed in their birthplace and embraced low-rank careers as office clerks or secretaries. To many, cultivating the language and literature of the partitioned country appeared the only way to counteract the uprooting cultural policies of the partitioning powers.

An additional and powerful support for Shakespeare's status came from the gradual dissemination of Polish Romantic literature (banned after 1830), composed largely in exile and fixated on the national tragedies of the preceding decades. Tinted with mysticism and messianism, Polish Romantic works, such as Adam Mickiewicz's *Forefathers' Eve* (*Dziady*), offered bitter anatomies of defeat, mingling images of devastation with declarations of trust in the redemptive power of suffering. Although the strongly religious dimension of Polish Romanticism found no direct counterpart in Shakespeare's plays, Shakespeare himself became the venerated patron-poet of the movement from its start. In 1822, Mickiewicz published his first volume of poetry in Vilnius entitled *Ballady i romanse*, featuring as its motto a translation of a dialogue from *Hamlet*, compressed into an introspective avowal: 'I see ... where? In my mind's eye.' The words became 'the quintessential declaration of Polish Romanticism' (Kujawińska-Courtney 2002–4), used to prioritize emotions and intuitive thinking over rational judgement. In a similar way, Juliusz Słowacki, interpolated into his major drama *Kordian* (1834) a loose translation of Edgar's description of the cliff in Dover (*King Lear* 4.6), apotheosizing Shakespeare's artistry of creating images for the blind. It also became Słowacki's ambition to convert Polish historiography and mythology into a monumental dramatic cycle, emulating the universal appeal of Shakespeare's plots. Indeed the structural parallels between Słowacki's *Balladyna* and *Macbeth*, his *Lilla Weneda* and *King Lear*, and *Horsztyński* and *Hamlet*, have been acknowledged and thoroughly examined in the critical discourse of the subsequent epochs. However, from the point of view of the early migration of Shakespeare, it was not the strength of conceptual borrowings, but the positioning and rhetorical effectiveness of the few citations embedded into the heart of national masterpieces which impacted on a wide readership and made them crave for complete translations.

Despite the proliferation of individual translating endeavours there was no publication of any complete edition of Shakespeare before the years 1875–7. The reasons for such a significant delay are manifold: the absence of any high-profile theatre venue which would stage Shakespeare; aesthetic disorientation in the face of a 'raw' Elizabethan playscript; tensions between cultural elites; and geographical peripheries without the means to disseminate their achievements. Typically, the best translators were often devoid of financial means to proceed with their projects, whereas affluent aristocrats published profusely, at their own expense. The translators with the greatest share in the national canon, Józef Paszkowski and Leon Ulrich, did not live to see all their translations in print and died unaware of the status they eventually achieved. Hence pivotal enterprises would advance in silence and isolation, sustained by aesthetic fascination, connoisseurship, escapism, rivalry and hope for final recognition.

The publication of the complete edition of Polish translations in 1875–7 can be interpreted as both the crowning and the closure of the first phase of Shakespeare's migration to Poland. A number of plays had established their presence in Poland by this time, though in a form exceedingly dependent on migration routes and mediating agents. Setting aside the cultural input of foreign companies, the first wave of Polish productions of Shakespeare, based on the rewritings of either French or German abridgments, comprised five core plays: *Romeo and Juliet*, *Hamlet*, *King Lear*, *Othello* and *Macbeth*. Most of these plays were first performed in Warsaw, Kraków and Lvov at the end of the eighteenth century, and continued to be staged, with varying intensity, until the 1830 uprising. In the subsequent decades, strict censorship in the Russian partition banished Shakespeare from the stage until the 1870s when the second wave of performances reached Warsaw. The choice of titles was virtually unchanged, based, however, on prior Polish translations, and comprising *Romeo and Juliet*

(1870), *Hamlet* (1871), *Othello* (1873), *Macbeth* (1878) and *King Lear* (1879).

In Lvov and Kraków the permissive policies of the Austrian empire allowed for a more challenging repertoire. In Lvov, the adapted adaptations (numerous abridgments of *The Taming of the Shrew* among them) enjoyed continuous popularity until the 1860s when they were replaced by playscripts based on Polish translations, an innovation originating in Kraków and propelled by the directorial talents of Stanisław Koźmian. The ultimate number of Shakespeare's plays introduced by Koźmian comprised one-third of the whole canon, but the choice of the pioneering titles looks conspicuously familiar. Prior to the publication of the canon, Polish theatre took little incentive in accommodating the plays from outside the core set, and only a few new titles briefly visited the stages in Kraków and Lvov. There was one play, however, which decidedly broke the pattern. In 1869 Warsaw saw the first performance of *The Merchant of Venice*, staged with minor exceptions for the next decade. The status of the play was even more conspicuous in Kraków, where *The Merchant of Venice*, performed first in 1866, was staged almost unremittingly until the end of the century.

The Polish response to *The Merchant of Venice* appears to fall in line with the pan-European tendency to single out this play and use it for a variety of strongly ideological purposes, such as ethnic slander, expiation or the means of collective therapy. Yet its centrality amongst Shakespeare plays performed on the Polish stage is clearly related to the specificity of local history. In the nineteenth century, the Polish lands held the largest Jewish population in Eastern Europe. The Jewish community was significantly diversified in their social status and the degree of assimilation with the local, usually Polish, but also Lithuanian, Ukrainian or Belarusian culture. This large settlement began in the thirteenth century – partially triggered by the policies of Edward I in England – when Jews expelled from western countries moved elsewhere, finding refuge in the vast spaces of Eastern Europe that had been recently abandoned by withdrawing Mongolian tribes. The subsequent centuries witnessed the establishment of a unique ethnic symbiosis, with Slavs benefiting from the economic and intellectual capital brought by the newcomers, and Jews free to observe their own way of life in what came to be called *paradisus Judaeorum*. With time, however, the tension increased. It was particularly the eighteenth and nineteenth centuries that bred ethnic hatred. With occasional acts of violence and new laws aimed at curbing the growth of the Jewish population, Jews were nevertheless an important part of the then Polish society, both in the urban and rural setting. It is precisely the presence of Jews and the ambivalent attitudes towards them which are the key to the early reception of *The Merchant of Venice*. As long as Shakespeare's Jews could be seen as projections of their situation throughout Europe, the play in translation entered cultural spaces full of live referents. Paradoxically enough, out of all of Shakespeare's characters, Shylock was to Eastern European audiences the only man whose identity seemed entirely local and familiar. In a way, the play was to find a home in a land which had taken part its ideological matrix.

The Merchant of Venice first received critical attention in 1841 when Andrzej Koźmian, the son of a leading poet of the Polish enlightenment, published an essay with a plot synopsis. With hindsight, Koźmian turned out to be a rather unsuccessful translator of *Macbeth* (1857), but in the 1840s his voice was, no doubt, augmented by the strength of his family background and societal ties with the literary elites of the time. His own son, Stanisław, would become the renowned director of the theatre in Kraków. In turn Stanisław Egbert Koźmian, Andrzej's cousin, was one of the three translators of the Polish canonical Shakespeare published in the years 1875–7.

Both the choice of the play and the profile of Koźmian's commentary appear indicative of the specific response *The Merchant of Venice* could generate in Poland. Koźmian placed the play among Shakespeare's greatest achievements although, regrettably, not free from some flaws which he in due course sought to expose and remedy. 'Shylock' – argued Koźmian – 'is a Jew besmeared with all the vices of his people. His greed equals his avarice, whereas his commitment to the prejudice and superstitions of his faith are equally as pervasive as his hate of Christians' (Koźmian 81).[5] The major weakness of the play was seen in the deficiencies of realism such as, for example, the improbable bond which Shylock had no reason to demand unless he had prior knowledge of the loss of Antonio's ships. Notwithstanding Koźmian's efforts to improve the plot, the play did not find its way onto the stage for the next twenty years or so, except for Lvov, where it was twice performed in 1844 and 1854 in a version so hybrid and derivative that it is impossible to agree on its provenance.

The absence of the play's performance in Polish was, to some extent, counterbalanced by the visits of foreign companies, Austrian and German in particular. A unique phenomenon, Ira Aldridge, a black American actor who toured Eastern Europe in the years 1853 to 1867, performed in an expressive style typical of the age. He excelled in the part of Othello and those of archetypal villains, such as Richard III and Shylock. Aldridge's Jew was savage and terrifying and yet capable of evoking compassion, partially due to the actor's superimposing his own otherness on Shylock's ethnicity (Sawala 349–73; Kujawińska-Courtney 2009). Thus the Jew's part became endowed with some tragic dimension, although mediated chiefly through non-verbal means. This referred in particular to the scenes of the elopement of Jessica and the enforced conversion, and the overall understanding of Shylock's villainy as a product of mistreatment covering many centuries. It is reported that following the production of *The Merchant of Venice* in one of the Russian towns, Aldridge was approached by a group of Jews who thanked him for the way he showed Shylock's terror upon hearing about the forced conversion (Marshall and Stock, cited in Kujawińska-Courtney: 288). But despite their artistic and interpretative merits, it is rather unlikely that Aldridge's guest performances featuring inevitable heteroglossia (he delivered his lines in English while performing with German and Polish companies) could truly anchor the play in the national consciousness.

The second production of *The Merchant of Venice* was staged again in Lvov in 1865 and was based on the three-act rewriting of Paris-based Count Krystyn Ostrowski. The translation was published in 1861 under the title *Lichwiarz* (The Usurer) which clearly demonstrated the shift of emphasis in the perception of the play's theme, further augmented by the vehemently anti-Semitic tirade in the preface, stigmatizing the 'parasitic tribe which has mingled with our people', infecting them with centuries' long 'leprosy' (Ostrowski ix–x). The text contained so many interpolations derogatory to Shylock that the Austrian authorities censored the promptbook for fear of igniting racial hatred. The negative perception of Jews was hardly rare at that time, even among those who would admit the iniquity of their persecution in past epochs. Such apparently compassionate observation, exemplified by the preface of the play in the later canonical edition of Shakespeare plays of 1877, in fact strengthened the already existing prejudice because the acknowledgement of the mistreatment of Jews went hand in hand with the conclusion that hardship had contaminated their character as a people:

> It would be all but superfluous to repeat that notwithstanding the consequences of their blood and religious doctrine, it was the thousand years of discrimination and exclusion from the law, and living in strange and hostile places which have undoubtedly shaped their revengeful, malicious, impious and cunning disposition, a disposition that this representative of their tribe [Shylock] so evidently displays.
>
> Kraszewski 403

Notwithstanding the appeal of the printed word, it was the theatre which held the strongest grip over popular imagination. Here the social and psychological design of the Polish Shylock became more ambiguous, though with the same tendency towards a domestication of the figure. The first fully fledged production of the play in Kraków, in 1866, exposed both the malice and the tragic dimension of Shylock, dressed in the daily apparel of local Jews, and speaking with an accent heard in the streets of the Jewish Quarter in Kraków (Żurowski 2001: 333–5). This common, underprivileged denizen was replaced with a more rabbinical figure in the Warsaw staging of 1869. The spectacular production resounded with music written by Stanisław Moniuszko, the father of Polish opera, whose score was also used in 1871 in the Warsaw production of *Hamlet*. The scenery followed an illusionistic trend in theatre productions and comprised large-scale illusionist paintings of sixteenth-century Venice. In the eyes of the reviewers, the Warsaw Shylock was supposed to embody 'the Jewish revenge for the persecutions of the whole tribe', whereas his speech oscillated between tuneful chatter and guttural rasping, 'typical of Semitic people', when the topic touched upon the subject of money or vengeance (Żurowski 2001: 232).

We can see how the two most influential Polish productions of *The Merchant of Venice* in the nineteenth century forged two complementary images of Shylock. One was patterned after a greedy money-lender from the neighbourhood, whereas the other was a proud Jew of the patriarchal type, challenging the authority of the judges. In both cases, however, Shylock was understood to be a familiar and realistic portrayal of the contemporaneous Jew whose villainy was interpreted in the light of our shared history. Hence the nineteenth-century Polish perception of Shylock was built on two different assumptions, one of which ignored the implications of dramatic fiction, whereas the other was a downright anachronism. Nonetheless, of all Shakespeare's characters and of all Shakespeare's plays in Poland, Shylock and *The Merchant of Venice* were initially most absorbed and naturalized. Interestingly enough, a similar urge to identify with and absorb permeates a well-known painting *Shylock and Jessica* (1876) by Maurycy Gottlieb, a Polish painter of Jewish origin. The poignant portrayal won a gold medal from the Academy in Munich and was displayed in Warsaw and Lvov. Significantly enough, the scenes from *The Merchant of Venice* appear to have been the most often explored theme in Polish visual arts of the time (Ciechowicz 197).

However the intensity of the initial absorption contributed to the strength of the subsequent ideological blockage: following the Second World War *The Merchant of Venice* disappeared from the Polish stage for decades.

Therefore, while acknowledging the intricacies of the ways by which Shakespeare began to enter a national or ethnic consciousness, it seems also tempting to challenge the underlying assumption that the process is, or should be, viewed as irrevocable. Do Shakespeare's plays enter national canons to remain there? If we agree that true embracement of foreign masterpieces calls for critical engagement rather than a hushed acknowledgement of status, can a play expelled from the stage and literary studies still hold its canonical status? And if not, can it nevertheless occupy a prominent place in the hosting land's culture? Naturally, there are numerous historical and aesthetic factors that affect the way a literary work drifts along through time. However, setting aside shifting preferences or topical interests, there are also potent ideological pressures which render critical inquiries and theatrical representation importunate or even ethically obtuse. Impeded and fragmented, the migration process endures, sustained by an alternation of lacunae and re-entries.

There are cases, however, when the immediate historical context facilitates migration but is soon exhausted and becomes irrelevant to the point of invisibility. Such an idiosyncratic pattern in Poland can be identified in the case of *The Winter's Tale*. In the 1870s – a decade which saw the publication of Shakespeare's complete works – the allegedly Slavic sources of *The Winter's Tale* stimulated national interest. The search brought rich but rather doubtful results, which nevertheless helped to solidify the perception of Shakespeare as a universal writer indebted to European culture at large. The inspiration (and scholarly credit) for investigations of Shakespeare's materials came from a German historian, Jacob Caro, who pointed to the similarities between Shakespeare's source, *Pandosto*, and the story of Zimovit III (*c.* 1320–81), the Duke of Mazovia, who likewise castigated his pregnant wife to find, years afterwards, a boy much like himself, his rejected infant son. It was also Caro who stipulated a historically viable path of transmission of the story by mentioning a large group of English knights (Henry Bolingbroke included) who at the end of the fourteenth century joined the crusades of the Teutonic Knights in the Baltics, and therefore could have heard about events in the neighbouring land. Caro's hypothesis was embraced by the first Polish translator of the play, Gustaw Ehrenberg, who in 1871 dedicated a lengthy preface to this question and strengthened arguments linking *Pandosto* with the Baltic region (23–6). The Slavic origin of the play soon became the subject of contemporary debate to the effect of including two other essays in the first collected edition of Shakespeare's plays: one in support, and another one undermining the hypothesis. The author of the latter offered a far more elaborate version of the story which bore but faint resemblance to *Pandosto*, but had its own sensational merits, adding to the attractiveness of the paratextual backup of the play (Kraszewski 695–9).

Setting aside the provenance of the plot, the immediate context of the Polish reception of *The Winter's Tale* appeared equally captivating. Ehrenberg was an illegitimate son of Tsar Alexander I and a Polish aristocratic woman. In his mid-twenties he began to operate as a political conspirator and an advocate for independence which eventually led to his trial and the death penalty in 1838. The sentence was commuted to hard labour in the Siberian mines where he spent approximately the next twenty years. In Nerchinsk (Transbaikal) where he was eventually relocated, Ehrenberg enjoyed more liberty and he could read Shakespeare's plays available from a local library, an interest well documented in his diaries. He returned to Poland in 1858 and published his only translation of Shakespeare: *The Winter's Tale*. The prose rendition was enthusiastically received and staged several times, the first ever performance taking place in Kraków in 1877. The productions of the play in Ehrenberg's translation – decades before Polish audiences saw *Twelfth Night* or *The Tempest* for the first time – drew covertly on the appeal of the translator's turbulent biography. Conversely, the status of Hermione as a Tsar's daughter, her trial, assumed death and return to life, invited parallels with Ehrenberg's life and added strength to his martyr-like fame. It was only in the twentieth century that the biographical context paled, letting the play live its own life.

Thus cultural affinities, be they imagined, assumed or actual, played a significant role in the early migration of Shakespeare's plays, enhancing the dynamics and intensity of naturalization. This was particularly true when productions targeted, for the first time, wide audiences who lacked expert knowledge about Elizabethan drama but were already aware of the playwright's high cultural status. Dependencies of this kind appeared less impactful for the earliest migration routes when the success of strolling companies hung on the sheer entertainment value of anonymous plots. Additionally, the itineraries of the first visiting companies were dependent on commercial networks and geographical conditions, an aspect less relevant for the migration mediated by the monarchy or literary elites, mobile and flexible in their pursuits. The agency of the latter, however, introduced Shakespeare to prestigious venues, rather inaccessible to popular audiences. It was only with the dissemination of printed editions and the development of public theatres, that the potential spectatorship and readership became more varied, allowing Shakespeare to truly settle into Polish culture.

Notes

1 This article incorporates the research results of the state-funded projects The e-Repository of the Polish 19th Century Shakespeare Translations: Resources, Strategies and Reception 2016–2018 (NCN Opus 9, UMO-2015/17/B/HS2/01784).

2 The term Polish lands refers here both to contemporary Polish territories (some of which in the eighteenth, nineteenth and early twentieth century were part of Prussia/Germany) and also to the regions which belonged to the Polish commonwealth in the said

period and now constitute parts of Ukraine, Belarus and Lithuania. The audiences in these regions were typically multi-ethnic, of varying national proportion.

3 Incidentally, Poniatowski could have shared his interest in Shakespeare with his then lover, Catherine II. See Kizima's chapter in this volume.

4 The identity of the author is the subject of a centuries' long debate in Polish Studies, with King Stanisław Poniatowski and Ignacy Krasicki (a leading poet of the age) among possible candidates, whereas the postulated source is a French review of Johnson's edition published in *Gazette littéraire de l'Europe*.

5 All translations into English are mine.

References

Bykowski, I. (1788), *Wieczory wieyskie*, cz. 2. Warszawa.

Cetera, A. (2009), *Smak morwy. U źródeł recepcji przekładów Szekspira w Polsce*, Warszawa: Wydawnictwa Uniwersytetu Warszawskiego.

Cetera-Włodarczyk, A. and A. Kosim (2019), *Polskie przekłady Shakespeare'a w XIX wieku: Zasoby, strategie, recepcja*, Warszawa: Wydawnictwa Uniwersytetu Warszawskiego.

Ciechowicz, J. (1993), 'Żydzi i chrześcijanie, czyli o *Kupcu weneckim*', in J. Ciechowicz and Z. Majchrowski eds, *Od Shakespeare'a do Szekspira*, Gdańsk: Centrum Edukacji Teatralnej, Fundacja Theatrum Gedanense, Wydział Filologiczno-Historyczny Uniwersytetu Gdańskiego.

Ehrenberg, G. (1871), 'Przedmowa' [do *Zimowej powieści*], *Przegląd Polski*, V: X, 23–37.

Gibińska, M. (2003), 'Enter Shakespeare: The Contexts of Early Polish Appropriations', in A. L. Pujante and T. Hoenselaars eds, *Four Hundred Years of Shakespeare in Europe*, 54–69, Newark and London: University of Delaware Press.

Komorowski, J. (2002), *Piramida zbrodni.'Makbet' w kulturze polskiej 1790–1989*, Warszawa: Instytut Sztuki Polskiej Akademii Nauk.

Komorowski, J. (2003), 'Czy angielscy komedianci grali w Polsce Shakespeare'a?', *Pamiętnik Teatralny*, 3–4, 5–14.

Koźmian, A. E. (1841), 'Rozbiory sztuk dramatycznych Szekspira' [*Kupiec wenecki*], *Biblioteka Warszawska*, 4, 74–99.

Kraszewski, J. I. (1877a), 'Przedmowa' [do *Kupca weneckiego*] in W. Shakespeare, *Dzieła dramatyczne*, trans. S. Koźmian, J. Paszkowski and L. Ulrich, vol. III, Warsaw.

Kujawińska-Courtney, K. (2002–4), 'Shakespeare in Poland', *Shakespeare around the Globe*, University of Victoria. Available online: https://internetshakespeare.uvic.ca/Library/Criticism/shakespearein/poland1/index.html.

Kujawińska-Courtney, K. (2009), *Ira Aldridge (1807–1867): Dzieje pierwszego czarnoskórego tragika szekspirowskiego*, Kraków: Universitas.

Limon, J. (1989), *Gdański teatr 'elżbietański'*, Wrocław: Zakład Narodowy im. Ossolińskich

Limon, J. (2009 [1985]), *Gentlemen of a Company: English Players in Central and Eastern Europe, 1590–1660*, Cambridge: Cambridge University Press.

Limon, J. (2016), 'Players and the Playing Business', in Bruce R. Smith ed., *The Cambridge Guide to the Worlds of Shakespeare. Shakespeare's World, 1500–1660*. Volume One, 83–8, New York: Cambridge University Press.

Marshall, H. and M. Stock (1958), *Ira Aldridge: The Negro Tragedian*, London: Rockcliff.

Ostrowski, K. (1861), 'Wstęp' in W. Shakespeare, *Dziełka dramatyczne*, trans. Krystyn Ostrowski, V–XII, Kraków.

Sawala K. (1989), 'Polskie losy afrykańskiego Roscjusza', in H. Marshall and M. Stock eds, *Ira Aldridge – ciemnoskóry tragik*, 349–73, Warszawa: Państwowy Instytut Wydawniczy.

Schulte, B. (1993), 'Shakespeare's Ways into the West Slavic Literatures and Cultures', in D. Delabastita and L. D'hulst eds, *European Shakespeare. Translating Shakespeare in the Romantic Age*, 55–74, Amsterdam: John Benjamins Publishing.

Shakespeare, W. (2006), *Hamlet*, ed. A. Thompson and N. Taylor, The Arden Shakespeare, London: Bloomsbury.

Szekspir, W. (1868), *Lichwiarz (Kupiec wenecki)*, trans. K. Ostrowski, Paris.

Żurowski, A. (2001), *Szekspir w cieniu gwiazd*, Gdańsk: Tower Press.

Żurowski, A. (2007), *Prehistoria polskiego Szekspira*, Gdańsk: Literatura net pl.

7

From migration to naturalization

Shakespeare in Russia

Marina P. Kizima

The world of Shakespeare's imagination embraced many lands and Russia had a place on its map: *Love's Labour's Lost*, *Measure for Measure*, *King Henry V*, *Macbeth*, *The Winter's Tale* show that Shakespeare had some inkling of the habits and ways of Muscovites and the cold climate of Muscovy. There is evidence that Shakespeare was not unknown to Russians in the seventeenth century, but the first recorded steps towards an acquaintance were made in the middle of the eighteenth through the influence of French and German cultures. A few decades later, with the confluence of Romanticism and the rise of nationalism, a more Russian Shakespeare emerged. The key figure instrumental in Shakespeare's 'naturalization' in Russia was Alexander Pushkin who embraced and embedded him in Russian literature and culture, paving the way to national acceptance and appropriation in the 1820s to 1830s.

Throughout the eighteenth century France and Germany were important cultural mediators in the migration of Shakespeare to Russia. French was the language the Russian élite learned in their childhood and could speak, read and write fluently. Initially Shakespeare was received through French adaptations and appeared in a classicist guise, which was almost inevitable, for classicism was the mode of the French theatre and prevalent all over Europe. In this respect the most significant roles were played by Voltaire and La Place. Voltaire's estimate of Shakespeare in the *Philosophical Letters, or Letters Concerning the English Nation* (Letter XVIII. *On Tragedy*), first published in 1733, remained dominant until the beginning of the nineteenth century. In 1745 the publication of French prose renderings of Shakespeare's plays by La Place in *Le Théâtre anglois* opened the way to a closer acquaintance for the reading public and gave rise to Russian theatrical adaptations. In the eighteenth century the reading public was growing and included, besides the aristocracy, many of the commoners. Russian theatre, too, developed rapidly in a variety of forms: there were privately owned theatres open to the general public for an admission fee and so-called 'school theatres' in educational establishments. The Land Forces Cadet School Theatre deserves to be mentioned here: in the 1740s its director was Alexander Sumarokov (1717–77), an outstanding Russian man of letters, poet and playwright, who was the first important figure in the Russian engagement with Shakespeare.

In 1748 Sumarokov published a poem 'Эпистола II. О стихотворстве' (Epistle II. On Verse-Writing) which paid homage to the great 'ancients', led by Homer, as well as the great 'moderns'; the English poets he mentioned were Shakespeare, Milton and Pope. This was the first time Shakespeare's name appeared in Russia in print: Шекеспир (another version of the name in the eighteenth century was Шакеспир; at present the accepted norm is Шекспир). However, the fact that Sumarokov included Shakespeare, 'though uneducated' (Сумароков [Sumarokov] 117),[1] among the great suggests that Shakespeare was not unknown to Russian readers.

In his notes to the 'Epistle' Sumarokov wrote: 'Shakespeare, an English author of tragedies and comedies, who has much that is very bad, but also much that is exceedingly good' (129). This mixed estimate of Shakespeare's achievements is generally attributed to the influence of Voltaire.

Obviously, Sumarokov was inspired by Shakespeare the dramatist, for that same year (1748) he published his Гамлет (Hamlet), based on La Place's prose version. Surprisingly, in this work Sumarokov did not even mention Shakespeare's name, a fact noted and criticized by his contemporaries. Vasiliy Trediakovsky (1703–69), a prominent man of letters, maintained that Sumarokov had used the works of others and that his *Hamlet* was a translation in verse of the French prose rendering, an argument rebutted by Sumarokov: 'My *Hamlet*, with the exception of the soliloquy at the end of Act Three and Claudius's falling on his knees, has hardly anything in common with Shakespeare's tragedy' (quoted in Алексеев [Alekseev] 23). Indeed, Sumarokov had changed the plot radically: the Ghost is suppressed; Claudius is a courtier, not the late King's brother; Polonius, his accomplice in the murder of the King, ends by committing suicide; Polonius's daughter Ophelia does not die and Hamlet becomes king. Ophelia and Hamlet love each other, but their mutual love is incompatible with their sense of duty to their fathers; this conflict between love and duty becomes central and the play is a triumph of virtue over vice, while the future of the mutual love remains uncertain. Nevertheless, it is difficult to accept Sumarokov's claim to originality without reservations. The most Shakespearean moment, as he himself admitted, is Hamlet's soliloquy ('To be or not to be . . .') where the verse – in images and wording – is very close to the French versions of Shakespeare. However, in his efforts to render Shakespeare in Russian as best he could, Sumarokov extended the soliloquy to fifty-four lines, achieving emotional intensity and stylistic beauty. D. M. Lang takes the view that, in fact, Sumarokov was a pioneer in recognizing the dramatic potential of Shakespeare's play; it was staged nineteen years before the first French adaptation of

Hamlet was made by Ducis, who was no less un-Shakespearean than Sumarokov (Lang 67–72).

Sumarokov's *Hamlet* was successfully staged for ten years (1750–60) in Saint Petersburg and Moscow, and made up for the absence of a Russian translation from the English. Its disappearance from the stage in 1762 had little to do with its artistic qualities; it was caused by the undesirable coincidences between the play and the events that took place at the time: the assassination of Tsar Peter III and the accession to the throne of his wife, Catherine II. As Alexander Bardovsky observed, 'the real, not the stage tragedy of Prince Hamlet was taking place before the eyes of all Russian society' (147): Prince Paul, the son and heir to the throne, was Hamlet; Peter III – the assassinated King; Catherine II – Queen Gertrude; her lover, the murderers' accomplice, Grigoriy Orlov (a courtier, exactly as in Sumarokov's play) was Claudius. In these unfavourable circumstances Sumarokov did not lose his interest in Shakespeare: working on a tragedy based on Russian history Димитрий Самозванец (Dimitriy the Pretender, 1770), Sumarokov proclaimed in a letter to his friend, writer and journalist Grigoriy Kozitsky, that 'this tragedy will show Shakespeare to Russia' (quoted in Алексеев [Alekseev] 32). The plot was set at a turning point in Russian history – the Time of Troubles (1598–1613) – marked by a series of economic and political crises, natural disasters, violent social and dynastic conflicts, it culminated in the patriotic war against the Polish invasion; victory in the war consolidated the Russian nation and brought the Romanov dynasty to power. This crucial page of Russian history later inspired Pushkin to write his Shakespearean tragedy – *Boris Godunov*.

Shakespeare was quickly gaining ground in Russia, and Russia, in a way, contributed to the French efforts towards a better acquaintance with Shakespeare. In 1776–83 a new, twenty-volume edition of Shakespeare translated into prose by Pierre-Prime-Félicien Le Tourneur was published by subscription; the first volume opened with the list of subscribers, among whom were the names of Empress Catherine II and other prominent Russian lovers of literature. At the same time, Germany as a mediator in the Russian appropriation of Shakespeare came to the fore with German prose translations of Shakespeare, *William Shakespeare's Schauspiele von J. J. Eschenburg* (Shakespeare's Plays Translated by J. J. Eschenburg, 1775–82, revised edition 1778–83) reaching Russia and arousing great interest. In 1786 Empress Catherine II wrote in a letter that she was reading Shakespeare in German translation and 'had already devoured nine volumes' (quoted in Алексеев [Alekseev] 34). She herself composed several plays imitating Shakespeare, setting the scene in Russia and giving Russian names to the characters. In 1786 her adaptation of *The Merry Wives of Windsor* was staged at the court theatre in Saint Petersburg under the title *Вольное, но слабое переложение из Шакеспира, комедия 'Вот каково иметь корзину и белье'* (A Free but Weak Rendering from Shakespeare, a Comedy 'This 'tis to Have Linen and Buck-baskets'); it was the first production on the Russian stage to bear the name of Shakespeare. The next year the comedy and two histories were printed in part 14, vol. 5 of *Российский феатр, или Полное собрание всех российских театральных сочинений* (The Russian Theatre, or a Complete Collection of All Russian Theatrical Works), published by the Imperial Academy of Sciences.

In the final decades of the eighteenth century more Russians were beginning to read Shakespeare in English and critical interpretation became less dependent on the accepted French appraisals. Mikhail Plesheev, who had been on diplomatic service in London and knew English, offered the public his translation of Hamlet's soliloquy ('To be or not to be . . .') and accompanied it with a letter signed 'Angloman' in 1775. Both were first published in the journal 'Works of the Free Russian Society at the Imperial Moscow University'; the Society was formed to promote the development of the Russian language. In the letter Plesheev remarked that it was important to translate the soliloquy into Russian, as not all Russians knew enough French to read Voltaire's translation; moreover, he found that 'Voltaire wrestled with Shakespeare more than translated him, and if his translation were translated back into English no one would recognize Shakespeare's work' (Шевченко [Shevchenko] 121). Plesheev believed that by reading foreign – especially English – writers, Russians would develop their imagination and the figurative qualities of their language.

Proto-romantic tendencies, in the wake of the *Sturm und Drang* movement in Germany, were growing in these decades and Shakespeare was seen as a source of a new art, free from the norms of classicism and true to nature, a force sharing in the general effort to reform Russian culture and Russian national literature. In 1787 a translation of Shakespeare's *Julius Caesar* was published anonymously in Moscow; its author, Nikolai Karamzin (1766–1826), was to become a major figure in Russian culture at the turn of the century. Undertaking an important reform of the Russian literary language in his poetry and prose he voiced the ideas of sentimentalism as a new literary trend. His multi-volume *История государства Российского* (History of the Russian State, 1803–26) was to exercise a strong influence on Russian society in general, and on Alexander Pushkin in particular.

In his literary approach Karamzin drew on contemporary German criticism and aesthetic thought including Herder, Goethe, Schiller and other writers of the *Sturm und Drang* movement. Jacob Lenz, one of the *Stürmer*, who lived for some time in Moscow, was a friend of Karamzin and may have stirred his interest in Shakespeare who became an integral part of Karamzin's inner growth as a man of letters. In the preface to his translation of *Julius Caesar* Karamzin boldly disagreed with Voltaire whom he called the 'famous sophist' (ii, 80) and, unlike the advocates of classicism, described Shakespeare's works as 'elegant and sublime' (ii, 79). He concurred with Herder and Goethe in stressing that the greatness of Shakespeare's genius was above conventional rules: 'His spirit soared like an eagle, and could not measure his flight with the same measure the sparrows measure their flight'; 'his dramas, like the immeasurable theatre of nature, are full of limitless variety' (ii, 81). The words echo passages in Herder's essay on Shakespeare.

Karamzin's was the first translation into Russian of a complete play by Shakespeare from the English original by a person who was a distinguished writer and, as such, he strove to make his prose version a work of art, true to the original and true to the Russian language – a decisive step forward compared with the usual practice at the time. Yet, in other respects, his translation of Shakespeare was untimely: the early 1790s were a time of persecution of Freemasonry in Russia, and *Julius Caesar*, a play about regicide (a very sensitive theme in Russia after the assassination of Tsar Peter III), translated by a former Mason and published by a leader of Russian Freemasons Nikolai Novikov (1744–1818) came under suspicion; in 1794 it was banned and disappeared from the public eye.

In the wake of censorship Karamzin did not translate any other works by Shakespeare, but allusions to Shakespeare and quotations from Shakespeare abound in his prose and poetry. The greatest number of these quotations can be found in his *Письма русского путешественника* (Letters of a Russian Traveller, 1791–2) published shortly after his journey to Europe when he visited Germany, Switzerland, France and Britain. Karamzin turns to Shakespeare in various contexts – reflecting on human passions and the destiny of nations, conveying his own feelings and emotions: he quotes Lear's monologue 'Blow winds . . . Rage, blow!' in English and then offers a translation; the lines from *The Tempest* he sees on the monument to Shakespeare in Westminster Abbey – the lines that he had quoted in his poem 'Poetry' (1787) – move him deeply and he quotes them again in an improved translation. 'Letters of a Russian Traveller' was a landmark in the history of Russian literature and very popular among readers; thus, through Karamzin as a mediator, Shakespeare was present in the Russian cultural discourse.

Indeed, Karamzin was not the only Russian writer who engaged in such intertextual dialogue with Shakespeare, for Shakespeare was becoming well known amongst men of letters and the general reading public. Shakespeare's migration to the Russian stage – as in other cultures – took quite a different path than that which led to his absorption into literary and cultural life. The situation in the theatre left much to be desired: the stage had to live by adaptations, at least twice removed from the original – Russian adaptations of free versions in French. Nevertheless, the role of these adaptations should not be underestimated, for they were instrumental in making the theatre-going public aware of Shakespeare. In this context two French playwrights were influential: Louis-Sébastien Mercier and, as already mentioned, Jean-François Ducis. Mercier, a prominent figure of the French Enlightenment and one of the founders of the new genre of social drama, was well known in Russia. One of his most successful adaptations was *Les Tombeaux de Vérone* (The Tombs of Verona, 1782) based on *Romeo and Juliet*. The adaptation was translated in 1790 by Vasiliy Pomerantsev, a famous actor, and staged in Moscow in 1795. Although he was translating Mercier, Pomerantsev gave the play Shakespeare's title and described it as a drama 'taken by Mercier from the works of Shakespeare' (Алексеев [Alekseev] 81). Ducis's verse adaptations of Shakespeare were also extremely popular. One of the most successful was *Othello* (1792); it inspired Ivan Velyaminov (1771–1837), an infantry general, a statesman and a man of letters, to write his own adaptation of the play in Russian (1808). Velyaminov felt free to cut and change the French source and mentioned neither Shakespeare nor Ducis. His prose version was fluent and free from archaisms, which ensured its longevity on the Russian stage: theatres in Russia used it until well into the 1830s.

The pan-European rise of Romanticism coincided in Russia with a flowering of its literature, the beginning of what was to be known as its Golden Age. In 1812 Russia triumphed in its patriotic war against Napoleon's invasion; the war consolidated the nation, as had occurred previously in the war against the Polish invaders, and reinforced its consciousness of national identity with the new cultural climate, giving an impetus to the development of literature, literary criticism and the theatre.

The young Romantic generation was rich in poetic talents, regarding Shakespeare as their great predecessor and appropriating him as a pillar in the construction of Russian national culture. This work culminated in the 1820s to 1830s in the towering figure of Pushkin whose genius expressed the Romantic vision and went beyond Romantic bounds.

In the narrative of Shakespeare's migration to Russia, the role of Alexander Pushkin (1799–1837) is seminal: he put Shakespeare, as it were, 'inside' Russian literature. He moved from translation and imitation to an artistic dialogue with Shakespeare as the 'father' figure; this dialogue embraced all aspects of his work (poetry, prose, drama, criticism) and had a great influence on the cultural scene, for Pushkin became the cornerstone of modern Russian literature, the fullest and noblest expression of the Russian mind. Pushkin's engagement with Shakespeare was a source of his own growth as an artist and a person; his appropriation of the English poet resulted in original and innovative works of Russian literature. Such was the nature of Pushkin's genius: it 'enabled him to imbue himself with the spirit of one writer after another, take all he could from each, and then return to his own writing enriched by new experiences and with a widened literary horizon' (Wolff 104).

Brought up on French literature, Pushkin knew of Shakespeare through the works of Voltaire and Jean-François de La Harpe, and in his growth as an artist he had to overcome French critical attitudes. The distinguished Russian scholar B.V. Tomashevsky noted that Pushkin came to understand Shakespeare by comparing him with Racine and Molière (1960: 91–2). Though such comparisons did not lose their importance, very quickly Pushkin's aesthetic tastes grew to embrace European literature in its variety; Shakespeare along with Dante, Calderón and Goethe were among his favourite authors. With Byron, Shakespeare was the poet who prompted Pushkin (around 1824) to start learning English in order to read both writers in the original, and in a few years he knew it well enough to read his favourite poets. The first documented evidence of Pushkin's serious interest in Shakespeare is his letter from Odessa (spring 1824) to his friend and distinguished poet Pyotr Vyazemsky (1792–1878) where he writes: '... reading Shakespeare and the Bible, the Holy Spirit is sometimes to my liking, but I prefer Goethe and Shakespeare' (xiii, 92). The combination of Goethe and Shakespeare is telling, considering Goethe's role in the European reappraisal of Shakespeare.

However, it is important to remember that in Pushkin's time French writers, too, were in growing opposition to the aesthetics of classicism. In 1821 a new edition of Le Tourneur's translations of Shakespeare, revised by François Guizot and Amédée Pichot, was published; a copy of this edition was in Pushkin's library (Модзалевский [Modzalevsky] 337, no. 1389). Guizot's introduction 'Vie de Shakespeare' gave, besides the biographical information, an analysis of Shakespeare's dramatic principles and the art of drama in general. Much of what Guizot wrote had been prepared by earlier criticism, particularly August Wilhelm Schlegel's lectures *Vorlesungen über dramatische Kunst und Literatur* (On Dramatic Art and Literature, 1809–11) which was translated into French in 1814. Pushkin had a copy of the French edition and in spring 1825, when he was in Mikhailovskoye, asked his brother to send it to him (Пушкин [Pushkin] xiii, 151, 163; Модзалевский [Modzalevsky] 331, no. 1356). No less important, the works of Madame de Staël, who was also a disciple of the German thinkers in general, and Schlegel in particular, were well known in Russia; in 1825 when her *Dix Années d'exil* (Ten Years of Exile, 1821) was published posthumously, Pushkin read and defended it against its Russian critics. Although the conservative Guizot was regarded by the young Romantic Victor Hugo as a political enemy, his introduction was in line with the romanticism of Hugo's 'Préface' to his play *Cromwell* (1827) and Stendhal's *Racine et Shakespeare* (1823–5). Pushkin's views on the art of drama and on Shakespeare developed under the influence of ideas expressed by Guizot, who contended that the art of drama had its roots in folk entertainments and only gradually became an entertainment for the élite, losing its spontaneity and variety. Pushkin expressed similar views: 'Drama was born in the square and was a folk entertainment' (xi, 178).

Shakespeare inspired Pushkin to undertake a reform of the Russian theatre. 'The spirit of the age demands major changes on *the dramatic stage*', he wrote; 'what becomes our theatre are the folk laws of Shakespeare's drama' (xi, 141). Not all Russian critics agreed that Shakespeare should be taken as a model; Faddey Bulgarin, for example, an important figure at the time, took a different line: 'Shakespeare must be for our age *not a model* but only a historical monument' (quoted in Алексеев [Alekseev] 174 n.). But Pushkin refused to view Shakespeare as a 'historical monument'; on the contrary, he found his inspiration for Борис Годунов (*Boris Godunov*) in Shakespeare's histories and tragedies and used them as his model.

Boris Godunov was the beginning of Pushkin's search for new principles of dramatic art and a significant intervention in European efforts to create new drama. The idea to write a tragedy based on the history of the Russian people came to Pushkin at the end of 1824, and the first five scenes of *Boris Godunov* were drafted early in 1825. Pushkin dedicated his play to the memory of Nikolai Karamzin whose *History of the Russian State* he drew on. 'A study of Shakespeare, Karamzin and our old chronicles led me to the thought of giving dram[atic] form[s] to one of the most dramatic epochs of modern history', he wrote in a draft preface to *Boris Godunov* (xi, 140). Pushkin explained that he tried to follow Karamzin in 'a clear development of events', that in the old chronicles he strove 'to guess the mind set and the language of those times', and that he imitated Shakespeare in his 'free and bold portrayal of characters' (xi, 140). It was this quality of Shakespeare's genius that Pushkin greatly valued, believing that Shakespeare made his characters speak with complete naturalness, fitting the language to the character (xiii, 198).

In a draft letter to the publishers of the *Moskovskiy Vestnik* (*Moscow Messenger*) Pushkin wrote that, since he was sure 'the outdated forms of Russian theatre were in need of reform', he had constructed his tragedy 'in accordance with the system of our Father – Shakespeare, and brought as a sacrifice before his altar two of the classical unities, barely keeping the third' (xi, 66). He included mass scenes, folk speech and comic episodes. Pushkin mentioned, with irony, that in some scenes he even 'stooped to humble prose' (xi, 67); scenes alternating between prose and verse give us reason to believe that Pushkin had seen the texts of Shakespeare's plays in English even before he had learned the language. Instead of alexandrine verse (preferred by the French), which did not allow for a variety of individuated speech, he chose an iambic blank verse (preferred by Shakespeare and other English poets) which was used for the first time in Russia. Although Pushkin's choice of Shakespeare's poetics in *Boris Godunov* did not effect the reform of Russian theatre that Pushkin had in mind, it made an impact on subsequent Russian drama, and the blank verse he introduced was later used by many Russian translators of Shakespeare (Левин [Levin] 379).

Pushkin stressed that in his play he aimed at a 'faithful portrayal of persons, times and the development of hist[oric] characters and events – in a word, wrote a tragedy that was truly romantic' (xi, 67). However, a close study of Shakespeare made him critical not just of classicism; the romantic approaches did not satisfy him either: 'How shallow compared to him [Shakespeare] is Byron the tragedian! Byron who created only one character . . .' (xiii, 197). In his letter to N. N. Rayevsky, Junior, in 1825 he viewed tragedy as the most misunderstood genre and argued that both the classicists and the romantics aimed at verisimilitude but misunderstood it: 'The true rule of tragedy is the verisimilitude of situations and the truth of dialogue' (xiii, 197). In his 1829 letter to Rayevsky he wrote that, 'following Shakespeare's example', he had confined himself to 'a portrayal of the epoch and historical persons' without 'stage effects, romantic pathos and the like' (xiv, 46). In other words, Shakespeare inspired Pushkin with realistic aesthetic principles.

Pushkin came to Moscow in autumn 1826 with the manuscript of *Boris Godunov* and read it to his friends. The so-called 'Moscow readings' of the play from September to October 1826 were his true literary triumph – but at an inopportune time: less than a year after the December 1825 uprising, when, in the confusion of the interregnum after the death of Tsar Alexander I, the liberal opposition forces among army officers convinced some of the troops in Saint Petersburg not to swear allegiance to Tsar Nicholas I. The uprising was suppressed, its leaders were tried, five were executed, others imprisoned or exiled to Siberia. In this context Pushkin's tragedy looked politically loaded, all the more so because it dealt with the tragic events of the interregnum at the Time of Troubles. *Boris Godunov* was published in Saint Petersburg only four years later, in December 1830 (dated 1831) and was given a cool reception. Karamzin, to whom the play was dedicated, was not popular with the rising generation of middle-class intellectuals; moreover, the second half of the 1820s saw the publication of new Romantic dramas, such as Victor Hugo's *Cromwell* (1827) and *Hernani* (1829) which were well received. In this context the innovative qualities of *Boris Godunov* were not appreciated and the disconnected scenes were regarded as faults in its dramatic structure. In contrast with the negative reviews, Vissarion Belinsky (1811–48), an uncompromising young literary critic and social thinker, grasped the true significance of the play as a 'folk tragedy' and, in 1841, acclaimed it as a 'work worthy to occupy the first place after Shakespeare's dramas' (v, 59).

By the time of *Boris Godunov* it is evident that Shakespeare had become invaluable to Pushkin in his literary and theatrical work, shaping his response to the course of history and the fortunes of men. Reflecting on the defeat of the December 1825 uprising, Pushkin wrote to his friend the poet Anton Delvig (1798–1831) on 15 February 1826: 'Let us be neither superstitious, nor one-sided – like the Fr[ench] tragedians, but let us look at the tragedy [of the Decembrists] with the eyes of Shakespeare' (xiii, 259). Shakespeare's objective historical vision, his deep understanding of social conflicts inspired Pushkin and helped him understand the historic events he witnessed.

Pushkin continued looking for new forms in drama; his *Маленькие трагедии* (The Little Tragedies, 1830), seemingly completely different from Shakespeare's plays, in fact have much in common with them. 'The truth of passions and the verisimilitude of feelings in the imagined circumstances – this is what our mind demands of a dr[amatic] writer', Pushkin wrote in 1830 (xi, 178) developing ideas he first formulated in connection with *Boris Godunov*; these 'Shakespearean' principles form the core of 'The Little Tragedies'. Belinsky described *Скупой рыцарь* (The Covetous Knight) as 'a great work of art, worthy of the genius of Shakespeare himself', an accolade based on the characterization and on 'the formidable force of pathos, wonderful verse, fullness and finish' (vii, 563). Since then, scholars have discovered similarities between 'The Little Tragedies' and Shakespeare's plays in the structure of some scenes, for instance the seduction of Donna Anna in *Каменный гость* (The Stone Guest) and the scene between Richard Gloucester and Lady Anne in *Richard III*; interesting intertextual connections in 'The Covetous Knight', and Shakespeare's use of 'covetous' in *King Henry V* (Долинин [Dolinin] 97–8).

Pushkin's engagement with Shakespeare – and with history – was not confined to dramatic forms (either Shakespeare's or his own), or to grand and tragic pathos. A month after he had finished *Boris Godunov* Pushkin wrote his long poem *Граф Нулин* (Count Nulin, 1825), entitled 'New Tarquin' in the first draft version. In his notes, Pushkin remembered that, in 1825, when he was re-reading *The Rape of Lucrece*, a thought came to his mind: what would have happened if Lucrece had slapped Tarquin in the face? It might have stopped him and he might have retreated. Then Lucrece would not have died and Roman history would have been quite different. An incident, somewhat similar to such an inverted version of ancient history, had happened not long before in Pushkin's neighbourhood and prompted him to start working: 'An idea occurred to me to parody history and Shakespeare. I could not resist the double temptation and it took me two mornings to write this story' (xi, 188), a 'story' describing, with irony, Russian provincial mores and manners.

Pushkin was inspired to enter into a dialogue with Shakespeare in different ways. In 1833 he began translating *Measure for Measure* from the English original. The theme of justice and mercy, the image of Angelo, whose words and actions contradict his secret passions, touched him so much that he dropped the translation and started writing *Анджело* (*Angelo*), a narrative poem in the style of a novella. The fact that the plot of Shakespeare's play was derived from Giambattista Cinzio Giraldi's novella may have prompted Pushkin to choose the form of narrative poem. B. V. Tomashevsky suggests that Pushkin was interested in developing the psychological portrayal of a character in its complexity, and so far he had done so only in drama: *Angelo* was his first attempt at a poem (1961: 407–8). The comical element is omitted; the plot is condensed to its core; and the scene of action is moved from Vienna to a city in Renaissance Italy re-created masterfully, following Shakespeare's example of a poetic reconstruction of time and place.

Pushkin always focused his attention on those aspects of Shakespeare's writings that were particularly relevant to his own work. Commenting on *Romeo and Juliet* he noted that it reflected sixteenth-century Italy, 'with its climate, its passions, festivals, voluptuousness, sonnets, with its luxurious language full of brilliance and *concetti*. That is how Shakespeare understood the dramatic locale' (xi, 83). Pushkin described Mercutio as 'a model of a young cavalier': Shakespeare 'chose him to represent the Italians who were then the fashionable nation of Europe, the French of the sixteenth century' (xi, 83). Shakespeare's imagination encompassed many lands and nations, this poetic worldview was congenial to Pushkin and he learned from Shakespeare how to re-create in verse different lands, idioms and cultures. J. Thomas has shown that in *Boris Godunov,* following the example of Shakespeare's poetic strategies in *Romeo and Juliet*, Pushkin used the sonnet as a marker of local colour when he incorporated it – 'camouflaged' – into a conversation between two Polish noblemen (191–219).

There are many allusions to Shakespeare in Pushkin's poetry and prose; his remarks show the depth of his insight into the nature of Shakespeare's genius. Some of his notes were gathered in 'Table-Talk' – a collection of anecdotes, miscellaneous thoughts, aphorisms recorded in 1834–6. In choosing this title, Pushkin was following in the footsteps of William Hazlitt and Samuel Taylor Coleridge whose books were in his library (Модзалевский [Modzalevsky] 246, no. 974; 198, no. 760). Notes on Shakespeare from this collection were first published in the *Sovremennik* (Contemporary) in 1837. Pushkin commented in them on some of Shakespeare's plays and characters: 'Othello by nature is not jealous – on the contrary: he is trusting' (xii, 157). *Othello* had a personal appeal for Pushkin, one of whose ancestors was of African origin, and – like Othello who served Venice – had served Russia under Peter the Great; in 1827–8 Pushkin was working in the archives writing a history of his dark-skinned ancestor, *Арап Петра Великого* (The Moor of Peter the Great). He drew on *Othello* when some critics of his narrative poem *Полтава* (Poltava, 1828–9) found it unbelievable that a beautiful young girl could fall in love with Mazepa, an old man: 'And what about Othello, an old negro, who captivated Desdemona with stories of his voyages and battles?' (xi, 164). The implication is that Shakespeare's precedent legitimizes his poem no matter how implausible the narrative may seem to the literal-minded.

Comparing Shakespeare and Molière, Pushkin juxtaposes two literary approaches and finds Shakespeare's realistic approach more attractive: 'The persons created by Shakespeare are not, like Molière's, types of a certain passion, a certain vice; but living creatures, full of many passions, many vices; the circumstances develop in front of the spectator their various and many-sided characters' (xii, 159–60); 'Molière's Miser [Harpagon] is miserly – and that is all; Shakespeare's Shylock is miserly, clever, vengeful, child-loving, witty. Molière's Hypocrite [Tartuffe] is wooing his benefactor's wife – hypocritically; accepts the keeping of the estate – hypocritically; asks for a glass of water – hypocritically. Shakespeare's hypocrite [Angelo] reads the court verdict with conceited severity but with justice; he justifies his cruelty with the thoughtful judgement of a statesman; he seduces innocence with strong captivating sophisms, not a ridiculous mixture of piety and philandering' (xii, 160).

Though Pushkin did not choose translation as his mode of engagement with Shakespeare, he understood its importance and asserted its new principles: 'At last the critics have come to their senses. They begin to suspect that m. Le Tourneur might have had a wrong view of Shakespeare and did not act altogether sensibly when he corrected *Hamlet*, *Romeo* and *Lear* to his own liking. The translators are now required to be more faithful and less prudish and subservient to the public – there is a desire to see Dante, Shakespeare and Cervantes in their own likeness and in their national attire' (xii, 137). These words reflected the changes in the aesthetic tastes of the public and encouraged translators to free themselves from old conventions. By the 1830s the Russian public could no longer be satisfied with Ducis-like adaptations and there was a demand for more adequate Russian versions of Shakespeare's plays; a new translation of *Hamlet* by Nikolai Polevoy (1796–1846), a prominent writer and literary critic, helped to fill the gap. The play was staged in 1837/38 in two major Russian theatres and the part of Hamlet was played by two great actors: Pavel Mochalov (1800–48) in Maly theatre in Moscow and Vasiliy Karatygin (1802–53) in Alexandrinsky theatre in Saint Petersburg. When Mochalov informed the actors that he was planning to take *Hamlet* for his benefit performance, his elder colleague, the famous actor Mikhail Schepkin (1788–1863) was indignant: he thought that Mochalov wanted to offer the public 'Ducis's rotten stuff' (Ласкина [Laskina] 236). But Mochalov announced that it was another *Hamlet*, translated by Polevoy, that the play was excellent and the style free and colloquial. Polevoy attended the rehearsals, and the cooperation between the actor and the translator was beneficial for both: it helped Mochalov to understand *Hamlet* better and it helped Polevoy to adjust his prose translation to the stage.

Karatygin and Mochalov were quite different in their appearance and style of acting. Mochalov broke with the norms of classicism; relying on inspiration he looked for a style that could reflect man's inner life and tragic loneliness; his acting was uneven but its psychological depth was overpowering. Unlike Mochalov, Karatygin had an imposing physique and wonderful enunciation; he was a master of impressive, often monumental, postures suited best for the classicist tragedy. Both were outstanding actors, and each had his admirers. This spontaneous competition between the two theatres and the two actors was very fruitful for Russian theatrical life, while the reviews put Shakespeare at the centre of public discourse; Alexander Herzen (1812–70) was so impressed and enthused by Karatygin's acting that he declared: 'to understand *Hamlet*, one must see it on stage' (Гостынская [Gostyinskaya] 15).

In the final analysis, Mochalov touched hearts at a deeper level and opened to the Russian public a Hamlet they had not known before, a Hamlet they could identify with. Mochalov's acting inspired Belinsky to write his seminal essay '*Гамлет, драма Шекспира. Мочалов в роли Гамлета*' (*Hamlet*, a drama by Shakespeare. Mochalov acting the part of Hamlet). The essay was published in full in the journal *Moskovskiy Nablyudatel* (Moscow Observer) in March–April 1838. Belinsky had worked on it for almost a year, from the end of January (the first night was on 22 January 1837) to the beginning of December 1837. He offered an analysis of Shakespeare's play and from this angle analysed the nine performances he attended, observing that Mochalov had grasped the mystery of Hamlet's character and expressed it in his acting.

Two aspects of Shakespeare's art were of particular interest to Belinsky: realism and the tragic hero. Belinsky distinguished two types of poetry – 'ideal' and 'real' – and thought that Shakespeare was one of the founders of the 'real'. He wrote that realism was based on an objective approach to reality and Shakespeare's was that of an objective genius who never sacrificed reality to his favourite ideas. Belinsky stressed that Shakespeare's genius was above the aesthetics of Romanticism, though Romanticism found in the English poet a kindred spirit, and he criticized Romanticism for its failure to come to grips with reality.

In the essay Belinsky pointed out that Shakespeare's art was founded on his great knowledge of the life of different layers of society – the high and the low, the complexity and variety of human beings and their relations. 'Each person in Shakespeare is a living image, with nothing abstract about him', he wrote (ii, 290). In his analysis Belinsky shows that the content of *Hamlet* is not confined to the destiny of the main hero, that it lies in the interplay of the relationships and interests of all characters, though Hamlet is the centre, that Hamlet's evolution is connected with the events in the play and the impressions he receives, and his central problem is the incongruity of reality with his ideals (ii, 293).

Belinsky wrote his essay at a time when the outlook for Russian literature and thought was bleak. After the publication of his first 'Философическое письмо' (Philosophical Letter, 1836) in the *Telescope* Pyotr Chaadayev (1794–1856), the most promising Russian thinker who aimed at giving a philosophical view of world history, was declared mad by Tsar Nicholas I and banned from social life, and the journal was closed; in January 1837 Pushkin was wounded in a duel and died. Mikhail Lermontov (1814–41) was banished to the Caucasus for the poem 'Смерть поэта' (Death of a Poet) he wrote on the death of Pushkin, in which he dared to include a direct invective against the powers that be, for Pushkin's death was cleverly pre-arranged through intrigues on the part of some of the courtiers. In this oppressive atmosphere Shakespeare's *Hamlet* acquired a special poignancy, a direct relevance and appeal, as Belinsky was well aware when he wrote: '*Hamlet*! . . . do you understand the meaning of this word? It is great and deep: it is human life, it is man, it is you, it is me, it is every one of us, more or less, in the high or ridiculous, and always in a sense that is sad and pitiful' (ii, 254).

The lasting effect of Belinsky's essay and the 1837 productions of *Hamlet* in Moscow and Saint Petersburg was to establish Shakespeare in the Russian theatre. These efforts continued Pushkin's work; by the end of the 1830s Russian literature, literary criticism and the theatre converged in their development, bringing about a decisive breakthrough in Russia's engagement with Shakespeare: Shakespeare became an integral part of Russian culture and has been in its bloodstream ever since.

Notes

1 All quotations from Russian works appear here in translation by Marina P. Kizima.

References

Алексеев, М. П., ред. (1965), *Шекспир и русская культура*, Москва–Ленинград: Наука.

[Alekseev, M. P., ed. (1965), *Shakespeare and Russian Culture*, Moscow and Leningrad: Nauka.]

Бардовский, А. А. ([1923] 2014), 'Русский Гамлет: Восемнадцатый век', в В. Ф. Шевченко (ред.), *Hamlet эпохи русского классицизма*, 135–49, Москва: Изд-во «Лабиринт», 2014.

[Bardovsky, A. A. ([1923] 2014) 'Russian Hamlet: The Eighteenth Century', in V. F. Shevchenko ed., *Hamlet in the Epoch of Russian Classicism*, 135–49, Moscow: Publishing House 'Labyrinth'.]

Белинский, В. Г. (1953–1958), *Полное собрание сочинений: В 13 т.* Москва: Издательство АН СССР.

[Belinsky, V. G. (1953–1958), *Complete Works: in 13 vols.* Moscow: Publishing House of the Academy of Sciences of the USSR.]

Долинин, А. (2007), *Пушкин и Англия: цикл статей.* Москва: Новое литературное обозрение.

[Dolinin, A. (2007), *Pushkin and England: A Cycle of Essays*, Moscow: New Literary Review.]

Гостынская, Л., ред. (2014), *Гамлет на сценах русских театров*, Москва: Галерея.

[Gostyinskaya, L., ed. (2014), *Hamlet on the Stages of Russian Theatres*, Moscow: Gallery.]

Карамзин, Н.М. (1964), *Избранные сочинения в двух томах*. Москва, Ленинград: Художественная литература.
[Karamzin, N. M. (1964), *Selected Works: In two volumes*, Moscow and Leningrad: Hudozhestvennaya Literatura.]
Lang, D. M. (1948), 'Sumarokov's *Hamlet*: A Misjudged Russian Tragedy of the Eighteenth Century', *Modern Language Review*, 43(1): 67–72.
Ласкина, М.Н. (2000), *П. С. Мочалов: Летопись жизни и творчества*. Москва: Языки русской культуры.
[Laskina, M. N. (2000), *P. S. Mochalov: A Chronicle of Life and Work*, Moscow: Languages of Russian Culture.]
Левин, Ю. Д. (2004), 'Шекспир', в *Пушкин: Исследования и материалы. Т.XVIII–XIX: Пушкин и мировая литература. Материалы к «Пушкинской энциклопедии»*, 376–83, Санкт-Петербург: Наука.
[Levin, Yu. D. (2004), 'Shakespeare', in *Pushkin: Research and Materials*, vol. XVIII–XIX: *Pushkin and World Literature. Materials for 'Pushkin Encyclopedia'*: 376–83, St Petersburg: Nauka.]
Модзалевский, Б. Л. (1910), 'Библиотека Пушкина: Библиографическое описание', в *Пушкин и его современники: Материалы и исследования*, Вып. 9–10, СПб.: Типография Императорской Академии Наук.
[Modzalevsky, B. L. (1910), 'Pushkin's Library: A Bibliographical Description', in *Pushkin and His Contemporaries: Materials and Research*, Issues 9–10, St Petersburg: The Printing House of the Imperial Academy of Sciences.]
Пушкин, А. С. (1937–1959), *Полное собрание сочинений: В 16 т.*, Москва; Ленинград: Изд-во АН СССР.
[Pushkin, A. S. (1937–1959), *Complete Works: in 16 vols*, Moscow and Leningrad: Publishing House of the Academy of Sciences of the USSR.]
Shaw, J. Th. (1994), *Pushkin's Poetics of the Unexpected: The Nonrhymed Lines in the Rhymed Poetry and the Rhymed Lines in the Nonrhymed Poetry*, Columbus, Ohio: Slavica Publishers.
Шевченко, В. Ф., ред. (2014), *Hamlet* эпохи русского классицизма, Москва: Изд-во «Лабиринт».
[Shevchenko, V. F., ed. (2014), *Hamlet in the Epoch of Russian Classicism*, Moscow: Publishing House 'Labyrinth'.]

Сумароков, А.П. (1957), *Избранные произведения*. Вступительная статья, подготовка текста и примечания П. Н. Беркова, Ленинград: Советский писатель.

[Sumarokov, A. P. (1957), *Selected Works, edited and with an Introduction and Notes by P.N. Berkov,* Leningrad: Sovetsky Pisatel.]

Томашевский, Б. (1960), *Пушкин и Франция*. Ленинград: Советский писатель.

[Tomashevsky, B. (1960), *Pushkin and France*, Leningrad: Sovetsky Pisatel.]

Томашевский, Б. (1961), *Пушкин: В 2 кн. Книга 2. Материалы к монографии (1824–1837),* Москва и Ленинград: Издательство АН СССР.

[Tomashevsky, B. (1961), *Pushkin: in 2 Books. Book 2. Materials for a Monograph (1824–1837),* Moscow and Leningrad: The Publishing House of the Academy of Sciences of the USSR.]

Wolff, T. A. (1952), 'Shakespeare's Influence on Pushkin's Dramatic Work', in Allardyce Nicoll ed., *Shakespeare Survey 5: Textual Criticism*, 93–105, Cambridge: Cambridge University Press.

8

Trade routes, politics and culture

Shakespeare in Sweden[1]

Per Sivefors

On 20 January 1787, the local newspaper *Götheborgska Nyheter* announced a royal event at the theatre in Gothenburg, the Comediehuset:

> The Esteemed Public are hereby notified, that the upcoming Wednesday, which is the 24th of Jan., in humble celebration of our Most Gracious King's high birthday, a Prologue will be performed at the Opera House, written and suited for this Great day; after which follows Hamlette, Tragedy in 5 Acts, translated from the English, written by the famous Shakesear [*sic*]. This great Play, for the first time performed at a Swedish Theatre, has gained acclaim in all languages.[2]

To further publicize this event, a nearly identical advertisement was placed in another newspaper, *Götheborgs Tidningar*, the day before the premiere, with the additional information that 'the spectacle begins tomorrow at 4 sharp in consideration of the length of the Play and the many changes in the new Decorations'.[3] Both advertisements moreover informed the public that the play would be followed by a 'redoute', a ball with costumes for rent at the theatre, and the first one, in *Götheborgska Nyheter*, was signed by the new twenty-year-old director and rising star of the theatre, Andreas Widerberg, who would also play Hamlet.

Widerberg was right in making this assumption as this is indeed the first documented performance of *Hamlet* in Sweden – or indeed in Scandinavia – a short general overview of which can be found, with a focus on early translations, in the works of Ruud, Molin, Smidt, Einarsson, Sorelius and Keinänen. At this point, Shakespeare was a recent arrival in the Nordic countries. In Sweden's neighbour Denmark, there had been a prose translation of *Hamlet* by Johannes Boye in 1777, but the first performance of Shakespeare in Danish – also of *Hamlet* – did not come about until 1813 (Ruud 1920: 84–5). Finland, Iceland and Norway, none of which would gain their independence until the twentieth century, are different and generally much later cases, although there is some evidence of performances of *Romeo and Juliet* in Finland as early as 1768 (Keinänen 2015). The troupe then was led by the itinerant impresario Carl Gottfried Seuerling, who would go on to introduce *Romeo and Juliet* to a Swedish audience in the industrial town of Norrköping in 1776. Seuerling's troupe had performed occasionally in Gothenburg from 1762 through early 1767, although no plays by Shakespeare are mentioned among their performances there (Berg 35–42). It has been variously conjectured that this first Shakespearean performance in Sweden was based on a French or German version of the play (Molin 10; Skuncke 1981: 36).

Similarly, circumstantial evidence suggests that when *Romeo and Juliet* was performed in Gothenburg in 1781, the text was a Swedish translation of the French adaptation by Jean-François Ducis, who is discussed extensively in other chapters of this volume. In fact, advertisements in the local press repeatedly describe *Romeo and Juliet* as a 'Tragedy in 5 acts, from the French', with no indication whatever that Shakespeare was the author or that the play was English (*Hwad Nytt?*, 13 and 30 November 1781). The advertisement for a revival in 1790 describes the same settings and stage arrangement as Ducis' version (Molin 13) which strongly points in his direction.

By contrast, the advertisements for *Hamlet* in the local newspapers in Gothenburg suggest, conspicuously, that the play was translated from English: a turning point in the history of Shakespeare in Sweden since this translation is the first that is explicitly said to be directly from the original language. (Unfortunately, but not surprisingly, it is lost and the identity of the translator remains unknown, although various names have been suggested, including Widerberg himself, who later translated plays for the Royal Theatre in Stockholm.) Later advertisements also insist on the English connection. For a revival on 4 March 1791, *Götheborgs Tidningar* announced that the play was to be performed using 'a new translation, closely following the English original' (Berg 345). What, then, lay behind the occurrence of this momentous theatrical event at this point, and at this particular place? As this chapter will contend, the migration of *Hamlet* to a town in western Sweden in the late eighteenth century was not a simple coincidence. My argument addresses three interrelated points. Firstly, the rise of a provincial bourgeoisie with economic links to England was one of the most significant historical processes of the Swedish eighteenth century, making economic change and class restructuring crucial factors in the migration of Shakespeare to Sweden. Secondly, the choice of *Hamlet*, with its Danish setting and troubled politics, may have had a particular significance to audiences in Gothenburg, which was geographically close to Denmark and was affected by the political conflicts between Sweden and Denmark in the late eighteenth century, such as King Gustaf's far-reaching plans to attack Copenhagen in the 1780s. Audiences would, moreover, have followed the very recent events at the Danish court, which included a rebellious crown prince and a deposed queen imprisoned at Hamlet's very castle of Elsinore. Thirdly, at the national rather than strictly international level, the Gothenburg production closely reflects the discrepancies in taste between different parts of the country. While *Hamlet* was staged in Gothenburg in 1787, the play had to wait until 1819 to reach Stockholm, and what we know of the repertoires of theatres in the provinces suggests that they were in general much quicker to adopt Shakespeare than in the capital, where more conservative, classicist influences prevailed.[4] As will be demonstrated, this difference may be connected to my first point: that Gothenburg had strong economic links with Britain.

In other words, the migration of Shakespeare's reputation and plays was never a question of just one country's relation to another: the Gothenburg production of *Hamlet* was, as we shall see, the result of a dense web of influences and connections at the national and international levels, and cultural, economic and political factors intermingled in the reception of Shakespeare. In contrast to other contributions to this book, then, this one focuses more on a single theatrical event. However, the Gothenburg *Hamlet* was not just the first performance of the play in Scandinavia or the first Swedish translation of Shakespeare that was stated to be directly from English. Shakespeare's Nordic play made its first appearance during a period which has been described as possibly the most significant in Scandinavian history, and the relations to England, France and the rest of Scandinavia are all arguably part of the early reception history of Shakespeare in Sweden: 'it is hard to discern a more momentous half-century in the entire history of the North', Barton (383) writes of the years 1760–1815. Rather than seeing the *Hamlet* production as an isolated event, this chapter therefore locates it in the wider historical arena of the time.

Gothenburg, theatre and literary culture

When *Hamlet* was performed in Gothenburg, playgoing had been a regular activity in the town for only a few years. Since its foundation in 1779, before which itinerant companies like Seuerling's previously mentioned troupe had been active in other venues, the theatre, Comediehuset, had become established as a scene with a permanent company. The celebration of King Gustaf III's birthday, stated as the occasion of the performance of *Hamlet*, was a recurring event every January, with a patriotic prologue followed by a performance of a more classical play than the light fare – comedy and French opera – that otherwise dominated the repertoire. Comediehuset was located on what is now a quiet pedestrian street in Gothenburg but was a busy thoroughfare at the time. (The street then was called 'Sillgatan', which translates as Herring Street – a suggestion of the bustle and smell that characterized life in the neighbourhood.) The theatre itself was erected and later rebuilt at the expense of the baron Patrik Alströmer, a known patron of the arts; it is said to have had an interior lavishly decorated with crystal chandeliers and three rows of booths. The local newspaper *Hwad Nytt?* gives a detailed description of the newly refurbished theatre (15 August 1783; reprinted in Berg 280–1). Already by 1780, the theatre was such a success that the local authorities issued a set of special traffic regulations, reported in *Götheborgska Nyheter* (9 December 1780), in the area around the theatre when plays and shows were performed. In August 1786, Widerberg – the first Hamlet – took over as director of the theatre from the previous owner Johan von Blanc, and his first season in 1786/7 featured re-runs of material performed under von Blanc as well as a number of new plays, including the proudly announced *Hamlet*.

Shakespeare's play was by all accounts a great success. Artistically, that is: Widerberg's gains from his first season as director were so poor that he had to borrow money to make ends meet and was later unable to pay it back (Berg 390). Advertisements indicate that *Hamlet* was performed again – including the Prologue – two days after its premiere, and then at least three more times until early March. We know also that the play was encored by popular demand and that Widerberg received praise for his interpretation. On 2 February 1787,

Götheborgs Allehanda announced that 'next Sunday, Mr Widerberg is pleased to perform *Hamlet*, at the request of several Honourable people', then four days later, exhorted 'one should not forget the Tragedie which has been thrice performed here to general acclaim, as Mr. Widerberg in the role of Prince *Hamlett* has so pleasantly shown his capacities in the Theatrical way that the Play is now for the fourth time requested' (Berg 344–5). In all, the only play to have a longer run during the season was another classic: Beaumarchais's *Mariage de Figaro*, possibly in a Swedish translation by Daniel Engelbert Pilgren (Berg 345–6), which was performed six times.

The documentation we have of the *Hamlet* production leaves many questions unanswered. There is no theatrical poster preserved (the earliest ones from Gothenburg are from the beginning of the nineteenth century) and, as already pointed out, the translation of the play, whoever was responsible for it, is also lost. But even so, some relevant conclusions can be drawn. Regardless of who the translator was or whether the information is even true, the advertisement stresses the English connection, as if it were a selling point in its own right. Indeed, the advertisements for the Gothenburg *Hamlet* quoted at the beginning of this chapter are full of conventional bardolatry that only makes sense if England is already acknowledged as a significant cultural influence. From a broader political and historical context, such a connection is understandable, for *Hamlet*, with its Scandinavian prince who embarks westward, may have had a particular significance for a Gothenburg audience who were steeped in commercial and cultural relations with Britain. The migration of *Hamlet* into Sweden reflects not only links between Sweden and Western Europe, but also political relations between Sweden and much of the rest of Europe.

Britain in the eighteenth century was a crucial trading partner. In 1800, 78 per cent of the bar iron exported from Gothenburg had England as its destination, while America became an increasingly important trading partner during the early nineteenth century (M. Andersson 72–3). The role of British investors in the Swedish East India Company, with its offices and port in Gothenburg, had been strong from its inception in 1731; it was the Scottish merchant Colin Campbell who was appointed director during its first charter (1731–46). While such British elements were quickly assimilated, second-generation immigrants with Scottish and English names continued to hold important positions in the Company throughout the century (Therborn 88; Söderpalm 43). For example, the Company's supercargo in Hong Kong at the time of the *Hamlet* production was William Chalmers, born in Sweden to Scottish parents and known today as the donor to what later became the Chalmers University of Technology (Frängsmyr 102–3). While a royal decree of 1741 had formally prohibited the employment of foreigners in higher positions, there were ways enough of circumventing such restrictions (Söderpalm 44). That the British economic influence on Gothenburg continued throughout the century can be gleaned from contemporary accounts. Although Mary Wollstonecraft, writing in 1795, claimed of the people she encountered in western Sweden that 'their tables, like their compliments, seem equally a caricature of the French', she also observed that the Scottish merchants had been the most successful ones in Gothenburg (Wollstonecraft 15; 13). According to Jacques-Louis de Bougrenet de la Tocnaye (Chateaubriand's companion in exile), in his *Promenade d'un Français en Suède et en Norvège* (1801), almost all imported goods in the town were from England and affluent citizens even had their shoes made in London (La Tocnaye 18). In fact, the available documentation on the theatre in Gothenburg sometimes offers tantalizing glimpses of such economic relations: for example, after a masquerade at Comediehuset on 4 March 1783, an English silver watch by the fashionable watchmaker Martineau was announced as lost or stolen (Berg 261), illustrating the prestige attached to English goods. Indeed, material wealth and trade would also be referenced in the productions themselves. On the king's birthday in 1784, the customary patriotic prologue had featured Andreas Widerberg's future wife Anna Catharina Widebäck – in the role of the Göta river, whose estuary was also the location of the port – wishing prosperity and Godspeed for the ships of Gothenburg: 'May trade, shipping, arts and crafts / Flourish, grow from year to year' (Berg 289). Judging from such well-wishings, in the minds of the Gothenburg audiences, trade and culture literally went hand in hand.

A further index to the relation between economic change and the consumption of culture is the extent to which the economic élite of Gothenburg were orientated towards England in their reading habits. The presence of books in English on the shelves of the affluent middle class was notable, as suggested by inventories and auction sales (Östman). And while novelists like Richardson and Fielding were predictably well-represented, we know that works by Shakespeare were also sold. This seems especially to be the case in Gothenburg, among people that also embodied the new wealth: for example, the earliest evidence of the first edition of Shakespeare on Swedish ground points to Magnus Lagerström, author of an English grammar, translator of Bunyan's *Pilgrim's Progress* and director of the East India Company from 1746, who possessed a copy of the 1623 Folio of Shakespeare's works.[5] The subsequent whereabouts of this volume are unknown, although it is tempting to imagine that it will show up some day, just like the single surviving copy of the first quarto of *Titus Andronicus* that surfaced in southern Sweden in 1904 (Swärdh). Other directors of the East India Company seem to have nursed similar literary interests: the very first one, the Scotsman Colin Campbell, owned a copy of *The Beauties of the English Stage* (1737), an anthology which included excerpts from Shakespeare (Molin 5). Hence, although France was – as Wollstonecraft's disparaging remark suggests – still a dominant cultural role model in late eighteenth-century Gothenburg, English literature would more and more reach the reading public directly in English rather than through translations. Östman observes that 'there has been a tendency to underestimate the direct flow of English literature coming into the country; to assume that the bulk of it reached eighteenth-century Sweden through French translation' (19). As shown by the example of Gothenburg and the 1787 *Hamlet*, there is reason to concur with this estimation. Such books would also be advertised in the local press: for example, in the *Götheborgs Allehanda* of 3 May 1785, the bookbinder and seller Nathanael Ekroth announced *Macbeth* and *Romeo and Juliet* for sale, bound together with a number of other plays in English. The volume was the most expensive among the advertised books, which included such varied fare as *The Pilgrim's Progress* and the Earl of Rochester's *Works*, all in English. This relatively broad interest in English culture, including some of the leading figures in Gothenburg's economic boom, may have paved the way for a more general receptiveness to 'the famous Shakespeare'.

It is true that English plays, including but not limited to Shakespeare's, were sometimes transmitted to Swedish audiences through translations of German or French adaptations; this was the case with Henry Brooke's *Gustavus Vasa* (1739), which had reached Gothenburg in a translation from a German adaptation and was performed on the king's birthday in 1781, and the previously mentioned *Romeo and Juliet*, staged later the same year, probably derived from Ducis. But, increasingly, there were direct translations from English, as indicated by advertisements and letters to the editors in the local press. Moreover, this was a period when people travelled to England and attended performances of Shakespearean plays; Jacob Wallenberg, a clergyman who joined one of the merchant ships from Gothenburg to Kanton and wrote a much-read account of his journey, saw David Garrick perform *Hamlet* in London in 1769. Wallenberg apparently liked Garrick, but was less appreciative of English drama, exemplifying a degree of resistance to the English influence and a lingering respect for French classicism. 'Generally, one might claim that the Englishman is excellent in the execution and elaboration, but his lack of taste causes him mostly to fail in the design or plan', Wallenberg asserts; yet this seeming ambivalence did not keep him from writing a play of his own, *Susanna*, which was performed in Gothenburg in 1779 and was reputed to be the first play in Swedish to show influences from Shakespeare (Berg 189; Molin 20–1, 49). As Molin claims, Wallenberg was particularly influenced by Voltaire's 'Appel à toutes les nations'.

While the form of this play was that of French classical tragedy and its content derived (as the title suggests) from the Old Testament, it also had similarities with *Othello*, particularly close parallels between the characters of the plays, including not only the protagonists but also figures like Emilia and Cassio (Molin 50). Specific influences from Shakespeare can be hard to prove, nevertheless, there are occasional examples of authors who show familiarity with his plays. Such knowledge, though, often continued to be mediated through French culture, particularly through Voltaire: one example is the poet Bengt Lidner, who was born in Gothenburg (although most of his literary career was spent elsewhere, including Stockholm) and whose play *Erik XIV*, written in the early 1780s, has been characterized as a hybrid between classicism and Shakespearean tragedy (Molin 52).

The first Swedish *Hamlet* and, indeed, most of the early productions of Shakespeare appeared at a cultural crossroads in a town where the British economic influence had been strong for more than half a century and where British cultural influence was gradually becoming more significant, even if, as we have seen, French taste had a lingering dominance. With the Revolution of 1789, France would become a much less important political ally and it is reasonable to assume that the political instability on the Continent also reflected back on the repertoire and preferences of the theatre and its audience. It has been asserted that 'this period, and particularly the years between 1780 and 1792', was 'marked by radical changes in favour of the middle class, a word that now begins to appear in political debates in place of the old-fashioned "middle Estate"' (Östman 18). Indeed, Gothenburg has even been claimed as the birthplace of the modern Swedish bourgeoisie (Therborn 88–9). Therborn points to the period 1802–1816, citing the position of Gothenburg as a hole in Napoleon's blockade against Great Britain, with its resulting influx of Scottish capital and the concentration of wealth from the export of wood from other parts of the country (91–2). However, these processes, and the related changes in cultural preferences, had arguably been in the making throughout the eighteenth century. Widerberg's troupe was catering to the taste of this emergent bourgeoisie while to an extent reflecting the social upheaval that was brewing in France. As previously stated the only play to exceed *Hamlet* in the number of performances during the 1786/7 season was *The Marriage of Figaro*, which Napoleon himself would later call 'the revolution already put into action' (Las Cases 55). However, even if the 'folle journée' of Beaumarchais' comedy plays fast and loose with the classical unities and class hierarchies of pre-Revolutionary France, this is not to suggest that its staging in Gothenburg carried a 'revolutionary' agenda – far from it. The royalist tendency of the *Hamlet* performance – held in celebration of Gustaf's birthday – is obvious. Moreover, the king himself was quick to harness the new bourgeoisie to his own political schemes, and; this link between the king and the middle class in Gothenburg was to become more and more influential. As Östman comments, 'it is one of the many paradoxes of the era that the king chose to rely on representatives of this new, rising class in order to achieve his aims. For the most prominent and remarkable feature from the late 1780s onwards is the rise to political importance of the middle class' (18).

Shakespeare and the Swedish Academy

In a certain sense, then, if not exactly radical in its politics, the Gothenburg audience can be seen as aesthetically ahead of their Swedish contemporaries. Arguably, the delay in bringing Shakespeare to the capital was to some extent a consequence of the strong preference for French classicism among the leading critics of the day (who were invariably based in Stockholm). It is plain that the predilection for Shakespeare at provincial theatres was not shared by the élite in the capital, because the aesthetic ideals they adhered to were mostly at odds with what they considered to be a disordered and tasteless type of drama. Indeed, Shakespeare would have been less than easy to yoke together with the enlightenment ideals embraced by the members of the Swedish Academy (founded only the year before the *Hamlet* performance, in 1786). The occasional judgements that members of the Academy pronounced on Shakespeare were ambivalent at best, and there was sometimes a political undercurrent to their preferences. For example, the poet, Carl Gustaf af Leopold, a founding member of the Academy and a staunch defender of French taste, would provide a colourful example of the ambivalence towards Shakespeare when, in 1792, he thus described him as

> the altogether raw, singular man of the woods, who, even in his external appearance, differs quite from the others. He may otherwise have many great advantages: doubly powerful sinews, doubly sharp senses, double liveliness of movement, but his body is semi-hairy, his gait sometimes upright, sometimes on all fours, his facial muscles strangely formed, and his voice makes noises that hurt the ear.
>
> Molin 30

To Leopold, Shakespeare is symbolic of popular vulgarity, full of vigour but also marked out as deformed and subhuman – in short, as an anthropoid ape. Some thirty years later, close to the heyday of Swedish literary Romanticism, Leopold seems to have been embarrassed by this portrait. A letter of his to a Shakespeare enthusiast and translator, Bishop Olof Bjurbäck, contains a clear – and hilarious – attempt at disavowing his earlier disparaging judgement:

> Since I have in some of my writings claimed that Shakespear is the Man of the Woods in literature, I did not thereby mean a forest animal, an Ourang-Outang, but on the contrary honour and justice. I believed I had found in this Poet a higher degree of the power and liveliness of Natural genius, but also a greater lack of culture and judgement than in any other modern Author.
>
> Molin 32

It is possible to see Leopold's earlier remarks as haunted by the events that had taken place just three years earlier, when the 1789 revolution had made France an impossible political ally although it had not disarmed its cultural influence. In 1789, King Gustaf had used the same simian metaphor to describe the revolutionaries in France: 'they are the ourang-outangs of Europe' (Lönnroth 2008: 354). By implication at least, 'natural genius' also seems to connote 'revolutionary' – and 'ape'.

Widerberg's *Hamlet* and Scandinavian politics

The contemporary aesthetic debates taking place amidst the political turmoil in Europe are crucial to understanding the conditions under which Shakespeare's *Hamlet* migrated to Sweden. The predilection of the Gothenburg audience for Shakespeare's play was in many respects founded on their identity as middle class and, as the new economic élite, their ties to England. What remains to be considered, however, is the significance, on arrival, of Shakespeare's Danish play from a Scandinavian perspective. This is admittedly more speculative ground as it forces us to consider potential audience reactions to the play. We know that when *Hamlet* was staged in Stockholm in 1819, all political material including the Fortinbras subplot was excised (Marker and Marker 105). Whether this was true also of the Gothenburg *Hamlet* more than thirty years earlier we do not know, but the announcement of 'new Decorations' and the fact that the play was unusually long suggests a fairly full-scale production with relatively few cuts. At any rate, if the audience in 1787 were inclined to see parallels between the play and the current situation in Scandinavia, they could certainly have done so. 'Something is rotten in the state of Denmark' (1.4.90): if they were included in the play, Marcellus's words to Horatio may, for example, have struck a chord with royalist spectators in Gothenburg whose king had harboured far-reaching plans to attack Copenhagen as late as 1783. Anti-Danish sentiment was prevalent throughout Sweden. In the year before the production of *Hamlet* it had been whipped up in Stockholm by Gustaf's opera project, *Gustaf Vasa* (1786), where the extras who played Danish soldiers even attempted to sell their parts – using drinks – to those who played Swedes (Lönnroth 1991: 18).

It has been claimed that there are similarities in staging and plotting between *Gustaf Vasa* and Shakespeare's *Richard III* (Molin 58–61). More specifically, Shakespeare's rebellious prince could have spawned comparisons with the contemporary Danish court that in 1784 had seen a *coup d'État* at the initiative of, among others, King Christian VII's stepmother, Juliane Marie, and the Crown Prince, Frederik. Christian himself was not without Shakespearean connections: back in 1768 during a visit to England he had seen Garrick perform, not the too-close-to-home *Hamlet* but *Richard III* (Langen 262–3). Stella Tillyard notes this parallel: 'If Christian VII was obviously no Hamlet, the British imagination nonetheless slipped easily into the idea that Juliane Marie was a perfidious Gertrude' (Tillyard 229). Perhaps even Christian himself was more of a counterpart to Shakespeare's prince than Tillyard admits: at least they certainly had in common a reputation for madness and a love for theatrical show. At any rate, in the wake of the coup London newspapers had been quick to pick up on the irony and Shakespearean significance inherent in the fact that the ousted Queen of Denmark, George III's sister, Caroline Mathilde, had been imprisoned at the castle of Elsinore. And if the Fortinbras subplot was included in the Gothenburg *Hamlet*, it may have suggested another oblique allusion to the political situation in Denmark, where a Norwegian peasant, Christian Jensen Lofthuus, had appeared as leader of an abortive insurrection against the Danish Crown in late 1786 and early 1787, coinciding with the *Hamlet* premiere. Lofthuus and his delegation had even made their way from Norway through western Sweden on their way to Copenhagen in October 1786 (Barton 151–3).

Arguably, then, the hostilities between Denmark and Sweden may have been read into *Hamlet*, even if this was not intended by Widerberg's troupe when they selected the play for performance on the king's birthday. However, the play might have elicited other reactions among its Swedish audience than just that of hostility to Denmark. For example, Gustaf himself was not devoid of similarities with Shakespeare's prince: his flair for theatrical show was ubiquitous, his aloofness in relationships – including estrangement from his Danish consort, Sofia Magdalena, and bitter conflicts with the widow queen, Lovisa Ulrika – was often alluded to in libels and pamphlets, and his attempts at showing himself a resolute warrior king would bring about an invasion from Norway within little more than a year of the first performance of Shakespeare's play. There is a certain historical irony inherent in the fact that the threat of war was soon to become grim reality. 'Am I a coward?' (2.2.506): Gustaf was ever anxious to answer Hamlet's question with a 'no', even to the point of violating his own constitution, and so would embark on a war with Russia in 1788, the very next year (Lönnroth 2008: 193–389). The inevitable result was an attack from Russia's ally Denmark, or rather the then-Danish Norway. Bohuslän, the strip of land between Gothenburg and Norway, may have been 'a little patch of ground / That hath in it no profit but the name' (4.4.17–18), nevertheless, the invasion took place and troops recruited in Norway advanced down the Swedish coast and on the inland, requiring that Gothenburg yield to them on 6 October 1788. The fact that a ceasefire was quickly negotiated may serve as another example of the importance of Britain to the politics of western Sweden: it was the English ambassador in Copenhagen, Sir Hugh Elliot, who led the negotiations (Apenes and Dyrhaug 104–17). Ironically, the war later became known among historians as the Theatre War. 'He that plays the King shall be welcome' (2.2.285): Hamlet's words to Rosencrantz arguably have a bearing also on the Swedish monarch who never tired of casting himself as the great man of action. Indeed, the title of Erik Lönnroth's biography on Gustaf from 1986 translates *The Great Part: King Gustaf III Played by Himself* (Lönnroth 2008).

These events would, of course, still lie in the future in 1787, but just exactly what significance they may have had for audiences in Gothenburg when *Hamlet* was revived in 1791 is a tantalizing question. It is axiomatic that plays acquire new meanings each time they are performed and this is particularly true of works which migrate from one culture to another in different historical circumstances. Not unlike Marlowe's *Massacre at Paris* two centuries earlier, with its French king whose real-life counterpart had turned Catholic between the two first-known performances of Marlowe's play, the rapid political development in Europe may have given *Hamlet* a rather different weight to its audience when it was revived in Gothenburg only four years after its initial production. In one sense, the 1787 and 1791 *Hamlet* were two distinct plays: as the context changed, so would the meaning of the text.

What is certain, at any rate, is that the first *Hamlet*, which initiated or helped to initiate Shakespeare's migration to Sweden, must be understood – as do acts of migration in general – in the broader context of the changing political and economic landscape in Europe and Sweden at the time. As this chapter has suggested, social upheaval, court politics and trade relations are all crucial in order to understand this seemingly insignificant event at a provincial theatre. The theatre itself would be dismantled and the boom period of Gothenburg would be over not long after the events described here (Berg 391–474). As for the dissemination of Shakespeare, this would soon take other, more direct routes. While Shakespeare was only occasionally performed during the rest of the eighteenth century, after 1800 translations directly from English were becoming increasingly common, much as a result of the emergence of Romanticism which in turn was bound up with further political developments in Europe. A case in point is *Macbeth*, which was famously translated in 1813 by Erik Gustaf Geijer, one of the foremost Romantic poets in Sweden. Geijer's translation was made with the help of Schiller's German version, although Geijer is far from slavishly dependent on it and frequently is closer to Shakespeare than Schiller is (Molin 141). And when *Hamlet* finally reached the stage in Stockholm in the already-mentioned production of 1819, the event was explicitly hailed as the final blow to French classicism: in the enthusiastic words of another, less known Romantic poet, C. F. Dahlgren, 'The French whore, with whom the Swede has so long fornicated, is locked up in the spinning-house or sent to [the asylum] Danviken' (Molin 102). As elsewhere in Europe, Shakespeare would come to be seen as a counterweight to the perceived stiffness of classical ideals. Yet the Gothenburg *Hamlet* demonstrates that the early history of Shakespeare in Sweden was not simply one of dependence on French and German models followed by a turn towards the Romantic ideals embraced by Geijer or Dahlgren. The production of *Hamlet* cannot be seen in such schematic terms: it had little or nothing to do with an emerging Romantic movement and all the more to do with the rise of a provincial élite with close ties to England, and it came about in the celebration of a king who, paradoxically, was one of the country's foremost defenders of French taste. Conceivably, the Gothenburg *Hamlet* could be dismissed as a quirk, an exception, but it demonstrates that Shakespeare's early history in Scandinavia resists easy divisions and periodization, and arguably shows how important economic and political ties are to changes in literary taste and ideals.

Notes

1 Some early ideas for this chapter were presented in the form of a lecture in the Kingston Shakespeare Seminar series at Kingston University in 2017; my warmest thanks to Richard Wilson for inviting me.

2 All translations are mine, unless otherwise stated. I have tried to preserve the idiosyncratic syntax and capitalization of the Swedish. Much of the scant documentation of the *Hamlet*

production is reprinted, although not always wholly accurately, in Berg.

3 *Götheborgs Tidningar*, 23 January 1787; cf. Berg 343, who does not mention the earlier advertisement in *Götheborgska Nyheter*.

4 For the Stockholm *Hamlet*, see Marker and Marker 105–7; also, Molin 98–101 and Nordensvan 178–81.

5 For Lagerström's life and work, see the account in Frängsmyr 105–7; for his ownership of the Folio, see Molin 4.

References

Andersson, B. (1988), *Göteborgs handlande borgerskap 1750–1805*, Gothenburg: University of Gothenburg.

Andersson, M. (2016), *Den europeiska varu- och kreditmarknaden under 1700-talet: Handel och sjöfart med Göteborg som utgångspunkt*, Möklinta: Gidlunds.

Apenes, G. and T. Dyrhaug (1988), *Tyttebærkrigen: Det norske felttog i Sverige 1788*, Oslo: Aschehoug.

Barton, H. Arnold (1986), *Scandinavia in the Revolutionary Era, 1760–1815*, Minneapolis: University of Minnesota Press.

Berg, W. (1896), *Anteckningar om Göteborgs äldre teatrar*, vol. 1, Gothenburg.

Einarsson, S. (1940), 'Shakespeare in Iceland: A Historical Survey', *ELH* 7(4): 272–85.

Frängsmyr, T. (1976), *Ostindiska Kompaniet: Människorna, äventyret och den ekonomiska drömmen*, Höganäs: Bra Böcker.

Keinänen, N. (2010), 'Suomalaisen Shakespeare-perinteen syntyvaiheista' [An Early History of Shakespeare in Finland], in Nely Keinänen ed., *Shakespeare Suomessa* [Shakespeare in Finland], 15–33, Helsinki: WSOY.

Keinänen, N. (2015), 'Finland', in M. Dobson et al. eds, *The Oxford Companion to Shakespeare*, second edn, Oxford: Oxford University Press.

Koninckx, C. (1980), *The First and Second Charters of the Swedish East India Company (1731–1766)*, Kortrijk: Van Ghemmert.

La Tocnaye, J. -L. de Bougrenet de (1801), *Promenade d'un Français en Suède et en Norvège*, Brunswick. Available online: https://archive.org/details/8SCSUP84109-1-NOR.

Langen, U. (2008), *Den afmægtige: En biografi om Christian 7*, Copenhagen: Jyllands-Postens Forlag.
Las Cases, E. -A. -D., comte de (1894), *Memoirs of the Life, Exile, and Conversations of the Emperor Napoleon*, vol. 3, New York. Available online: https://archive.org/details/ MemoirsOfTheLifeExileAndConversati2
Lext, G. (1950), *Bok och samhälle i Göteborg 1720–1809*, Gothenburg: University of Gothenburg.
Lönnroth, E. (1991), 'Prologue', in Inger Mattsson, ed., *Gustavian Opera: An Interdisciplinary Reader in Swedish Opera, Dance and Theatre 1771–1809*, 15–18, Stockholm: Royal Swedish Academy of Music.
Lönnroth, E. (2008), *Den stora rollen: Kung Gustaf III spelad av honom själv*, Stockholm: Atlantis.
Marker, F., and L. -L. Marker (1996), *A History of Scandinavian Theatre*, Cambridge: Cambridge University Press.
Molin, N. (1931), *Shakespeare och Sverige intill 1800-talets mitt: En studie av hans inflytande*, Gothenburg: Elanders.
Nordensvan, G. (1917), *Svensk teater och svenska skådespelare från Gustav III till våra dagar*, vol. 1, Stockholm: Bonniers.
Östman, H. (1983), *English Fiction, Poetry and Drama in Eighteenth Century Sweden 1765–1799: A Preliminary Study*, Stockholm: Acta Bibliotecæ Regiæ Stockholmiensis.
Ruud, M. (1917), *An Essay Toward a History of Shakespeare in Norway*, Scandinavian Studies and Notes.
Ruud, M. (1920), *An Essay Toward a History of Shakespeare in Denmark*, University of Minnesota.
Shakespeare, W. (2006), *Hamlet*, A. Thompson and N. Taylor eds, London: The Arden Shakespeare.
Skuncke, M. -C. (1981), *Sweden and European Drama 1772–1796: A Study of Translations and Adaptations*, PhD diss., Uppsala University.
Skuncke, M. -C. (1990), 'Theatre and Drama in Sweden under Gustaf III (1771–1792)', in *Changes in Two Baltic Countries: Poland and Sweden in the XVIIIth Century*, 157–63, Poznań: Uniwersytet im. Adama Mickiewicza w Poznaniu.
Smidt, K. (1993), 'The Discovery of Shakespeare in Scandinavia', in D. Delabastita and L. D'hulst, eds, *European Shakespeares: Translating Shakespeare in an Age of Romanticism*, 91–104, Antwerp: John Benjamins.

Söderpalm, K. (2000), 'SOIC – ett skotskt företag?', in K. Söderpalm, ed., *Ostindiska Compagniet: Affärer och föremål*, 36–61, second edn, Gothenburg: Göteborgs stadsmuseum, 2000.

Sorelius, G. (2002), 'Introduction', in G. Sorelius, ed., *Shakespeare and Scandinavia: A Collection of Nordic Studies*, 9–16, Newark: University of Delaware Press.

Swärdh, A. (2016), 'The 1904 Discovery of Shakespeare's *Titus Andronicus* First Quarto in Sweden', *The Library* 17(4): 424–45.

Therborn, G. (1989), *Borgarklass och byråkrati i Sverige: Anteckningar om en solskenshistoria*, trans. G. Sandin, Lund: Arkiv.

Tillyard, S. (2007), *A Royal Affair: George III and His Troublesome Siblings*, London: Vintage.

Weibull, J. (1992), 'The Swedish East India Company and the East Indiaman *Götheborg*', in B. Johansson, ed., *The Golden Age of China Trade: Essays on the East India Companies' Trade with China in the 18th Century and the Swedish East Indiaman Götheborg*, Hong Kong: Hong Kong Viking.

Wollstonecraft, M. (2009), *Letters Written in Sweden, Norway, and Denmark*, T. Brekke and J. Mee, eds, Oxford: Oxford University Press.

9

The mirror and the razor

Shakespeare's arrival in Spain[1]

Keith Gregor

'In France Shakespaar [*sic*] has only ever been seen in disguise or spruced up. The quill of the French has proven more a razor than a mirror to this English poet.' Coming in 1764 as part of his riposte to a series of articles ridiculing the Spanish Golden Age *comedia* in the pro-Enlightenment periodical *El Pensador* (The Thinker), this testy comment by journalist Francisco Mariano Nipho is the earliest written evidence we have of any acquaintance with Shakespeare amongst Spain's cultural elite. And though Nipho is not unique in misspelling the name, he wholeheartedly endorses the English author as the exponent of a particular *kind* of drama that mixes ideas that are 'noble, great, vast and sublime' with expressions that are 'low, some lofty and a few gigantic' – the complete opposite, presumably, of the way his work is currently being served up in France. Nipho evinces a sense of a Shakespeare beyond or prior to the sanitized versions of contemporary French adaptations; a Shakespeare who has outlived the assaults of the *philosophes* and their Spanish epigones and who 'even today, some two hundred years later, is the idol of all his nation' (Nipho 125–7).[2]

As in other European countries, Shakespeare's early migration to Spain was inextricably linked to debates already raging in the country about the proper path the drama should be taking. Nipho's comments have been shown to be part of a broader cultural war raging in late eighteenth-century Spain between defenders of the traditional Spanish *comedia* (verse drama of the seventeenth century) and proponents of the 'new' approach to drama inspired by their Enlightenment colleagues in France (Pozuelo and Aradra 89–90). Typically, Shakespeare is nationalistically presented as the innocent victim of French-inspired literary revisionism – yet another casualty of the neo-classical war of attrition on the aureate tradition which was already laying waste the cream of Spain's own historic dramaturgical talent. Nipho's defence of Shakespeare proceeds from an account of *Coriolanus* and the acknowledgement that such emotionally wrenching narratives cannot possibly be subjected to the 'tyranny of the rules', that by disobeying them as Shakespeare does, one can actually create 'beauties more essential and more exquisite' (Nipho 125). As even Voltaire had ventured over three decades earlier, an excessive respect for the rules can prove incompatible with the effects tragedy is supposed to produce. In this respect, though English dramatists like Shakespeare 'have produced some frightful spectacles ..., we French, as scrupulous as you were reckless, tend to hold back lest we go too far, and at times we do not attain the tragic, for fear of overstepping the mark' (Voltaire 149). Though it is hard to determine how much (if any) of Shakespeare's work Nipho had read in the original or how familiar he was with English attitudes to Shakespeare himself, clearly it is the more constructive early vein of Voltaire's criticism and its particular conception of 'the tragic' that are being echoed in his own appraisal.

Although Nipho's praise would be more or less explicitly reiterated in a number of late eighteenth-century critical interventions, a measure of what he and they were up against can be gauged by a succession of authoritative calls for more 'enlightened' modes of dramatic composition. In 1784 the exiled Jesuit thinker, Juan Andrés,[3] published the second of his ambitious ten-volume *Origen, progresos y estado actual de toda literatura* (Origin, Progression and Present State of All Literature) where he declares his inability to find the supposed beauties of Shakespeare's work 'amid the much and almost constant tastelessness and foolishness' by which it is deformed. And though there is a recognition of the few genuinely excellent and 'divine' passages in *Hamlet, Julius Caesar, Othello, Macbeth* and other tragedies, who, he wonders, could possibly have the patience

> to see the appearance of a mouse, a wall, a lion, a moonlight that talk, act and address each other; to hear the low and vulgar speeches, to witness the play-acting of shoemakers, tailors, gravediggers and the meanest, most despicable riff-raff; to hear princes and the most respectable personages utter vulgar pleasantries, indecencies and plebeian buffoonery; in short, to read such continual eccentricities and insufferable extravagances?
>
> 4: 229–30

Certainly not the advocates of an 'enlightened' Spain in *El Pensador*, who took their cue from the idea of Tragedy which had been long considered the most dignified form of drama, spelt out as early as 1737 in Ignacio de Luzán's vastly influential *Poética*. Here the substance of the tragic plot is restricted to 'a great shift of fortune befalling kings, princes and characters of the utmost quality and dignity', whose falls, deaths, disasters and dangers should serve as a lesson to all, 'but especially to kings and persons of the highest authority and power' (443).

If taste is, as Theodor Adorno once noted, 'the most accurate seismograph of historical experience' (95), Spanish reformers like Luzán saw drama, especially *tragic* drama, as the last bastion against the popularization of culture, a tendency frequently ascribed not just to the work of Shakespeare, still largely unknown, but to that of Spain's own Golden Age authors. In the name of good taste, also demanded by other European readers, some of the *Poética*'s heaviest invectives are levelled against Lope de Vega, whose impressive dramatic output needed to be set against the fact that many of the plays appear improvised, disregard the unities, threaten verisimilitude, are philosophically vacuous and, most obnoxiously, lack decorum. From such a total disregard for the classical rules there could, for Luzán as for his followers, be but one conclusion: 'if a Lope de Vega, a don Pedro Calderón, a Solís, had added study and art to their naturally lofty talents, we would have such well-written plays in Spain they would be the envy and admiration of the other nations, whereas in the main they are the butt of their criticism and mockery' (402). It was this repudiation of Spain's own national dramatic tradition by Spanish critics themselves that, indirectly, led to the arrival of Shakespeare. The failure of the *comedia* to adhere to the 'rules' of classical dramaturgy set down by Aristotle and perpetuated throughout mainland Europe by critics like Boileau, Muratori and Luzán, required either its adaptation to the new aesthetic, the urgent composition of fresh and more 'orthodox' work or, as became frequently the case, the translation of foreign, mainly French, plays.

Of the latter, Jean-François Ducis's rewriting of Shakespeare's *Hamlet* was a relatively early arrival. Premiered just three years previously in Paris, Ducis's trimmed-down classicist version of the tragedy would be singled out by Andrés as an example of how, if properly 'corrected and reformed', certain passages of Shakespeare could acquire added value (309). Correcting and reforming are, as Michèle Willems shows in her chapter, an understatement when it came to Ducis's adaptations of *Hamlet* and other Shakespearean dramas. The play performed on 4 October 1772 at the Corral del Príncipe theatre in Madrid, generally attributed to playwright Ramón de la Cruz, followed Ducis's text almost to the letter – albeit adapting Hamlet's name to the more Spanish-sounding 'Hamleto', squeezing the

French alexandrines into classic Spanish hendecasyllables and, most strikingly, appearing to give actual physical presence to the ghost of Hamleto's father. For the rest, apart from the obvious attempt to work in certain allusions to contemporary Spanish politics (Pujante and Gregor), the translation deviates very little from the original, removing what Ducis referred to as Shakespeare's 'wild irregularities' (above all scrupulously avoiding the flexible time frame and shifts of location, the comic characters and interludes, the unseemly marriage between Gertrude and Claudius).The result was a drama that, in line with Ducis's intentions, strove to build Shakespeare's closet scene into a study of a 'parricidal queen' and, in the figure of the prince, a portrait of a 'pure and melancholy soul' who is 'a model of filial tenderness' (Albert 8).

Though by the theatrical standards of the day the production seems to have been moderately successful (Andioc and Coulon 17, 312–13), it was soon caught up in the debate between traditionalists and neo-classicists, making Shakespeare a pawn in a contemporary cultural conflict. A warning shot was fired that same year by the poet, playwright and essayist, José Cadalso, who in a provocative piece entitled *Los eruditos a la violeta* (or 'wise men without learning', false wits over-dependent on second-hand, predominantly foreign models of thought), dismissed the work as a play about a 'poor fellow' continually startled: 'His being startled was made into a tragedy in England; this spawned another tragedy in France, and the French one led to still another being miscarried in Spain' (40). Though undoubtedly a classicist at heart, Cadalso was in his own provocative way not only hinting at the poverty of the Spanish translation but also correctly defining the way in which Spanish culture had too readily opened itself to non-Spanish, particularly French, influences. Earlier in *Los eruditos* he counsels his pupils to acquire a 'French-style' contempt for English poets, particularly Shakespeare, whose 'gloomy, funereal, blood-soaked, spleenful dramas, laden with dense vapours from the Thames and black particles of soot', are precisely the kind of material the wise unlearned man should be familiar with, if only to 'astound' listeners with his erudition. An actual knowledge of the plays is not required (22).

Shakespeare's migration into Spain through predominantly French cultural channels was inevitable in a country whose ruling elite, even after the Revolution of 1789, continued to see French cultural paradigms as the model to be adopted in the fully modernized, though by no means secular, state of which they dreamed (Aguilar Piñal 2005). Such an enlightened, if unrepentantly Catholic view of contemporary Spanish society flashes through a report commissioned by the Academy of History on the present state of spectacles and public entertainments in Spain, drawn up in 1790 by the jurist and future minister Gaspar Melchor de Jovellanos. Having already declared his admiration for French tragedy as the natural heir to the Greek and Roman, and reiterated the familiar complaints about the moral defects of Spain's aureate drama in the prologue to his play *La muerte de Munuza* (The Death of Munuza) (1772), Jovellanos called for the production of new work in which could be seen

> heroic examples of reverence for the Supreme One and for the religion of our forebears; of love of the homeland, the sovereign and the Constitution; of respect for hierarchies, for the law and the depositories of authority; of conjugal fidelity, paternal love, filial tenderness and obedience; a theatre which presented good and magnanimous rulers, humane and incorruptible magistrates, citizens full of virtue and patriotism, prudent and zealous parents, true and constant friends; in a word, heroic and hard-working men, lovers of the public good, jealous of their liberty and their rights, protectors of innocence and the ruthless enemies of iniquity.
>
> 114

The kind of moral policing he had in mind was aimed primarily at promoting a theatre which, 'having honestly and agreeably entertained the audience, would also serve to refine its heart and cultivate its spirit; that is, which would serve to improve the manners of the nobility and wealthy youth that are wont to frequent it' (115). The critical studies which make any reference to Shakespeare in the period could be said to share Jovellanos's Voltaire-inspired distaste for the social content and potential addressees of his drama. 'When one reflects upon the enormous faults the English poet's scrupulous exactness in imitating nature gives rise to', wrote the Jesuit philosopher Esteban de Arteaga in 1789,

> when one sees transgressions, not merely of the rules of unity of place, action and time, but of those of geographical and historical accuracy; when one notes the barbarism and indecency with which the most distinguished personages comport themselves, though both may be taken from history; when one considers the immoderate and irregular nature of most of his compositions; when one observes his style, now bloated and pompous, now lax and diffuse, now heavy and opaque, now cold, puerile and laden with antitheses and confusions, the reader cannot help but feel disgust, as he sees before his eyes such representations of imperfection and baseness. And this is why the cultivated nations of Europe [such as Spain], though appreciative of the fact that in Shakespeare is to be found a far more original and fertile wit than in the French dramatists, have almost totally abandoned him and turned to the imitation of the latter.
>
> 207–8

Jovellanos's recommendations, which though appealing to the middle-class values of family, friendship and hard work, were aimed specifically at upper-class audiences, would be developed further by Leandro Fernández de Moratín. Himself a successful playwright, and son to Nicolás, one of Boileau's many mid-century Spanish epigones, Moratín would be made director of the Junta formed to oversee the repertoire of plays performed in end-of-the-century Madrid, and later '*corrector de comedias antiguas*', or censor of older plays, a role he seems to have fulfilled with relish (Oliva and Torres Monreal 247). Moratín's 1793 letter to Manuel Godoy, recently appointed prime minister to the Bourbon Charles IV, is a merciless assault on the quality of contemporary acting, the poverty of Spanish playhouses and the neglect of both local and national authorities with respect to the importance of the stage. 'Bad theatre is capable of corrupting behaviour, and when the latter goes awry it is extremely hard to maintain the rule of law', he would write in 1792:

> In the older *comedias* it is as though the playwrights had summoned up all the strength of their imagination to paint the fairest picture of every conceivable vice, every crime, and to do so not just by beautifying their deformity, but by presenting them to the public gaze under the name and appearance of virtue.
>
> Andioc 117

Bitterly opposed to what he termed the 'relaxing of customs, false ideas of honour, Quixotism, boldness, complacency, disobedience of magistrates, scorn for the law and the highest authority' (117–18), Moratín thus helped wage a short-lived crusade against popular theatrical tastes, culminating in 1799 in a government decree approving the *Idea de una reforma de los teatros de Madrid* (Idea for the Reform of the Theatres of Madrid), to be implemented in the season 1800/1, the publication of exclusive collections of mainly French tragedies and even a catalogue of plays, the *Teatro Nuevo Español*, considered worthy of the stage.

It is Moratín who was responsible for the first translation of Shakespeare's work more or less direct from the source, his 1798 rendering of *Hamlet*. Strikingly, however, the idea was neither to honour Shakespeare nor to legitimize *Hamlet* as a remotely performable play. Market strategies do not always coincide with consumer realities. For theatre audiences at least, tragedy, French or otherwise, remained a minority genre in the late eighteenth/early nineteenth century. In his prologue, like Arteaga before him, Moratín expounds the reasons why the English author is unworthy of the Spanish stage.[4] 'Lacking the sense of good judgement,' he would assert, 'art can never attain perfection'; and though capable of painting the full range of human characters and failings, of handling delicate issues of politics and morality 'with the utmost intelligence', filling his plays with 'interest, movement, variety and pomp', expressed by the most graceful and witty of styles, Shakespeare could never be a model for the budding playwright. Bereft of principles and forced into writing 'out of necessity rather than choice, dragged into it by the bad example set by his century and doomed to offer spectacles to a rude and ignorant public, whom he sought to please rather than to instruct', the migrant Shakespeare would, after two centuries, remain in the role of mere entertainer 'until someone else, gifted with the same sensibility and imagination, but more delicate taste and greater instruction ... might give new shape to the drama of his age' (n.p.). Rather surprisingly for such a prolific playwright, Moratín did not contemplate doing the job himself. Like Voltaire before him, his fear or contempt aroused by the monster he risked unleashing prevented him from seeing his text through to performance.

Symptomatic of Shakespeare's ambivalent position in Spanish culture this translation, largely considered both faithful to the original and an improvement on Pierre Le Tourneur's first full French version (García Martínez), is accompanied by a 'critical apparatus' arguing why the play cannot be considered worthy of the native stage. In fifty or so pages of endnotes, Moratín brings to bear all the classicist objections to Shakespeare's idiosyncrasies. Accordingly, though at times felicitous (the 'To be or not to be...' soliloquy is hailed as an example of truthful and 'eloquent simplicity' [352]), Shakespeare's use of speech is seen as generally marred by a tendency to brutishness, bawdy and inconsistent choice of verse or prose. Equally inconsistent and, in a number of cases (Polonius, the actors, the gravediggers) inappropriate to the world of tragedy, is his drawing of character, which is further encumbered by a profusion of minor roles (Rosencrantz and Guildenstern, Fortinbras, Laertes) allegedly with little or no 'bearing' on the action. The unities of time, place and action – and so an ideal audience's suspension of disbelief – are constantly undermined, an effect aggravated by the author's blatant disregard for historical and geographical accuracy. Shakespeare may well have been a fine imitator of Nature, but too often he fell into the trap of copying it too 'slavishly, as it really is' or, worse, following simply his own imagination to paint 'ideal and monstrous portraits that resemble no-one' (374). This, he argues, is the fault not just of Shakespeare or of *Hamlet*, but (here again the gravediggers' scene is chosen as a particularly scabrous example) the taste of a whole nation which, despite the best efforts of actor-impresarios like Garrick, took pleasure in 'horror shows and buffoonery, inebriated kings and emperors, philosophical discourses, pomposity, battles and burials, witches, apparitions, face-slapping, triumphs, music, torture and dead bodies'. Shakespeare, Moratín suggests, may well enjoy the esteem of his co-nationals but these excesses will surely help to cool the 'envy of those nations that haven't produced a Bacon or a Newton' (371), fathers of the *true* English enlightenment.

How much Moratín's translation either advanced or stemmed the migration of the original Shakespeare in Spain is unclear. On stage, it was the 'adapted' Shakespeare that Moratín, following Andrés, so eagerly encouraged with the result that it continued to reign supreme until the 1830s. Here again Ducis led the way, with translations amongst others by Manuel Garcia Suelto, Antonio de Saviñón, José María de Carnerero, José María Díaz and, even as late as 1872, Carlos Coello, based mainly on his late eighteenth-century adaptations. Of these the most popular proved to be his *Othello* which, in a version by an author calling himself 'Teodoro de la Calle', was attacked by scholarly critics. The play's Frenchness was stressed in an anonymous review in the normally pro-Enlightenment periodical *Memorial Literario*, which complained that 'according to our inviolable custom, this tragedy has not come straight from its native soil, but through the custom-house of the Pyrenees' (Anon. 60). Nevertheless De la Calle's version dominated Spanish theatrical life for nearly two decades and extended the fame of Shakespeare throughout the country and from there to Latin America.[5] Spain's early nineteenth-century 'Othellomania', boosted by the charisma of the actor, Isidoro Máiquez, who made the part his own practically up to his death and by the enterprising French-born theatre manager Jean Grimaldi (Calvo 2006), confirmed the play as commercially the most successful of the Shakespeare adaptations. So popular did the play prove, and so firmly entrenched in the pre- and post-War of Independence repertoires, that it eventually became an object of burlesque, spawning at least three different versions of a 'tragical *sainete*' called *Caliche* (1828) which transfers the characters and the action of the play to a variety of unmistakably Spanish, low-life urban settings. Even as late as 1873, it is the 'Máiquez' *Othello* that the novelist Benito Pérez Galdós invokes in *La Corte de Carlos IV* – a tribute, as Clara Calvo has suggested, less to the original playwright than to the actor (121–4).

With the end of the war and, consequently, of the French occupation of Spain, the cause of the French-inspired neo-classicists did not dampen, but a new kind of audience and reading-public sought projections of their own preoccupations in the literature that was being performed or published. No longer predominantly the 'nobility and wealthy youth' targeted by Jovellanos, cultural consumers in the Fernandine period sprang from a wide range of social groups and classes, though it was the urban middle classes that appeared to have the biggest say as to what was produced and how. They relished the influx of new types of drama (many of them also of French origin) which, as Guillermo Carnero has shown, handled seriously or in a sentimental way aspects of contemporary everyday life and private familial issues of marriage, family and friendship, featuring middle- or lower-class protagonists or else high-ranking ones engaging 'not in the exercise of their prerogatives, but in their human, personal and private dimension' (123).

Without quite spelling the end of the neo-classical project of reform, the new French *drame* began to occupy an important place in the repertoires and publishing-houses of the new post-independence Spain. Theatrically speaking, Shakespeare continued to be presented in strict classical form, but outside the theatres, and especially in the criticism that proliferated in the early part of the nineteenth century, the 'Enlightenment' Bard was giving way to visions of his work that tended to reflect the new bourgeois consciousness.

Part of this new set of concerns was the desire to *read* Shakespeare in something approximating his original form. Perhaps symptomatically it was a German, the former consul to Cadiz, site of the 1812 liberal Constitution, Johann Nikolaus Böhl von Faber, who set the tone when he suggested that the obsession with reducing the original creations of both Spanish and English drama to the tyranny of the unities had had disastrous consequences for the genre. A follower of Schlegel, many of whose ideas he reproduces verbatim, Böhl von Faber urged respect for the 'organic' relationship not just between form and content but between literature and society as a whole – a belief, that is, in the unmistakably 'national' characteristics of literature that had been disfigured by the artificial imposition of the Aristotelian rules and virtually outlawed in the process. In the case of Spanish literature, Böhl von Faber waged a Schlegelian defence of Golden Age drama, particularly Calderón, whose religious pieces and *autos* had been the targets of classicist prejudice, rewriting and even prohibition. If only the Spanish were able to attend to their hearts and awaken from the errors of their submission to the false god of Reason, they would, assures Böhl von Faber, 'learn to admire by conviction what hitherto they have loved by inclination; and paying no heed to the bastardized criticism of the philosophical century, will put all their efforts into composing in the same way as the great models of their Golden Age' (n.p.). As far as the English were concerned, the temporary triumph of Reason, as exemplified in the criticism of Pope and Johnson, should not be allowed to efface the spontaneous and 'passionate' nature of that nation's character, whose true representative was none other than Shakespeare. The former classicist José Joaquín de Mora, whose correspondence with Böhl von Faber provides a fascinating insight into the way the ideals of the Romantics began to permeate Spanish soil, would in 1814 confess his admiration for 'the most beautiful genius that has ever existed':

> I love it when people say he is a barbarian, a savage, a ruffian; because if these men understood and praised him, would he be what he is? The further he strays in his poetry from everything which smacks of drama in this country, the better. He is the greatest of poets. His only rule was his inspiration, he created another nature, he penetrated human nature as if he had discovered himself in his creation, and no one can match him in the way he encases in one line of verse a series of ideas that would provoke whole hours of meditation.
>
> Cited in Llorens 19

A complaint frequently levelled by later classicists at the Romantic cult of Calderón and Shakespeare was that it reeked of nostalgia for the ages long-dead that had little to do with modern 'civilized' culture. 'There is a sect of German *littérateurs*,' warned the critic and grammarian, José Gómez Hermosilla, in 1821, 'whose principles in matters of poesy are opposed to those that in the most civilized nations have been set down by good taste' (131). Coinciding, as the Romantic turn did, with the restoration of Ferdinand VII as the legitimate monarch, there could not, as Carnero (237–8) has argued, help but be a whiff of the old regime in the defence of the older *comedia* and Shakespearean drama. Radically opposed to established 'taste', such a defence seemed to invite association with a whole string of postulates, none of which were based on Reason. First, the existence of a peculiar national character was posited, epitomized by a seigniorial concept of honour, fanatical religiousness, extreme patriotism and hatred of anything foreign. Second, the notion of a 'true' enlightenment was promoted, embodied in the ideals of the old regime, as opposed to the 'false' enlightenment, exported by the French government. Third, it hailed the revelation of a national character in the 'popular' uprising against Napoleon, insisting on the need to reproduce seventeenth-century forms of political organization as the highpoint of Spain's splendour. Fourth, it underlined the essentially conservative nature of Spanish politics, religion, customs and literature versus the inappropriateness of 'modern', foreign-inspired political experiments such as those tried out at Cadiz. Finally, it appeared to identify liberalism with *afrancesamiento*, a necessary collusion with the enemy, and the defence of neo-classical precepts as a political crime.

With the end of Ferdinand's iron grip on the nation's liberties following his death in 1833, the time seemed right for many of the liberals who had fled the absolutist purges of the 1820s and early 1830s to return to Spain, thus opening a new migratory route for Shakespeare. With the liberals came not just a first-hand knowledge of the tastes and customs of their adoptive countries, notably France and England, but a sense that 'modernity' now lay beyond the cramping strictures imposed by the neo-classicists, which had continued to beset cultural production under the Bonapartes and Ferdinand. A measure of how thinking about the drama in particular had moved on in these years is the career of Antonio Alcalá Galiano. A former deputy at the liberal court of Cadiz who had been violently opposed to the romanticized nostalgia of thinkers like Böhl von Faber, Alcalá Galiano seems to have undergone a radical transformation during his exile in London, writing that the Restoration had been 'doubly damaging' for Spanish letters, by punishing writers and putting multiple obstacles in their way to discourage literary aspirations (37). If, on his return, the country still looked to France for intellectual, if no longer political, orientation, it was now to the Romantic revolution of Hugo and his twin belief in '[l]iberty in art, liberty in society', rather than to the waspish censures of the enlightened Voltaire, that the intelligentsia were prepared to turn. Mariano José de Larra, one of the most influential critical voices in the period, would adapt Hugo's rallying cry in *Hernani*: 'Freedom in literature, as in the arts, as in industry, as in commerce, as in conscience. This is the sign of the times, this is our insignia, this is the yardstick we shall use to measure things' (cited in Flitter 103). In dramatic art such freedom was nowhere more evident than in the forgotten work of Calderón and Shakespeare. As the critic Eugenio de Ochoa would put it in the fiercely pro-Romantic journal *El Artista* (The Artist), for men who judge the arts on instinct rather than codes,

> the works of Calderón and Shakespeare will be a constant source of pleasure, regardless of the fact that all their comedies and tragedies last more than the mysterious twenty-four hours, which, like ancient cabalistic signs, have the virtue of making good a play which (oh! the power of white magic) would be hateful if it lasted twenty-four hours and three minutes.
>
> 88

Lurking beneath the irony is what rings like a Coleridgean trust in the flexibility of the imagination and the critical recognition of the intrinsic value of such long-neglected work. The contribution of other returning émigrés like José Blanco White, for whom if Shakespeare was to blame for anything, it was 'not so much in the want of the Unities, as in the novelty and boldness of his Metaphors' (288), was, as Ángel Luis Pujante has shown, equally decisive here.

That said, the out-and-out rejection of a predetermined standard of 'taste', based on the play's degree of conformity to the 'rules' of classical dramaturgy, and the appeal to the critic's 'instinct' as a criterion must have sounded, at best, hopelessly subjective, at worst, dangerously anarchic in a cultural formation still densely populated with the heirs of the eighteenth-century defenders of the rules or '*preceptistas*'. The classical model persisted through the first few decades of the century, with the performance of Golden Age drama continuing to be filtered through the theatrical tastes of pre-Revolutionary France and, as Vicente Llorens (386) has shown, with the application of the adaptor's razor to shorten scenes or suppress 'unnecessary' characters or, if required, the replacement of passages in the original text or the insertion of 'whatever he saw fit'. In the case of Shakespeare, and despite the critical clamour for productions that reflected the 'true spirit' of the originals, theatre managers preferred not to take risks, favouring previously expurgated versions rendered, with very few exceptions, from tried and tested, invariably French, adaptations, such as Casimir Delavigne's rewriting of *Richard III*, *Les Enfants d'Edouard* (The Children of Edward), or Ducis's own version of *King John*, *Jean sans Terre* (John Lackland), unequivocally attributed by Spanish translator, José María Díaz, to the immortal 'Shecspeare' [*sic*] (cited in Par 180).

Significantly, these versions outlived by at least two decades the most adventurously Shakespearean theatrical version of the period – the first time an original text formed the basis of an actual production. The 1838 premiere of *Macbeth*, as translated by José García de Villalta, has a not uncontested place in Shakespeare's Spanish stage history. The work of a committed liberal who had served his time in London as an exile of the Fernandine purges, the translated text was advertised as that of a play 'universally applauded throughout Europe', a drama which, it was important to point out, was nonetheless 'freer in its forms, less certain in its development and richer in adventitious adornments' than anything produced under the aegis of the Greco-Roman rules (cited in Llorens 379). Certainly, for the members of the audience not familiar with the original, the play would have spelt a radical departure from previous *Macbeth*s, those performed to moderate success in classical versions, when Shakespeare was still in thrall to neo-classical norms (Gregor and Pujante). Especially striking was the presence of the three witches, tactfully omitted from the previous versions to avoid any charges of indecency, poor taste, or the suggestion that Macbeth's actions may have had a supernatural motivation; the presence of the ghost of Banquo which, notwithstanding the appearance of a ghost in the 1772

Hamleto, must have sent murmurs of surprise amongst the spectators – especially as he was only visible to Macbeth and them; Macbeth's lack of remorse and determination to fight to the end – a shocking vindication of the callous disrespect for monarchic legitimacy and evoking the allure of tyranny; finally, the breakdown of Lady Macbeth, whose initial cruelty and ambition soon morphs into madness and despair. Away from established ways of presenting the play, an even more ambitious *mise-en-scène*, in the spirit of the Romantic *Gesamtkunstwerk*, incorporated richly painted backdrops produced by artist Francesco Lucini and a fourth-act witches' chorus composed by Basilio Basili, musically adorning a scene which, by its very existence, was an affront to some of the most cherished tenets of the older classicism.[6]

Perhaps predictably, the production was savaged by a still largely classically minded press. The least scathing response to the play came in a long review by Enrique Gil y Carrasco, who noted the complete 'incompatibility of Spain's theatrical resources with the pomp and circumstance that ought to accompany such lofty pieces': accommodating the play to the native stage was like 'laying a giant in a child's cot' (424). To the material difficulties of adapting such a production to the poorly equipped stage of Madrid's Teatro El Príncipe he adds the disorientation of the actors, whose previous knowledge of Shakespeare – the 'real' Shakespeare – was based on nothing more reliable than the 'ham-fisted and incomplete translation of *Hamlet*' by Moratín (425). More disquieting was the response of a sector of the first-night audience who, according to some reports, booed and hissed so loudly that much of the play was inaudible to an already bemused public.

The *Macbeth* stage experiment would not be repeated for a number of years, and the standard repertoire was carefully adjusted to suit the tastes of increasingly bourgeois audiences (Picoche 77–8). Still, Shakespeare had a considerable presence in the critical literature of the period: the first translations of works as yet unperformed reflected an interest in the English playwright that began to spell the end of the neo-classical grip on his work. As Evaristo San Miguel would put it in 1844 in an article published in *El Laberinto*:

> Some sixty years ago it would have been unthinkable to give a clear idea of the works of Shakespeare to an audience accustomed to the order, to the regularity of what was called classicism, to ousting from the stage whatever infringed the precepts of Aristotle which were so rigorously set down, so respectfully and even boastingly abided by. Now that those ideas and tastes have changed, the task is not so arduous, though always complicated by the nature, difficulty and range of genres which are mixed in his productions.

197

Without being a complete vindication of Shakespeare, and while continuing to reveal a certain ambivalence in mid-nineteenth-century attitudes to his work, the quoted passage is as close as any to an admission of his having gained a niche in Spanish culture.

It is one of the most compelling but underexamined aspects of Shakespeare's migration to Spain that, though most of the original plays were only available to the public in adapted form, 'Shakespeare' was to feature prominently as a fictional character in a number of early to mid-nineteenth-century stage plays. Moratín's biography, based on the English editor Rowe's, was arguably the trigger to a series of representations in which the author, almost always in the process of composing one of his (as yet untranslated) plays, emerges as a figure of dramatic interest in his own right. Alexandre Duval's *Shakespeare amoureux* was performed in Barcelona as early as 1810, when *Richard III* – the play Shakespeare has just finished in which his sweetheart is appearing – was unavailable in any form to Spanish audiences, adapted or otherwise. Though these first performances were in French, an entertainment aimed primarily at French troops and functionaries stationed in Spain during the period of the occupation, the play generated an interest in the English author that would eventually result in a Spanish translation, *Shakespeare enamorado*, by Ventura de la Vega (1831). Even by the date of de la Vega's version, only four of Shakespeare's plays had been produced in Spain, all of them tragedies and all of them, with the exception of Moratín's *Hamlet*, available textually only in adaptation. Of these, *Othello* seems to have made the biggest impression, by 'explaining' the protagonist's jealousy in *Shakespeare enamorado* – *Othello* is the play he is currently working on. *Othello* is also cited liberally in Enrique Zumel's later *Guillermo Shakespeare* (1853) and virtually dictates the plot of Manuel Tamayo y Baus's Romantic, self-reflecting piece, *Un drama nuevo* (1867).

How influential these works were in the consolidation of Shakespeare as Spain's best known, most widely criticized and translated cultural immigrant, is unclear. What is certain is that by the 1870s, with the publication of the first full prose translations of the complete works by the Naples-born Jaime Clark, the mist surrounding the author's written work had lifted considerably. Promoting Clark's translation, the novelist and former diplomat, Juan Valera, could, citing Emerson, glumly admit that '[n]ow, all our philosophy and thought are Shakespearized. His mind is the horizon beyond which we do not see' (xviii). The location of Shakespeare at the centre of the cultural debate following the 1868 revolution that ousted Isabel and on which the succession of Italian theatre companies visiting Spain were able to capitalize (Puigdomènech), was still greeted with dismay and scepticism by sectors of society. The unmediated reception of plays which dealt with threats to political legitimacy and shamelessly foregrounded violence and such ignoble desires as ambition was regarded as an unacceptable reminder of those revolutionary events. For many critics, the 'naturalism' of the Italian productions, and their respect for as much of the original texts as it was possible to perform, ran counter to the 'proper' task of theatre which was 'the representation of native customs and ... [of] moral values traditionally associated with the Spanish character' (Rodríguez Sánchez de León 1881). For others, it was a sign that the mirror had at last begun to replace the razor.

Notes

1 I am grateful to the Spanish Ministry of Economy and Competitiveness for funding the research for this essay as part of project FFI2014-53587P 'The reception of Shakespeare's work in Spanish and European culture'.

2 All translations from the Spanish are my own.

3 The Jesuits had been expelled from Spain in 1767 on account of their alleged support for an uprising, the so-called 'motín de Esquilache', against the government of Charles III. Andrés, who made his home in Ferrara, first published the *Origen* in Italian. It was subsequently translated and published in Spanish by his brother, Carlos.

4 Moratin's preface, which includes a so-called 'Life' of Shakespeare, is heavily indebted to Nicolas Rowe. The translation as a whole is written under the pseudonym 'Inarco Celenio'. Writing under an assumed name was a common tactic amongst writers not wishing to be associated with the work they were translating.

5 For brief accounts of the play's impact in countries like Argentina, Uruguay and Chile, see Modenessi and Gandara, and Versiani and Stegh.

6 For a full account of the text and the production, see Zaro (49–66).

References

Adorno, Theodor (2005), *Minima Moralia: Reflections on a Damaged Life*, London: Verso.

Aguilar Piñal, Francisco (1990), 'Las refundiciones en el siglo XVIII', *Cuadernos de teatro clásico* 5: 33–41.

Aguilar Piñal, Francisco (2005), *La España del absolutismo ilustrado*, Madrid: Espasa.

Albert, Paul, ed. (1879), *Lettres de Jean-François Ducis*, Paris: G. Jousset.

Alcalá Galiano, Antonio (1969), *Literatura española siglo XIX: de Moratín a Rivas*, Madrid: Alianza.

Álvarez Barrientos, Joaquín (1990), 'Sobre el cambio del concepto de imitación en el siglo XVIII español', *Nueva Revista de Filología Hispánica* 38, 1: 219–46.
Andioc, René, ed. (1973), *Epistolario de Leandro Fernández de Moratín*, Madrid: Castalia.
Andioc, René and Mireille Coulon (1996), *Cartelera teatral madrileña del siglo XVIII (1708–1808)*, vol. 2, Madrid: Anejos de Criticón.
Andrés, Juan (1784–1806), *Origen, progresos y estado actual de toda literatura*, Madrid: Antonio de Sancha.
Anon. (1802), 'Teatros. Juicio general del año cómico de 1801 a 1802', *Memorial Literario* III: 54–61.
Arteaga, Esteban de (1789), *Investigaciones filosóficas sobre la belleza ideal, considerada como objeto de todas las artes de imitación*, Madrid: Antonio de Sancha.
Blanco White, José (1845), *The Life of the Reverend Joseph Blanco White Written by Himself with Portions of His Correspondence*, ed. J. H. Thom, London: Chapman.
Böhl von Faber and Johan Nikolas (1814), 'Reflexiones de Schlegel sobre el teatro, traducidas del alemán', *Mercurio gaditano* 121, 16 September, n.p.
Cadalso, José (1772), *Los eruditos a la violeta*, Madrid: Antonio de Sancha.
Calvo, Clara (2006), 'De-foreignizing Shakespeare: *Othello* in Romantic Spain', in J. M. González, ed., *Spanish Studies in Shakespeare and His Contemporaries*, 117–29, Newark: University of Delaware Press.
Calvo, Clara (2008), 'Shakespeare, Napoleon and Juan de Grimaldi: Cultural Politics and French Troops in Spain', in P. Franssen, J. de Vos and D. Delabastita, eds, *Shakespeare and European Politics*, 109–23, Newark: University of Delaware Press; London: Associated University Presses.
Carnero, Guillermo (1997), *Estudios sobre teatro español del siglo XVIII*, Zaragoza: Prensas Universitarias de Zaragoza.
Flitter, Derek (1992), *Teoría y crítica del romanticismo español*, trans. J. C. Mainer, Madrid: Akal.
García Martínez, Isabel (1987), 'Estudio comparativo entre dos traducciones dieciochescas y dos actuales de *Hamlet*', *Archivum* 37–8: 529–52.
Gil y Carrasco, Enrique (1954), 'Macbeth', in *Obras completas de don Enrique Gil y Carrasco*, ed. J. Campos, 419–27, Madrid: Atlas.

Gómez Hermosilla, José (1821), 'Reflexiones sobre la dramática española en los siglos XVI y XVII', *El Censor* 38, VII, 21 April, 131–41.

Gregor, Keith and Ángel-Luis Pujante, eds (2011), *Macbeth: las versiones neoclásicas*, Murcia: Edit.Um.

Jovellanos, Gaspar Melchor de (1967), *Espectáculos y diversiones públicas*, Salamanca: Anaya.

Llorens, Vicente (1979), *El romanticismo español*, Madrid: Castalia.

Luzán, Ignacio de (1977), *La poética o Reglas de la poesía en general, y de sus principales especies*, ed. R. P. Sebold, Barcelona: Labor.

Modenessi, Alfredo M. and Margarida Gambara Rauen (2016), 'Shakespearean Tragedy in Latin America and the Caribbean', in M. Neill and D. Schalkwyk eds, *The Oxford Handbook of Shakespearean Tragedy*, 864–80, Oxford: Oxford University Press.

Moody, Jane (2003), 'Shakespeare and the Immigrants: Nationhood, Psychology and Xenophobia on the Nineteenth-Century Stage', in G. Marshall and A. Poole, eds, *Victorian Shakespeare, Volume 1: Theatre, Drama and Performance*, 99–118, Basingstoke: Palgrave Macmillan.

Moratín, Leandro Fernández de (1798), *Hamlet. Tragedia de Guillermo Shakespeare*, Madrid: Oficina de Villalplana.

Nipho, Francisco Mariano (1764), *La nación española defendida de los insultos del Pensador y sus secuaces*, Madrid: Gabriel Ramírez.

Ochoa, Eugenio de (1836), 'Literatura', *El Artista* VIII: 88.

Oliva, César and Francisco Torres Monreal (1990), *Historia básica del arte escénica*, Madrid: Cátedra.

Par, Alfonso (1936), *Representaciones shakespearianas en España. Vol. 2: Época realista, y tiempos modernos*, Madrid: Librería Victoriano Suárez; Barcelona: Biblioteca Balmés.

Picoche, Jean-Louis (1995), 'Dramaturgias románticas', in J. Canavaggio ed., *Historia de la literatura española*, vol. 5, 77–96, Barcelona: Ariel.

Pozuelo, José María and Rosa María Aradra Sánchez (2000), *Teoría del canon y literatura española*, Madrid: Cátedra.

Puigdomènech, Helena (1998), 'Il recupero di Shakespeare attraverso le compagnie italiane a Barcellona nella seconda metà del'ottocento', in J. Espinosa Carbonell ed., *El teatro italiano:*

Actas del VII Congreso Nacional de Italianistas, 567–76, Valencia: Universitat de Valencia.

Pujante, Ángel Luis (2012), 'Discovering Shakespeare in Exile: Spanish Emigrés in England (1819–1840)', *Miscelánea* 46: 83–98.

Pujante, Ángel Luis and Keith Gregor (2008), 'Conservatism and Liberalism in the Four Spanish Renderings of Ducis's *Hamlet*', in P. Franssen, J. de Vos and D. Delabastita, eds, *Shakespeare and European Politics*, 304–17, Newark: University of Delaware Press; London: Associated University Presses.

Rodríguez Sánchez de León, María José (2003), 'Teoría y géneros dramáticos en el siglo XIX', in J. Huerta Calvo, ed., *Historia del teatro español*, vol. 2, 1853–1894, Madrid: Gredos.

San Miguel, Evaristo (1844), 'Biografía. Shakespeare', *El Laberinto* 1, 15: 197–9.

Valera, Juan (1873), 'Prólogo', in Jaime Clark trans., *Obras de Shakespeare*, 5 vols., Madrid: Medina y Navarro.

Versiani, María Clara and Anna Stregh Camati (2017), 'Shakespeare in Latin America: Appropriation Politics and Performance Practices', in J. L. Levenson and R. Ormsby, eds, *The Shakespearean World*, 78–96, London and New York: Routledge.

Voltaire (1835), *Œuvres complètes de Voltaire*, vol. 1, ed. M. Beuchot, Paris: Furne.

Zaro, Juan Jesús (2007), *Shakespeare y sus traductores: Análisis crítico de siete traducciones españolas de obras de Shakespeare*, Bern: Peter Lang.

10

Migrating with migrants

Shakespeare and the Armenian diaspora

Jasmine H. Seymour

When Shakespearean texts emerged in the Armenian language in the nineteenth century, the Kingdom of Armenia had long been divided between Western and Eastern territories by successive foreign invaders. After the fall of the last Armenian Kingdom of Cilicia in the fourteenth century, Western Armenia was conquered by the Ottomans, and the vanquished Armenians existed in perpetual fear of further persecution. Meanwhile, the Eastern Armenian provinces, under Persian rule since the early Middle Ages, were annexed in 1828 to the Russian empire following the Russo-Persian wars. A section of these formed the first independent Republic of Armenia in 1918, however, it was reconquered and declared the Soviet Republic of Armenia in 1920. Unsurprisingly, Shakespeare's texts initially flourished not on the historical Armenian soil, but in foreign realms, where Armenian migrants, in search of safety, had gradually established economically and culturally prosperous communities.

Within Armenian schools across their dispersed communities, 'scholastic theatres' inspired by European prototypes sprung up, where during festivities students displayed their oratory skills reciting selected extracts from classical plays. One of those renowned establishments was the Mekhitarist seminary in Venice, which played a vital role in safeguarding the Armenian literary, religious and cultural heritage. Its founder, Abbot Mekhitar of Sebaste, when fleeing Ottoman persecutions, was granted the small island of San Lazaro in the Venetian lagoon in 1717. To celebrate Shakespeare's tercentenary in 1864, students of the Venice seminary staged an 'adaptation' of *Macbeth* in classical Armenian, Grapar, based on Jean-François Ducis's version of the play. Ducis's reworking of Shakespeare's tragedy was further amended by Father Kaisserian to suit the limitations of the all-male Catholic school: Lady Macbeth was converted into Macbeth's son Edgar, and the number of characters contracted from twenty-four to nine (*Bazmavep* 1964: 287–9). However, this was an isolated case of importing Shakespeare via French abridgements by Ducis into Armenian, while this student production bore but superficial resemblance to Shakespeare's masterpiece (Samvelian 63).

Since Shakespeare's legacy among Armenians is little known outside Armenia, this chapter will explore the historical circumstances in which Shakespearean drama was introduced by Armenian migrants in Calcutta, Smyrna, Constantinople and Tiflis, pioneering Shakespearean drama in their adoptive countries.[1] The aim here is to examine the contribution of Shakespeare as poet and dramatist, first to the development of the modern language and the national theatre under foreign power, and second to the renewal of national identity throughout the nineteenth century which eventually led to self-determination: the first independent Republic of Armenia, founded in 1918.

Early translations into classical Armenian

The early translations of Shakespeare into Grapar were attributed to Armenians in India. Initially, these were merely 'birds of passage', according to historian Jacob Seth, merchants who had been travelling 'from the Kingdom of Armenia through the fertile Indian lands on their way to China since antiquity' (Seth 1). Valuing their trading and negotiating skills, the Mughal emperor, Akbar I, invited Armenian traders from Persia to settle in Agra in the sixteenth century. Thus Armenian settlements were gradually formed across the peninsula. According to the official historiographer of the East India Company, Sir John Bruce, Armenians were the first settlers in Calcutta, preceding the English by at least sixty years, serving 'as political stepping-stones of the English in India', playing a vital role in the expansion of the Company (Seth 281). Their community in Calcutta, which never exceeded a few thousand, prospered due to its firm commitment to their ancient language, religion and distinct culture. To safeguard their language and ancestral heritage, Armenian philanthropists, who had accrued considerable wealth and transnational reputation, subsidized schools in Indian and European metropolises to educate Armenian children from the first half of the nineteenth century. For instance, Moorat-Raphael College in Venice was subsidized in 1836 by Mkertich Murat and Edward Raphael from India. At the Armenian Philanthropic College in Calcutta, established in 1821 (today a thriving international college), Shakespeare among other European authors was taught in order to improve the students' rhetoric skills, essential for future merchants and negotiators.

The first mention of Shakespeare and his works among Armenians was recorded in Joseph Hovsep Emin's (1726–1809) autobiography published in London in 1792. Against the will of his merchant father, Emin left his paternal home in Calcutta to study at the Royal Military Academy of Woolwich. Through his aristocratic connections, the charismatic young émigré was introduced to London's high society, where he met the actor, David Garrick, who, with his Shakespearean performances at the Drury Lane theatre in the 1750s, undoubtedly fuelled his bardolatry.[2] Passages of his autobiography on Othello, Shylock and Hamlet express his veneration for Shakespeare. Invited to the house of the naval officer Mr Thomson, alluding to valiant Othello, Emin narrated his own battles in foreign lands to the host, his French wife and their young gullible daughter: 'Emin, like the Moor of Venice, Mrs. Thomson hearing his tale like a tender mother; and the young lady, resembling the lovely Desdemona, drinking up each word with thirst, and with tears in her eyes, pitying him, and fetching deep sighs' (Emin 135). After his graduation, Emin joined the English army in the Prussian wars, gaining valuable experience for his forthcoming campaigns in Armenia. Later, he raised an army for the liberation of Karabagh from the Turks, thus becoming one of the pioneers of the Armenian self-determination movement. In the wake of Emin, Shakespeare was gradually introduced by Armenian translators, intellectuals and theatre practitioners who, in their separate ways, fought for the survival of the Armenian language and cultural identity in exile.

The rhetorical power of Shakespearean speeches stimulated Armenian editors in Emin's native Calcutta. Mixing with English settlers, they had learnt English from an early age, and were able to translate Shakespearean texts from the original. While the identity of the first Indo-Armenian translators was concealed under various pennames (Bachelor, Veraks, Himenos, Humanist), it was assumed that the initiator of those works was the editor Martiros Mkrtchian, who apotheosized the Shakespearean canon as the most significant text after the Bible. Translated passages from *The Two Gentlemen of Verona, Hamlet, Twelfth Night, Measure for Measure, Much Ado About Nothing, Othello, A Midsummer Night's Dream* and other plays were published in the periodical *Shtemaran* between 1822 and 1823 (Hovhannisyan 2011: 26). Articles conveying didactic declarations on love, friendship, honesty and integrity were reinforced by quotations from Shakespeare, 'the greatest judge of human nature', wrote the editor (*Shtemaran* 371). For example, criticizing the vanity of certain local statesmen who abused their positions, the translator quoted from *Measure for Measure* (2.2.117–22) to demonstrate the culpabilities of the ruling classes:

Մարդիկ սեպհականողք մի փոքրիկ կարողություն
Այնպես ցնորական գործես գործեն առաջի
Բարձր երկնքից,
Մինչ հրեշտակած լացուցանեն:

The passage, a word-by-word translation, was remarkably close to the original: 'Men possessing a slight authority, / Commit such senseless acts against Heaven,/ That they make angels weep'.[3] Furthermore, Shakespeare's style was emulated here (even the original run-on lines were reproduced), indicating the linguistic potency and the flexibility of the adoptive language. Elsewhere, the extract 'The lunatic, the lover and the poet' (5.1.5–9) from *A Midsummer Night's Dream*, translated by so-called 'Veraks' in blank verse, again, successfully emulated the original: 'Lovers and madmen have such hot brains, / Such vivid imagination, that they make / Cold reason a mystery. The lunatic, the lover and the poet / Are equal in imagination' (*Shtemaran* 554–5). The translator has skilfully maintained the enjambements and the iambic pentameter of the original. However, as Armenian words are generally longer than their English equivalents, Shakespeare's metre was stretched to fifteen syllables here and in subsequent translations.

If the initial extracts from Shakespeare published in *Shtemaran* served didactic purposes, more radical and political objectives were pursued a quarter of a century later by the well-known poet, writer and educator, Mesrovb David Thaliadian (1803–58) from Calcutta, who translated Brutus's speech to the Roman crowd (*Azgaser*, no. 130). Welcoming the liberation of Eastern Armenia from Persian rule in 1828, Thaliadian played a significant role in introducing Indo-Armenians to the burgeoning liberal ideologies that swept through Russia and Europe. His translations from Homer, Euripides, Dante, Byron and Firdausi were intended to illustrate the stories of heroic battles in different cultures. Later, Thaliadian's translation from English of the entire Act Three of *Julius Caesar* – including Brutus's soliloquies (in prose) and Antony's (in verse) – was printed by the Venice Mekhitarists in *Bazmavep* (1853: 163), one of the oldest periodicals in Europe. Introducing the plot, the translator unambiguously defended the viewpoints of Brutus and his allies as 'burning with the love of freedom', thus justifying Caesar's assassination, since he was perceived as a threat to democracy. Through Shakespeare's Roman tragedy, Thaliadian was prompting his readers to stand up against foreign oppression.

However, those initial Shakespeare translations by English-speaking editors from India were targeted chiefly at the educated elite: students, intellectuals and affluent members of the Armenian society, proficient in classical Armenian. Shakespeare had yet to reach the ordinary people, who spoke the modern Western or Eastern Armenian, which gradually replaced the rather complex Grapar.[4] The obstacles to Shakespeare's delayed arrival in modern Armenian were manifold, but the main cause was certainly the dispersed geography of a stateless nation.

Shakespeare's challenge to the Ottoman regime

The socio-economic conditions of Christian communities living under the Ottomans improved marginally thanks to the reforms brought about by the efforts of pro-European Abdülmecid I to save the empire from discontented minorities. A growing number of Armenian printing houses produced new translations of European authors which stimulated the penetration of liberal ideologies into the national consciousness. Free schools (both for boys and girls) were opening across communities for children of varied background, not just for the descendants of the aristocratic and bourgeois elite. Apart from the scholastic theatres, since the 1800s dramatic performances were delivered in small auditoriums belonging to affluent Armenian households in the capital city. Thus, from the 1850s the first designated theatres in the empire were owned principally by Greek and Armenian minorities predominantly showcasing local and visiting opera acts. The first professional theatre in Constantinople – the Eastern Theatre, founded by Petros Maghakian – opened with a French melodrama in 1861 (Stepanian 219). A dozen promising young actors joined the artistic director Maghakian, including the first female actor in the Near East, Arusiak Papazian. Other talented young women followed, viewed as obnoxious and immoral by the ruling autocracy. In despair, several actors committed suicide, while Arusiak Papazian was separated from her children and locked in an asylum. Nonetheless Armenian actors, who were able to perform in several languages (Armenian, French, Greek or Turkish), rapidly gained a widespread reputation. When the celebrated black tragedian, Ira Aldridge, arrived in Constantinople to perform *Othello* in 1866, he appeared on stage with the leading actor, Stephan Ekshian, and other Armenians, who delivered their parts in French so fluently, that they were misidentified as French players by Aldridge's own biographer (Samvelian 90).

However, Shakespearean drama never appeared in the repertory of the Eastern Theatre. Instead *Macbeth* premiered in 1867 at the second Armenian establishment, the Asian Theatre, founded by actor-manager, Hagop Vardovian (1840–98). The chosen appellations (Eastern and Asian) aimed to conceal the ethnicity of the cast and their Armenian-language repertories for fear of censorship, which ultimately happened. To publicise his adaptation of *Macbeth*, Vardovian wrote in the Armenian press: 'Shakespeare's name has become immortal with this sublime and exceptional tragedy, and to support our endeavour, we anticipate that our theatre-loving audience would encourage the troupe with their attendance and, simultaneously, relish a sublime and entertaining drama' (Stepanian 312). Despite the significance of Shakespeare's launch on the Armenian stage, the press remained silent. The only testimony came from the national playwright, Hagop Baronian, who solely commented on Vardovian's 'exaggerated' interpretation of Macbeth: 'if there was a susceptible young girl in the audience, she would have fainted' (Samvelian 88). Another eminent author, Arshag Chobanian, in his article on the national theatre, described Vardovian as 'a skilful impresario, average actor, limited mind and a profit-driven character'. A century later, the Shakespearean scholar Samvelian echoed Chobanian's opinion that Vardovian lacked the artistic assets to handle one of the most complex roles and that Shakespeare's tragedy was selected rather inadvertently (Samvelian 88).

However, the development of Armenian-language theatres, and the growing reputation of Armenian actors, displeased the vigilant Ottoman authorities. Staging politically insightful plays not only threatened to mirror the murky reality of oppressed minorities, but also injected 'anti-government' moods amongst citizens. After the opening night, *Macbeth* was hastily removed from the repertory and censored thereafter for decades. But the worst was yet to come: immediately after the sudden death of Sultan Abdülaziz in mysterious circumstances and the coronation of Sultan Abdul Hamid II in 1876, Armenian theatres were banned altogether. Shakespearean tragedies, exposing murders in royal households, were unsolicited reminders of the bloodshed in the Ottoman palaces. When Vardovian opened the first Turkish-language theatre – the Ottoman Theatre – with a small group of Armenian actors, he chose an inconsequential repertory of light-hearted operettas and melodramas that gratified Abdul Hamid's taste. A majority of leading Armenian actors refused to participate in the Turkish-language theatre, once again taking the road of exile: 'the Ottoman Theatre, although founded by Armenians, directed by Armenians with an all-Armenian cast, nevertheless accelerated the decline of the Armenian theatre in Constantinople and contributed to the creation and development of the Turkish theatre', dismally chronicled Chobanian from his Paris exile (*Luma*, no. 7).

The trials and tribulations of Shakespeare's entry in Western Armenian

The first complete versions of Shakespeare's plays in modern Western Armenian emerged in Smyrna, once the Hellenistic multi-cultural port on the Aegean Sea, which after the Turkish invasion became the Ottoman empire's window to Europe. In the nineteenth century the city was divided into five well-defined areas (Jewish, Greek, Muslim, Armenian and European Quarters), with the Greek population an enduring majority. The stylish Armenian Quarter (known as Haynotz) inspired by Italian baroque architecture, grew into the second-most prosperous Western Armenian community after Constantinople (Hovhannisian 2012). Despite their significant contributions to the prosperity of the empire, Christian Armenians were treated there as second-class citizens, labelled as *gâvur*, infidels. The Teteyan Brothers' Publishing House, launched in 1851, made a significant contribution to the Golden Age of Armenian Smyrna. The cultural resourcefulness of the Teteyan brothers served the community for decades: firstly, through their printing enterprise, they promoted the standardization of the Western Armenian tongue, replacing Grapar by publishing modern grammar, dictionaries and much-needed textbooks (Seferian). They were also actively engaged with local Armenian schools for boys and for girls, supporting educational reforms. Finally, fluent in several European languages, the brothers published hundreds of new translations from European authors (exclusively from the original) including Homer, Dante, Molière, Voltaire, Hugo, Dumas, Goethe, Schiller, Byron, Walter Scott and Shakespeare. Each publication required authorization from the authorities in Constantinople which was frequently refused, ultimately causing the closure of the Teteyan publishing house in the early 1890s.

Upon his return from England in 1851, Aram Karapet Teteyan (1822–1901), found himself 'under the spell' of Shakespeare's plays he had watched in London, embarking on Shakespearean translations without delay. His preliminary translation of Act One of *The Comedy of Errors* was published in the journal *Arpi Araratian*, alongside Tigran Teteyan's translation of Molière's *L'Avare* (*The Miser*, *Arpi Araratian*, no. 1). The publication of Shakespeare's comedy was suspended possibly owing to the cold reception from subscribers, who preferred the French playwright. Nine years later, Teteyan resumed his Shakespearean project in the journal, *Haverjahars*. His new editor, Sargis Papazian, had watched Shakespeare's 'immortal' plays in Europe and America, and was similarly eager to introduce Shakespeare to their Armenian readers (*Haverjahars*, no. 11). Teteyan's translation of *The Merchant of Venice* (from English) was presumably well received by subscribers, for the comedy was published in entirety on this occasion. In the introduction, Papazian expressed his distress at the thought that 'many praiseworthy translations, including of Shakespeare, were decaying unpublished due to the lack of support and funding' (*Haverjahars* 89). Although Teteyan had already translated several plays of the canon, the decision to print *The Merchant of Venice* was relevant: Shylock was perceived as a local and familiar character from the Jewish Quarter; Jews confined inside the Venetian Ghetto and Armenians demoted across the Ottoman empire were equally unwelcome by reigning authorities.

In the same year, Teteyan launched another journal, *Dimak* (Masque), which was undoubtedly stimulated by the opening of the first professional Armenian theatre in Smyrna, Vaspurakan, inaugurated in a splendid Italian-style auditorium in 1861. Teteyan's translation of Acts One and Two of *Hamlet* was published in the first two issues of *Dimak*, after which the journal was suspended, as the mandatory permission was not granted (Samvelian 54). His versions of Shakespeare were never staged at the Armenian theatre in Smyrna, for, after a few triumphant seasons, the Vaspurakan Theatre was likewise closed.

Teteyan's subsequent translation, *Romeo and Juliet*, (from the English) was printed as a separate volume in 1866 with the translator's extended introduction on the life and works of Shakespeare. Adopting François-Victor Hugo's word-by-word approach to translation, Teteyan aimed to convey the 'sweetness of the original text' (*Romeo and Juliet* 7). In the preface he acknowledged the interpretive hurdles he had confronted, including stylistic and semantic nuances such as homophones, metaphors and similes. A gifted poet himself (his poems in Grapar had been published previously), he nonetheless chose to translate *Romeo and Juliet* entirely in prose, except for the Chorus, elegantly executed in verse. The entire body of his translations was delivered in Smyrna vernacular: for instance, 'man' was translated as ապայար, 'my master' as աղաս and for 'my mistress' he employed խաթունս. While Teteyan's version was readily accessible to ordinary readers, his prose version in the local dialect indisputably lacked the lyrical excellence of the original.

During the Great Fire of Smyrna in 1922, known to Greeks as 'the Great Catastrophe', and to Armenians as the final chapter of the Armenian Genocide, the entire Hellenistic city with its inherently cosmopolitan communities, went up in flames. Of Aram Teteyan's Shakespearean translations, only *The Merchant of Venice* and *Romeo and Juliet* survived, having been previously dispatched to collections elsewhere (including the British Library and the Michigan University Library), as testimonials of Shakespeare's arrival in Western Armenian. With relentless dedication and resourcefulness, in an adverse socio-political setting, Aram Teteyan introduced Shakespearean drama to readers of Western Armenian.

The making of a national theatre in Tiflis

As the theatre project was eclipsed for Western Armenians under Ottoman rule, simultaneously yet autonomously, it was initiated by theatre devotees in the Caucasus. Following the Russo-Persian wars, parts of Eastern Armenia and Georgia were annexed to the Russian empire (Treaty of Gulistan, 1813), while Tiflis was proclaimed the capital of the Southern

Vice-Royalty of the Russian empire. By the early 1800s, Tiflis had developed into the cultural and economic centre for Eastern Armenians, who constituted three-quarters of the city's population. During festive celebrations, amateur performances, primarily historical dramas, were showcased from 1824 at the Nersisian School, where generations of notable Armenian authors, scientists and artists were educated. The growing popularity of these performances impelled the erection of purpose-built auditoriums to accommodate larger audiences with regular shows. The expansion of theatres in Tiflis was led principally by munificent Armenian patrons. Thus, the Shermazanian Gates (with around 350 seats), the foremost theatre at the residence of Lord Galoust Shermazanian (1814–91) – the mayor of Tiflis and a playwright himself – initially hosted Georgian and Russian ensembles. Additionally, at the Tamamshian Theatre, inaugurated in 1851 (with 800 seats), the Armenian troupe performed from 1858, which is considered the year of the foundation of the Armenian national theatre in Tiflis. Furthermore, in the final decades of the century, the Armenian troupe regularly performed at the Artzruni Theatre, owned by Lord Grigor Artzruni (founder of the periodical *Mshak*), the brother of Senekerim Artzruni who was the first translator of *Hamlet* and *King Lear* for stage productions. The Pitoewski Theatre (currently the home of the renowned Georgian State Theatre of Rustavelli), was subsidized by the industrialist Alexander Mantashev in 1887. Regardless of such significant investments in bricks and mortar by Armenian benefactors, the national theatre project turned out to be a gruelling mission: without external funding, the troupe's livelihood depended solely upon box-office revenues.

The Chmshkian years

The arduous task of advancing the cause of the national theatre was taken on by Gevork Chmshkian (1837–1915). First educated at the Nersisian seminary in Tiflis, he graduated from Saint Petersburg University as land surveyor for the Tsarist government in the Caucasus. It was after attending a performance by the Armenian theatre troupe in January 1863 that he abruptly quitted his secure public post to devote his entire life to the national theatre project. Regardless of perpetual financial hardships, with his three key associates – Mihrdat Amerikian, Stephanos Matinian and Artashes Sukiassian – Chmshkian, the newly appointed artistic director of the permanent troupe, undertook radical dramaturgical reforms. Since his student years in Saint Petersburg, Chmshkian had been deeply influenced by the democratic movement led by Vissarion Belinsky (1811–48), a great admirer of Shakespeare, who was considered the spiritual father of Westernizer Intelligentsia.[5] A permanent troupe of twelve actors, including five women (for the first time in Caucasus), was formed. Among them a promising young actress and soprano, Satenik (Chmshkian's future wife), was subsequently involved in virtually all Shakespearean productions. Ahead of his time, Chmshkian initiated the first 'ensemble theatre' with unwavering commitment to actor training, equal rights and wages for women and the backstage staff.

One of the theatre committee's pressing priorities became the renewal of the repertory, in order to raise the standards of the troupe and audiences alike. Shakespearean drama was considered an indispensable part of theatre reforms (Samvelian 105). New translations were commissioned to various linguists, while Chmshkian translated around twenty European and Russian dramatic masterpieces himself, including *Titus Andronicus*, *The Merchant of Venice* and *Othello*. Yet not everyone in the community agreed with the radical changes conducted by the theatre committee; traditionalists such as the journalist Alexander Yeritsian remained highly critical of theatre reforms, questioning the young troupe's abilities: 'We have heard that those gentlemen are even thinking of staging Shakespeare!', he wrote sardonically, perhaps causing Chmshkian to destroy his preliminary translation of *Titus Andronicus* in 1863 (*Meghu Hayastani*, 1863: 334). In his autobiography Chmshkian later expressed his anguish: 'The Armenian press – *Meghu Hayastani, Haikakan Ashkharh* – did not facilitate the development of the national theatre, quite the opposite. Critics did not extend their horizons, simply stating "this performance went well, that performance went badly", which proved rather unhelpful' (Chmshkian 84).

Shakespeare's delayed arrival among the nations of the Caucasus and the Near East finally occurred at the Tamamshian Theatre on 17 April 1866, with Acts Three and Four of *The Merchant of Venice* directed by Chmshkian, who also interpreted the role of Shylock. Chmshkian had completed his prose translation in 1864 from Benjamin Laroche's prose version (1839), regarded as one of the best French versions of the time. The sold-out premiere was attended by the local and European political, aristocratic and intellectual elite, including a high-ranking diplomat from the British Embassy in Batumi (Hovakimyan 2012: 301). However, this significant regional event was ignored by the press, except for Father Stepané's half-hearted eye-witness account: 'We share the inspirational idea of Mr. Chmshkian to introduce Shakespeare; Shakespeare is the God in the world of theatre. No other playwright could be more enlightening, sublime and inspirational than Shakespeare, but ask anyone, including the most erudite viewers, if they understand him.' The reviewer, however, commended Chmshkian's acting: 'It was apparent from Mr. Chmshkian's performance that he strived to portray the character realistically. We are pleased that Mr. Chmshkian is trying to accomplish his mission with a great sense of responsibility' (*Huis*).

Some insight into Chmshkian's interpretation of Shylock was conveyed through his article published in *Mshak* on the occasion of Shakespeare's inauguration on the Georgian stage by Kote Kipiani's troupe in 1878. The Georgian version mocked Shylock, presenting him as a malicious character with a strong Kutaisi accent. The Kutaisi Jews were one of the oldest communities on the eastern coast of the Black Sea. In the 1850s they were accused – in what became known as blood libels – of killing Christian children across Russia for their religious rituals, although on trial they were declared innocent. When serfdom was finally abolished in Russia in the 1860s, they were free to establish communities; however, anti-Semitic outbreaks continued. Following the infamous blood-libel trial in Kutaisi in 1875, violent clashes were recorded in the city with the largest Jewish community in Georgia. The adaptation of *The Merchant* opened during the hostilities. Acknowledging the complexity of Shakespeare's text, Chmshkian claimed that the character necessitated more intellectual groundwork: 'Even foremost European and Russian theatres handle Shakespeare with caution, particularly his monumental Shylock, who had embarrassed Christians for their past reprehensible actions, which have only recently been partially amended' (*Mshak* 1878, no. 56). According to Chmshkian, the Georgian director should have pondered more cautiously upon his key message to his audiences before executing ill-judged textual cuts. Vano Ter-Grigorian shared Chmshkian's viewpoint on the Georgian production: 'Shylock was the symbol of the Jews tortured for centuries, whose heart had toughened from continuous suffering, unable to pardon any longer' (*Mshak* 1878, no. 56). According to Ter-Grigorian, Kipiani's Shylock – with the distinct accent of Kutaisi Jews – reduced him to a grotesque character: 'Yet Shylock symbolises the entire Jewish nation, his inner turmoil is huge, his hatred of Christians overwhelming, therefore the role should not be interpreted in any dialect, as it risks ridiculing Shylock, instead, it should be presented in literary language to convey more gravity to the role'(*Mshak* 1878, no. 56).

In his own reduced version, Chmshkian had maintained Act Three, Scene One and the entire Act Four with Shylock as the central figure on the stage. Overwhelmingly angry, he voiced the dreadful condition of Jews under Christians and vehemently condemned their treatment by Venetian lawmakers as well as the reactionary Tsarist regime. Following in the footsteps of Russian revolutionary-democrats (many of whom perished in Siberian prisons, including the Armenian poet Mikael Nalbandian), Chmshkian condemned serfdom, social injustice and discrimination against minorities on and off stage. Defiantly supportive of the Jewish cause, he expressed his affection for the backstage employee, David, the Jew in his autobiography: 'I loved him more than some of the educated members of my own community!' (Chmshkian 73). Likewise, he fervently coached the Bremner sisters, of Jewish heritage, who were eager to join the Armenian troupe; Lisa Bremner even substituted Satenik Chmshkian in the role of Portia, which was echoed in the national press: 'her language, for a non-native, was very pleasing, but her acting was rather lifeless' (*Mshak* 1873, no. 50).

Chmshkian used the theatrical platform to express his views through his most successful roles, including Shylock. One of his subsequent articles clarified his standpoint: 'this should be the purpose of the theatre [. . .] a profound speech, that penetrates from the stage deep into viewers' hearts, and moves them so deeply that it accompanies them for the rest of their lives' (*Meghu Hayastani* 1871). Shylock's famous speech, 'Hath not a Jew eyes', profoundly moved Chmshkian's audiences. His highly partisan, philo-Semitic approach persisted through his performances for two decades and influenced the actor-directors who succeeded him, especially Gevork Petrossian and Ovi Sevumian.

Chmshkian's second Shakespearean production, *Othello*, premiered on 10 February 1867 at the Tamamshian Theatre, yet no critical response was recorded in the national press. His prose adaptation of *Othello*, rendered from Laroche's French and Weinberg's Russian versions, delivered in the local vernacular, was designed to bring Shakespeare closer to ordinary theatregoers. In his manuscript of *Othello* (in the national archives), Chmshkian had corrected the slang words and expressions previously used: for instance, 'handkerchief', in the Tiflis dialect այլուլու, was crossed out and replaced by բաշկնակ, 'husband', initially translated մարդ, was crossed out and replaced by ամուսին. Shakespeare's Moor, like Shylock, personified the outsider and outcast, and Chmshkian defended him just as unreservedly. But presumably, the role of

Othello, which he performed only a few times, including on Shakespeare's 320th birthday on 23 April 1884, did not resonate with the audiences as much as his portrayal of Shylock. During Chmshkian's directorship, regardless of persistent financial adversities and the absence of a supportive press, the Armenian theatre registered decisive achievements by embracing an effective dramatic repertory, including its first Shakespearean productions. Furthermore, discarding the outdated Romantic pathos, the troupe generated performances in Eastern Armenian, thus forging the path for the next generation of directors and actors.

Permanent adoption: the Petros Adamian decade

The 1880s, regarded as the Golden Age of the Armenian theatre in Tiflis, became pivotal for Shakespeare's adoption on the Armenian stage and ultimately for the national culture. Lord Napoleon Amatuni – a well-respected aristocrat, resolutely dedicated to the national theatre project – succeeded Chmshkian as the artistic director of the troupe, pledging himself to continue his reforms. The newly formed theatre committee delegated Chmshkian to travel to Constantinople to recruit leading actors, whose stage careers had been suspended following theatre closures there. In summer 1879, Chmshkian returned to Tiflis with Petros Adamian, the sisters Siranush and Astghik Gantajian, and the sisters Yearanuhi and Vergine Garagashian, who hugely contributed to Shakespeare's definitive triumph on the Armenian stage. Meanwhile tensions seemed unavoidable between Chmshkian, still one of the leading actors of the troupe, with his quixotic commitment to the theatre, and the newly arrived actors who demanded higher wages and were reluctant to take on secondary roles. Without external subsidy, the theatre's financial state worsened when the auditorium rents doubled from 1879, jeopardizing the entire project. Besides, the new recruits from Constantinople brought in a repertory dominated by French melodramas of highly Romantic pathos, against which Chmshkian and his associates had been fighting for decades. Nevertheless, after the first victorious theatrical season of 1879/80, the repertory was renewed with progressive Western and a few Russian dramas; Shakespeare was reinstated with the premiere of *The Taming of the Shrew* in the autumn of 1880.

Following the first theatrical season in Tiflis, Petros Adamian (1849–91) was unanimously acknowledged, both by audiences and the harshest critics, as the leading actor, ready to take on much – anticipated Shakespearean roles. Once Senekerim Artzruni's translation of *Hamlet* was hastily completed (within twenty-three days) from unidentified French and Russian versions, after two weeks of rehearsals, his five-act *Hamlet* opened on 20 November 1880 at the Summer Theatre, marking the arrival of Shakespeare's best-known tragedy among the nations of the Near East and the Caucasus. Adamian's highly acclaimed performance in the title role, attended by local and foreign audiences, brought him instant recognition and touring contracts across Russia. During those long tours, Russian critics and spectators alike were captivated by the actor from Constantinople, who performed either in French or Armenian. Critics compared him with the celebrated actors of the era – Ernesto Rossi, Tommaso Salvini and Aleksandr Lensky who similarly toured Russia in the 1880s. Reviews from Odessa, Kazan, Novosibirsk, Moscow, Saint Petersburg and other cities recognized that Adamian dealt with Hamlet's role in an entirely novel way (Yarishkin). The prevailing approach of his contemporaries was borrowed from Goethe's and Hegel's melancholic, passive and self-absorbed Hamlet, disengaged from his surrounding world (Zarian 1979: 92–106). According to the famous author Alexei Veselovski, 'This Hamlet does not correspond to the heartbroken grandee and intellectual martyr portrayed by his predecessors' (*Armianski Vestnik*). To another Russian reviewer, Adamian's Hamlet 'was a complete innovation' (*Elizavetgrad Vestnik*). Unlike Salvini or Rossi, who portrayed a remote, 'idealistic' Prince, Adamian's Hamlet was an ordinary and compassionate human being. 'Neither emulating nor following other reputable actors, he somehow created an unusual, yet a truly ground-breaking character, scrutinized in every single nuance', wrote a Moscow critic (*Iskusstvo*).

The source of Adamian's inspiration dated back to the 1830s, when the celebrated Russian actor, Pavel Mochalov, had reportedly played the Danish Prince with a Byronic touch; his 'volcanic' Hamlet, according to Belinsky, represented the Russian revolutionary moods of the era. Adamian, born after Mochalov's death, had not seen him perform, but he had read Russian critics, including Belinsky's well-known article on Mochalov's Hamlet of 1848 in Artzruni's translation. He frequently gave talks on *Hamlet* during his touring performances, and subsequently published his as critical study of Shakespeare's tragedy. Born and raised in Constantinople, he had experienced personal repression, unrelenting censorship and discrimination against minorities. Within his vast and varied repertory, no other character voiced Adamian's frustration and discontent as eloquently as Hamlet: when he vowed that Denmark was a prison (2.2.247), he hinted at the tyrannical rule of Abdul Hamid II. Thus, alongside Mochalov's revolutionary stance, Adamian's interpretation was further prompted by his ethnic background. Shakespeare's universality was once again tested on local, geopolitical margins of Europe; Adamian had reached his distinct version by combining the universal character with the national hero. Adamian *was* Hamlet: a kind, compassionate human being who stood against injustice and oppression, abuse and manipulation. 'From Hamlet's first entry, the spectator was watching an ordinary human being, not a pompous, self-absorbed Hamlet', wrote the acclaimed Russian critic, Yarishkin: 'Adamian's Hamlet was possibly the one that the great playwright had imagined himself' (Yarishkin 15). Critics unanimously agreed that he was particularly outstanding in the delivery of soliloquies, asserting that no actor could match him in 'To be or not to be . . .' (3.1.55–87). 'In our opinion, he hardly has competition in the soliloquy', testified one of the Russian reviewers (*Pchiolka*). "'To be or not to be" must be the supreme part, which he delivers magnificently', indicated another reporter (*Novoe Vremia*).

While Adamian's Hamlet, including his triumphant performances in Moscow and Saint Petersburg, was unanimously acclaimed, his Othello received a mixed critical reception. Translated by Stepanos Sulchasiantz from P. I. Weinberg's Russian version, the tragedy premiered on 17 February 1886 at the Artzruni Theatre. The national press reported that 'Mr. Adamian's acting, as always, was successful and triumphant, nevertheless, Mr. Adamian's voice and appearance did not match the character of Othello. As Hamlet, Mr. Adamian was outstanding, and we were keen to see him in the latter role during his benefit evening' (*Mshak* 1886, no. 20). Nonetheless, a few months later, an anonymous reviewer commended Adamian's Othello in the same magazine: 'from start to finish Mr. Adamian's interpretation was thought-provoking, meaningful and convincing ... he was calm but behind his composure, it was palpable in every second, that his heart and soul were in extreme turmoil, that he was suffering and burning inside' (*Mshak* 1886, no. 131). Adamian differed from the Moor portrayed by his celebrated contemporaries. During his Odessa tour, the actor explained that 'Othello is an outstanding general, influential, with massive willpower, and typically all great generals have been outstanding by their intellectual rather than physical attributes' (*Odesski Vestnik*). Accordingly, his reading of the role emphasized Othello's innermost virtues rather than his physical strength. Slender, of medium height, with expressive blue eyes and a soft velvety voice, he hardly resembled a fierce army leader, yet his opulent Venetian military outfit stressed his assimilation and devotion to the Venetian state. Another noteworthy aspect of the performance was Adamian's understating of Othello's ethnicity: as the Shakespearean scholar Ruben Zarian claimed, 'His Othello could have been of any race; for the Armenian actor, the blackness was merely a plot detail' (Zarian 1981: 81).

A triumphant five-year tour across Russia established Adamian's reputation as one of the great Shakespearean actors of his time. He returned to find his native Constantinople plunged into a deeper political crisis, and was refused permission to perform either his acclaimed Hamlet or King Lear under the lingering tyrannical rule of Abdul Hamid II. In his final year, Adamian relied on the generosity of his Armenian friends in Tiflis and Russian supporters for his hospital care; the great tragedian died in utter poverty, while working on new Shakespearean roles: he had commissioned his friend Vardgez Surenyantz in Tiflis to translate *Richard III* and *Macbeth* which he was hoping to stage, plays dealing with issues of power struggle, autocracy and the individual's duty to society that particularly attracted him to Shakespearean tragedies (Samvelian 210). With his Hamlet, Othello and Lear, Petros Adamian inspired his contemporary actors, authors and audiences, thus serving Shakespeare's definitive arrival on the Armenian cultural arena.

Shortly after Adamian's death, the persecution of Armenians culminated with the Great Massacres of 1894–6, when around 300,000 Armenian civilians lost their lives across the Ottoman empire by the orders of Abdul Hamid II. Under adverse political and socio-economic circumstances, translators, theatre practitioners and actors introduced Shakespearean drama not only to their dispersed communities but to their adoptive nations. They all shared similar values in rather dissimilar geopolitical sceneries: fierce opposition to autocracy, social injustice and discrimination against minorities. However, above all, these champions of the Shakespearean canon longed for peaceful collaboration and coexistence between nations in their uncertain times. Embracing the political implications and humanistic breadth of Shakespearean drama, they depicted Shakespeare as timeless and timely, opaque and transparent, universal and local. Migrating with Armenian migrants, Shakespeare stimulated and marshalled them in their long and arduous journey to protect their ancient language, theatre and cultural identity across scattered diasporas.

Notes

1 In this essay cities and regions are called by their officially recognized names of the period; in the 1920s Smyrna was renamed Izmir, Tiflis was renamed Tbilisi, Constantinople renamed Istanbul, and Calcutta changed its name to Kolkata in 2001.

2 Emin's letter addressed to Dr Mancy on 22 August 1757 was printed in the second edition of his autobiography in 1918.

3 All translations into English are mine.

4 Western Armenian is spoken in the Middle East, North Africa and Europe, and Eastern Armenian – currently the official language of the Republic of Armenia – is used by Armenians in Iran, Georgia, Russia, Ukraine and other diasporas.

5 Belinsky not only influenced prominent Russian authors (see Marina Kizima's chapter in this volume), but also the new generation of Armenian authors and artists, such as Khatchatour Abovian, Mikael Nalbandian and Gabriel Sundukian.

References

Primary bibliography

Ադամյան, Պետրոս (1887), Շեքսպիրը և յուր Համլետը, Թիֆլիս. [Adamian, Petros (1887), *Shakespeare and his Hamlet*, Tiflis.]

Армянский вестник (1916), no. 36, [*Armianski Vestnik*, *Armenian Herald*].

Արփի Արարատեան, Smyrna (1853), no. 1, Ձմիռնա. [*Arpi Araratian, Sun of Ararat*]. Available online: http://tert.nla.am/mamul/Arpi_araratean/Table.html

Ազգասէր, Calcutta (1848), no. 130, Կալկաթա. [*Azgaser, Patriot*]

Բազմավէպ, Venice (1853), no. 11, Վենետիկ. [*Bazmavep, Polyhistory*]. Available online: http://tert.nla.am/archive/NLA%20AMSAGIR/Bazmavep/1853%2811%29.pdf

Բազմավէպ, Venice (1964), Վենետիկ. [*Bazmavep, Polyhistory*]

Белинскій, Виссаріо́н (1848), 'Мочаловъ в роли Гамлета'. из книги *Школьный Шекспир* (1876), Санкт Петербургъ, 129–42.

[Belinsky, Vissarion (1848), 'Mochalov in the Role of Hamlet' in
  *Shakespeare: Biography, Hamlet, Critical Essays of Belinsky and
  Turgenev* (1876), St Petersburg, 129–42.]
Кавказ (1879). [Caucasus]
Չմշկյան, Գ-նորգ (1953), Իմ հիշատակարանը, խմբ.՝ Ս.Մելիքսեթյան,
  Երևան.
[Chmshkian, G. (1953), *My Autobiography*, ed. S. Meliksetian,
  Yerevan.]
Елизаветградский вестник (1888), no. 10 [*Elizavetgrad Vestnik,
  Elzavetzgrad Herald*]
Emin, Joseph (1918), *The Life and Adventures of Joseph Emin, an
  Armenian*, London, Calcutta, second edition.
«*Искусство*» (1884), no. 56 [*Iskusstvo*, Art]
«*Հույս*» (1 Dec. 2016), no. 229 [*Huis*, Hope]
«*Լումա*» (1906), n° 7 [*Luma*, Contribution]
«*Մեղու Հայաստանի*» (1863), Թիֆլիս, Tiflis, no. 38 [*Meghu
  Hayastani*, Armenia's Bee]
«*Մեղու Հայաստանի*» (1871), Tiflis, no. 4 [*Meghu Hayastani,
  Armenia's Bee*]
«*Մշակ*» (1873), Tiflis, no. 50 [*Mshak*, Cultivator]
«*Մշակ*» (1878), Tiflis, no. 56 [*Mshak*, Cultivator]
«*Մշակ*» (1886), Tiflis, no. 20 [*Mshak*, Cultivator]
«*Մշակ*» (1886), Tiflis, no. 131 [*Mshak*, Cultivator]
« *Նոր Դար* (4 Dec. 1886), Tiflis [*Nor Dar*, New Era]
«*Новое время*» (1884), no. 2846 [*Novoe Vremia*, New Times]
«*Одеский вестник*» (1887), no. 301 [*Odesski Vestnik*, Odessa
  Herald]
«*Пчёлка*» (1888), no. 44 [*Pchiolka*, Bee]
«*Շտեմարան*» (1822), Calcutta [*Shtemaran*, Repository]
Շեքսպիր, Վ. (1864), «Վենետիկի վաճառականը», թարգմ
  Գ.Չմշկյանի, Չմշկյանի արխիվ, Գրականության և արվեստի
  թանգարան.
[Shakespeare, W. (1864), *The Merchant of Venice*, trans.
  G. Chmshkian, Chmshkian archives, Museum of Literature and
  Arts.]
Շեքսպիր, Վ. (1889), «Համլետ» թարգմ. Ս. Արծրունու, Թիֆլիս.
[Shakespeare, W. (1889), *Hamlet*, trans. S. Artzruni,
  Tiflis.]
Shakespeare, W. (1865), *Hamlet*, in *Œuvres complètes,* tome 1,
  trans. François-Victor Hugo, Paris, Pagnerre.

Շեքսպիր, Վ. (1862), Վենետիկի վաճառականը, Հավերժահարս, no. 1–12, թարգմ. Ա.Կ. Տէտէեանի, Զմիռնիա.
[Haverjahars (1862), The Merchant of Venice, trans. A. K. Teteyan, Smyrna, no. 1–12.]
Շեքսպիր, Վ. (1866), Օթելլօ, թարգմ Գ.Չմշկյանի, Չմշկյանի արխիվ.
[Shakespeare, W. (1866) Othello, trans. by G. Chmshkian, Chmshkian archives.]
Shakespeare, W. (1877), Œuvres complètes. Tome neuvième, trans. Émile Montégut. Librairie Hachette et Cie, Paris.
Շեքսպիր, Վ. (1866), Հռոմէոս եւ Ճիիւղէդդա, թարգմ. Ա.Կ. Տէտէեանի, Զմիռնիա
[Shakespeare, William (1866), Romeo and Juliet, trans. A. K. Teteyan: Teteyan Publishing House, Smyrna.] Available online: https://archive.org/details/HromeosEwChiwleedda/page/n3
Shakespeare, W. (2006), Hamlet, ed. A. Thompson and N. Taylor, The Arden Shakespeare, London: Bloomsbury Publishing.
Ярышкин, А. (1887), П.И.Адамян в роли Гамлета, Одесса.
[Yarishkin, A. (1887), Adamian in the Role of Hamlet, Odessa.]

Secondary bibliography

Հովակիմյան, Բ. (2012), Շեքսպիրը հայ բեմում, Երևան, ԵՊՀ հրատարակչություն.
[Hovakimyan, Bakhtiar (2012), Shakespeare in the Armenian Theatre, Yerevan, YSU Press.]
Hovhannisian, Richard (2012), Armenian Smyrna/Izmir: The Aegean Communities, Costa Mesa, Mazda Publishers.
Հովհաննիսյան, Լյուդմիլա (2011), Թարգմանությունը որպես Շեքսպիրի հայացման միջոց, Երևան, ԵՊՀ հրատարակչություն.
[Hovhannisyan, Lyudmila (2011), Translation as a Method of Shakespeare's Adoption, Yerevan, YSU Press.]
Սամվելյան, Լուիզա (1974), Շեքսպիրը և հայ մշակույթը, Երևան, Հայաստան հրատարակչություն:
[Samvelian, Louisa, (1974), Shakespeare and the Armenian Culture, Yerevan, Hayastan.]
Սեֆերյան, Սոնա (2002), Շեքսպիրը հայ իրականության մեջ.
[Seferian, Sona (2002), Երևան, Սահակ Պարթև: Shakespeare in the Armenian Feality, Yerevan, Sahak Partev].

Seth, Mesrovb Jacob (1937), *Armenians in India*, Ray at Sri Gouranga Press, Calcutta.

Ստեփանյան, Գառնիկ (1962), Ուրվագիծ արևմտահայ թատրոնի պատմության», հատոր 1, Երևան, ՀՍՍՀ Ակադեմիայի հրատարակչություն.

[Stepanian, Garnik (1962), *Outline of the Western Armenian Theatre*, vol.1, Yerevan, State Academy Press.]

Юзовский Ю. (1947), *Образ и эпоха*.

[Yuzovski, Y. (1947), *Character and Era*.]

Զարյան, Ռուբեն (1979), Էջեր հայկական շեքսպիրապատումից, հատոր 1, Երևան, ՀՍՍՀ Ակադեմիայի հրատարակչություն.

[Zarian, Ruben, (1979), *Pages from Armenian Shakespearean*, vol. 1, Yerevan, State Academy Press.]

Ռուբեն Զարյան «Էջեր հայկական շեքսպիրապատումից», հատոր 2, ՀՍՍՀ գիտությունների ակադեմիայի հրատարակչություն, Երևան 1981.

[Zarian, Ruben, (1981), *Pages from Armenian Shakespeare Heritage*, vol.2, Yerevan, Academy of Sciences Press.]

11

Shakespeare in Greece

From Athens to Constantinople and beyond

Mara Yanni

The migration of Shakespeare to Greece took place in the second half of the nineteenth century, the time of nascent nationalisms and insurgent revolutions. Having been a part of the Ottoman empire for four centuries, Greece became an autonomous nation state in 1830, under the political surveillance of the foreign superpowers: France, England, Russia and, later on, Germany. With the protocol of London (1830) and the Treaty of Constantinople (1832) they declared Greece an autonomous state, choosing Otto I, prince of Bavaria, as its first monarch. The geographical boundaries of the new state included only Peloponnesus, the central part of the mainland, and the islands of Cyclades, leaving out a considerable portion of areas peopled by Greeks, including those in Constantinople and Asia Minor. A recently acquired freedom, a strong memory of Greek classical antiquity, a Byzantine heritage and the urgent need for national integration and European modernization created a set of unique historical circumstances. The discontinuities of the past, as well as new problems arising from the complexities of the present, infused the Greek national imaginary with an ambiguous vision of nationalism, merging two irreconcilable ideologemes: national continuity and European modernization.

The reconstruction of Greece was in the hands of a small circle of state officials and intellectuals educated in Europe, while a Bavarian king and court held the highest office of the state since there was no autochthonous nobility. Fluid boundaries among sections of the just-emerging middle classes, and a problematic relation between an ineffectual, large body of petty bourgeoisie and the ruling oligarchy were the main features of Greek society at that time (Jusdanis 33). During the third decade of the nineteenth century and past the middle of the twentieth a highly centralized system of state control decided on all matters pertaining to civil organization, including language, education, literature and the theatre. It was an age, as Hobsbawm put it, in which the primary meaning of the word nation was political, based on an equation of the people with the state 'in the manner of the American or French Revolutions' (18). Given the situation, the migration of Shakespeare to Greece began amid tensions arising from the struggles to advance the new state to a European level of civil and economic development.

Unlike other countries, Greece did not have to forge a Western history of origins – or call Shakespeare 'its own' in order to claim a position on the map of Europe: no one questioned the splendid role of the Greek classical past in the history of Western civilization. 'European romantic Hellenism provided the Greeks with an access to Europe unavailable to other nations' (Jusdanis 14). Accordingly, the Europeans continued to imagine Greece in terms of former classical glories, while they ignored its Byzantine legacy and expressed contempt for its present backwardness. Furthermore, political dependence on the dominant European powers and the imposition of a foreign monarchy apparently testified to its present ineffectuality. In fact, the new citizens of Greece were forced to see themselves as Europe saw them – that is, as the 'other' of a once glorious classical past. Under the circumstances, the appropriation of Shakespeare's European authority was a means towards the legitimation of the 'rightful' return of the country back to Europe. Shakespeare, in this case, was 'the place where European culture is supremely discovered' (Healy 226) and a visible proof that the modern Greeks were still worthy of their ancestors.

The story of Shakespeare's early migration to Greece, we shall see, suggests that his recruitment as an agent of European cultural advancement bore more fruitful and larger results at the nascent Greek theatre than in the closed circles of the literati. Rather than producing 'high art', the inexperience of the just-emerging professional acting companies constructed a populist aesthetics that addressed the aspirations of the Greek citizens on a nationwide scale. The appropriation of Shakespeare within the popular and national character of this new professional theatre functioned as a bridge between the elite's hegemonic Eurocentric vision of modernization and the living realities of a yet indefinable mass of bourgeoisie with a strong sense of local tradition.

Shakespeare and Greek literary culture

The systematic on-page reception of Shakespeare started approximately a decade after the inauguration of Greece into a free nation state and evolved within a small circle of intellectuals educated in Europe. At this early phase, two aesthetics dominated the Greek literary field, represented by a purist (called 'katharevousa') and a demotic (vernacular) linguistic register. The first epitomized the classicist and European-oriented ideology of the state, promoting an odd fusion of archaic and more recent vocabulary or syntax; it was established from the start as the official language of the government, education and other state-subsidized institutions. Purists did not see their classicist predilections as a backward movement, but as a purposeful act of modernization in line with the nineteenth-century European ideal of Hellenism, namely the goal towards which Greece should strive. However, the demotic, the spoken language of the Greeks, had direct links with Byzantine popular culture. Against the dominance of purism the demotists argued that the common language of the people was the true language of literature, and proof of national continuity and authenticity. The disagreement was to lead to confrontations: East *vs* West, tradition *vs* modernity, indigenous *vs* foreign, classical *vs* romantic, high *vs* low culture.

The most ardent followers of Shakespeare came from the demotist camp. They associated him with liberal politics, while praising the 'romantic' elements of his art: for them the English dramatist was a revolutionary invoking great passions and singular characters instead of decorous unities. The advocates of purism had ambivalent reactions. While most intellectuals and state representatives excluded Shakespeare from the national plan of cultural reform because of his alleged 'romantic' affiliation, a few others in the same faction produced translations in a purist idiom, with celebratory Prologues that described Shakespeare as a poet of nature and universal stature equal to Homer, Aeschylus, Sophocles or Euripides. Shakespeare's detractors came mainly from a minority of ethnocentric groups, who rejected foreign imitations and sought national authenticity either in the roots of classical antiquity or in the popular tradition of Byzantine orthodoxy:

> Shakespeare lived in cold climates and his audiences were reserved and unemotional. He had to resort to passionate and horrid scenes in order to move them. Conversely, the

Greek tragedians who lived under clear skies produced dramas without melancholy and physical violence on stage, because the emotions of their audiences were easily affected.

Neologos, 17 May 1889[1]

It is striking that Shakespeare was censured less for breaking the rules of classicist poetics than for being foreign to the Greek character and the Mediterranean predilections.

The neologism 'shakespearism' was coined early and it was used throughout the century to denote Shakespeare's influence on Greek writers or to designate romantic hyperboles in acting. The plethora of writers who quoted lines or drew inspiration from Shakespeare includes some major Greek poets. Dionysios Solomos – resident of the Ionian Islands – produced a free adaptation of Desdemona's song in *Othello* in the early 1820s and invoked scenes from *Romeo and Juliet*, as well as from *Cymbeline*, in his prose work *Dialogos* (1824) and the Italian prose poem 'Donna Velata' (1846), respectively. Kostis Palamas, moreover, composed 'Miranda' (1892), an original poem inspired by the heroine of the *Tempest*, while Konstandinos Kavafis refers to the situation at Elsinore in his long poem 'King Claudius' (1899). Most importantly, in the context of European Romanticism Shakespeare's works influenced a number of Greek dramatists, by offering an alternative to the current dominance of Greek classical tragedy or French neo-classicism.

Demetrios Vernardakis, an intellectual educated in Germany, first established the notion of 'romantic' Shakespeare as a model for the Greek writers of national drama, under the influence of the *Sturm und Drang* movement. The 'Prolegomena' (Prologue) of his drama *Maria Doxapatri,* published in Munich (1858) shortly before his return to Greece, is a true manifesto of 'shakespearism'. Vernardakis expresses his unbounded admiration for the English dramatist and theorizes the reasons for which the Greek writers should follow him in writing national dramas. As he explains, just as the Greeks abide by the British in politics, so they must follow Shakespeare in poetry, especially because the British are closer to their national character than the French, the Germans or the Spanish (Vernardakis νγ'). In *Maria Doxapatri* Vernardakis employed a variety of Shakespearean features: he dispensed with unities in the plot, used a mixture of prose and verse to indicate the social status of the speakers, and adopted the garden scene from *Romeo and Juliet*, as well as the theme of Ophelia's madness in *Hamlet*. He adjusted all of these elements into an indigenous setting drawn from Byzantine history, while the selective use of demotic idioms enhanced the plot with populist elements against a background coloured by nationalism and melodramatic intensity. Vernardakis continued to draw inspiration from Shakespeare, zealously incorporating stylistic effects and substantial parts or whole scenes from *Hamlet* and *King Lear* in his *Kypselides* (1860) and from *Macbeth* in *Efrosyni* (1876).

Maria Doxapatri appeared on stage with great success on 10 December 1865 and had sixteen performances during the same season – an unusual number for the stage practices of this period. Its overt 'shakespearism' set a precedent for a whole host of other dramatists. There was even a sequel to the play written by Sophocles Karydis, entitled *Ta Tekna tou Doxapatri* (1868). Additionally, Spyridon Vassiliadis incorporated elements from *King Lear* in his *Scylla* (1873), while the love story in *Galateia* (1873) merges a Victor Hugo type of romantic passion with elements from the second act *of Othello*. Among the playwrights who drew inspiration from Shakespeare are K. Rangavis, *Ioulianos o Paravatis* (1865); I. Mavromichalis, *Koriolanos* (1868) and *Alosis Tripolitsas* (1870); S. Lambros, *O telefteos Komis ton Salonon* (1870); A. Moraitidis, *Michael Komninos B'* (1872); and T. Theocharidis, *Petros o Synglitikos* (1875). The increasing popularity of this new type of national romantic drama eventually brought the best of these plays to the stage, with numerous performances in Athens and Constantinople. In spite of initial difficulties, during the last decades of the century the 'romantic' Shakespeare was gaining ground, along with Byron, Hugo and Schiller. Thus, in an 1887 poetic competition sponsored by the University of Athens – so far a stronghold of classicism and purism – the participants were asked to submit a tragedy in the manner of Shakespeare or Hugo.

The tensions and ambiguities generated by the Greek literary debates were no less present in the area of Shakespearean translations. The artificiality of the purist language and the lack of fixed grammatical rules in the demotic, as well as the tendency to mix both registers in the spoken language, were but a few of the problems facing the translators. Their general guidelines were similar to those practiced in the rest of nineteenth-century Europe: respect for the spirit of Shakespeare (in whatever way this was understood), additions of scholarly introductions or footnotes; *mot à mot* equivalence with the source text which most often was a French or German adaptation (notably by Le Tourneur, Ducis or Schlegel). It was natural for translators to want to promote their work at the theatre, but notions of performability did not greatly affect their treatment.

The earliest Greek translation of a Shakespeare play may have been the 1789 version of *Romeo and Juliet* by Georgios Sakellarios, but the text has never been found in either printed or manuscript form (Dimaras 18–22). The first extant translation is the unpublished *Macbeth* by Andreas Theotokis (dated 1842, but probably written in 1819), which was dedicated to Otto, the first king of Modern Greece, and is kept today at the National Library in Munich (Karagiorgos 1976: 230). *The Tempest* (1855) was the first Greek translation to appear in print, in the demotic prose version of Iakovos Polylas. It was issued outside the official boundaries of Greece on the British-ruled island of Corfu and remained an isolated attempt with no impact on the Greek theatre, probably because Polylas's language contained too many idiomatic expressions of his native island. *Hamlet* appeared next (1858) in the archaic purist register of Ioannis Pervanoglou, who used the Byzantine twelve-syllable iambic metre. The translator who had studied in Munich referred to Schlegel in his Prologue as the 'best German translator of Shakespeare's dramas'. In his own work, however, the artificiality of the purist registry failed to convey the subtle meanings of Shakespeare's poetry.[2]

Despite frequent complaints about Pervanoglou's archaic language, his *Hamlet* was used repeatedly in performances, until the publication of Demetrius Vikelas's translation in 1882. Most of the early translators of Shakespeare employed a purist idiom, among whom the most tenacious classicist was M. Damiralis. 'Translating *Hamlet* – the tragedy of intellect and a true royal drama – in vulgar demotic language, is the same as dressing a king in a peasant's attire', he declared in the Prologue of his own prose version of *Hamlet* (Damiralis δ´). Although he was the most prolific nineteenth-century translator of Shakespeare, with twenty-one translations, most of them remained unpublished during his lifetime and were rarely performed.

Vikelas published a triptych of *Romeo and Juliet*, *Othello*, and *King Lear* in 1876; *Macbeth* and *Hamlet* came next in 1882 and, lastly, *The Merchant of Venice* in 1884. He had been educated at University College in London, so he had direct access to the English editions of Shakespeare's plays, including the Cambridge Shakespeare (1863–6) and the Globe Shakespeare (1864). His erudition shines in the notes and the long Prologue of his 1876 edition of *Romeo and Juliet*, where he outlines the European critical history of Shakespeare and attempts to define his current position in what he calls 'the new school of Romanticism'. In his opinion Shakespeare was a poet of the universal, but also a superb creator of dramatic situations that could represent the living experiences of individual characters:

> When he wrote, he had in mind his audiences, not the upcoming generations. He was not restrained by pre-established rules and did not wish to develop philosophical theories in his dramas. Principally, his onstage representations are human beings and their various passions, presented as a true and lasting image of human nature. This is why his dramas are full of life and they will live forever.
>
> Vikelas ι´

As he further explains, his translation of Shakespeare aimed at a double goal: the faithful transcription of the source and, at the same time, its reproduction in a form that could transport the 'liveliness, the energy, and the truthfulness' of Shakespeare's dramas.

With this dual goal in mind Vikelas made the use of the best linguistic medium his primary concern. He chose what he called the 'middle way' – an odd demotic polished with simple forms drawn from the purist registry – which he hoped would 'make Shakespeare accessible to more people and thus contribute to the enhancement of the new Greek theatre' (ibid., ιδ'). In his attempt to domesticate Shakespeare, Vikelas went even further, using the fifteen-syllable iambic metre traditionally associated with Greek folk poetry and songs. Predictably, his bold linguistic endeavour raised a number of objections among the literati. Nevertheless, his works soon found their way to the stage: contributing to his success was the actor and theatre manager Nikolaos Lekatsas, who employed his texts in most of his Shakespearean performances in the 1880s. Vikelas's translations were used at the theatre throughout the early decades of the twentieth century, until replaced by the works of a new generation of demotist translators.

Shakespeare and the Greek travelling actors

More than a decade before the first appearance of a Shakespeare play on a Greek stage, Italian opera functioned as the earliest venue for the introduction of Shakespeare to the Greek audiences of the two major centres of Hellenism – Athens, the capital of free Greece, and Constantinople, part of the Ottoman empire. For instance, the Athenians watched in awe the chorus of the three witches in a performance of Verdi's *Macbeth*, the local paper, *Palligenesia,* reports on 10 March 1856: 'It is a shame that our readers in the provinces did not see the huge cauldron on stage, in which the witches dropped mysterious herbs, cooking in their imagination the future of Scotland'. Similarly, the recorded productions in Constantinople, during the frequent visits of Italian opera companies, include Bellini's *I Capuleti e I Montecci* (1865), Rossini's *Otello* (1865, 1866, 1870), as well as Verdi's *Macbeth* (1865, 1866).

It is also worth noting that the only time Athenian society had a chance to watch Shakespearean performances by a foreign dramatic company was during the visits of Ernesto Rossi in 1889 (*Hamlet, Othello, The Merchant of Venice*), and of Jean Mounet-Sully in 1899 (*Othello, Hamlet*). While Rossi was in Athens, he delivered a lecture in Italian at the literary club 'Parnassus', in which he declared his adoration of classical antiquity, and compared Shakespeare's art with that of the Greek tragedians *(Neologos*, 16 May 1889). Henceforth Rossi's great success in Athens would provide the measure for Greek actors' Shakespearean interpretations and a point of reference for an unqualified acceptance of the English dramatist. In Constantinople. *Othello* was produced with Ira Aldridge (1866) at the Crystal Palace and later on with Tommaso Salvini (1880), as well as Mounet-Sully and Adalbert Matkowsky (1899). The actor Dionysios Tavoularis mentions in his *Memoirs* (151) that he had to compete with the last two when he presented his Greek *Othello* at the same time.

The first recorded Shakespeare performances by professional Greek actors were *Hamlet* and *Othello* in Athens, by Pantelis Soutsas's company on 9 and 15 October 1866, respectively.[3] For both performances, Soutsas used the only Greek translations available at that time: the purist versions of Pervanoglou (*Hamlet*) and Kontopoulos (*Othello*). These initial attempts received scant notices in the daily newspapers, suggesting no particular enthusiasm on the part of the Athenian audiences. Shakespeare was also absent from all kinds of amateur or coterie performances in Athens committed to the cultivation of Greek classical tragedy and European high culture, mainly because of his controversial status in the aesthetics championed by the state during the early years of its constitution.

Four centuries of Ottoman rule had stunted the literary and theatrical progress of Greece, keeping it apart from the splendid developments that shaped the traditions of Europe. After the liberation, the learned intelligentsia and the ruling order argued respectively for either the revival of ancient Greek drama or the transplantation of the European poetic theatre and opera. However, the situation of the first professional Greek actors was not unlike that of the troupes in mid-eighteenth-century Germany. Like their German predecessors, they 'worked under conditions scarcely better than those tolerated by the English Comedians' and they 'had to travel from town to town, often performing and living in the most squalid of circumstances' (Williams 46). In spite, however, of differences in tastes and social status, a single unifying force conditioned the expectations of all agencies: the desire to upgrade the Greek theatre to an advanced European level through a well-founded theatrical education for actors and audiences alike.

The usual charges brought against those marginalized actors by the ruling order were targeted against their low origins, lack of formal theatrical training, inaptness of costumes or settings, and choice of plays that did not meet the criteria of an erudite culture. An additional source of bitter complaints was the inappropriate behaviour of the majority of the spectators who talked, smoked and consumed beverages during performances – not unlike the situation of working-class audiences at the peripheral theatres of nineteenth-century France (Hemmings 117–32).

> The Greek theatre, as it is today, is not prepared for performances of the great dramas of Shakespeare, Schiller, even of Hugo ... These dramas must be produced with elaborate settings, by established actors, in front of audiences with great historical and general erudition, and with translations that reproduce with fidelity the originals.
>
> *Efimeris*, 7 July 1878

The absence of state officials and the upper classes from the theatre was quite noticeable in Athens. In fact, with the exception of a few intellectuals and students, the larger part of the audience came from the middle and lower sectors of a nascent bourgeoisie, largely unschooled in theatrical matters. This contemptuous attitude towards the inexperienced actors and their audiences persisted until almost the end of the century, posing a serious obstacle to the revival of the Greek theatre.

The lack of state support and great financial difficulties made it impossible for the first professional acting companies to survive in Athens during the 1860s. The only alternative was travelling to the stages of the diaspora, namely to places with a Greek population that lay outside the boundaries of the free state: mostly Constantinople and Smyrna, as well as to major cities in Cyprus, Egypt, the Danubian principalities and Russia. Between 1866 and 1880 the acting companies chose to stay away from the Athenian capital more frequently and for longer periods, in search of more welcoming environments. In contrast to the negative attitude of the state officials in Athens, the Greek communities of the diaspora – especially those under Ottoman rule – received them in a spirit of affirmation and enthusiasm. For the Greek residents of Constantinople or Smyrna, the mere presence of the migrant actors and the sound of the Greek language on stage was enough to incite their fervour for freedom and unification with the motherland. And the same can be said about the reception of Armenian actors and companies by the respective ethnic community. Among the various foreign companies performing in the cosmopolitan milieu of Constantinople and Smyrna, the Armenian and Greek performances greatly enriched theatrical life throughout the century.

Following the unsuccessful performances of *Hamlet* and *Othello* (1866) in Athens, Soutsas's company left on a tour to the Eastern Mediterranean. Unlike the indifference they met with in Athens, the very same plays enjoyed a great deal of success in Smyrna – as did the first-known performance there of *Macbeth* (27 January 1867). The arrival of Shakespeare in

Constantinople was delayed until 1869, but performances continued steadily afterwards to the end of the century, through the alternation of several Greek companies who included Shakespeare in their repertories. Constantinople had better theatre buildings than Athens these were, better suited to host famous foreign actors and melodramatic groups: *Crystal Palace, Naum,* and *Verdi* (Stamatopoulou 363–9).

Apart from other concerns, the presence of Shakespeare on the stages of Constantinople was a politicized issue. The flourishing Greek community who lived there welcomed the migration of the English dramatist in an anglophile atmosphere. Because of the dominant position of England in the economic colonization of the Eastern Mediterranean – which opened up trade routes to India – the Greek diplomats, merchants and members of the upper classes had developed close relations with the Englishmen who often came to Constantinople. England then had the last word in the political game played among the superpowers with regard to the future of the subjugated populations of Greece on the coasts of Asia Minor. Shakespeare could not but be accepted, mainly because he was from England, 'the most enlightened country in the world', as opposed to France in which the Romantic dramas of Hugo represented 'the redundant debris of aged nations' (*Tilegragos ke Vyzantis*, 1 April 1861).

The scarcity of detailed descriptions about settings and costumes in the theatrical records of this period does not allow a clear view of the ways individual plays of Shakespeare were staged. Since there was no definite modern acting theory nor a pre-established acting tradition, the Greek actors used as a guide an antiquated native tradition of poetics and rhetoric that associated stylized body movements with particular emotions: not unlike acting practices in nineteenth-century Europe (Booth; Davis; Taylor). In addition to Shakespeare's, the repertory included an incongruous assortment of plays with different generic significations and cultural histories suited to the tastes of diverse audiences: European 'classics', melodramatic French plays, vaudeville, as well as Greek patriotic tragedies.

Although they were regarded as great art, the general opinion that Shakespeare's plays required costly elaborate settings and costumes as well as large casts, deterred the companies from frequently staging them. The play considered most problematic in this respect was *Macbeth*, 'because of its scenic complexity and other theatrical mechanisms that are readily available only in Europe' (*Neologos*, 28 November 1883). Moreover, the audience's demand for frequent changes of play made expensive productions unprofitable. Considering that the theatres were not always full and that the population in the small city of Athens was approximately 60,000 or 70,000 in the early 1880s, each play could not have had more than an average of two or three performances in the same season.

The small number of members in the acting profession was also an obstacle for staging plays that required a large cast. Cross-dressing was inevitable, but it was accepted with reticence in tragedies, since it was felt incompatible with the seriousness of the situation. Taking into consideration the prejudices towards actresses, the few who appeared on stage deserved to attract admiration not only for their talent but also for their courage. What is more, until the mid-1870s, women spectators were not allowed to sit with men in the auditorium and had to watch performances from a special part of the galleries (Hatzipantazis 2002: 43, 65–6).

Throughout the second half of the century, the travelling companies, by continuing to include Shakespeare in their repertoires, were instrumental in Shakespeare's migration. Pantelis Soutsas, Dionysios Tavoularis and Demosthenis Alexiadis led the earliest of these. As actors and managers of their companies, all three undertook leading roles. Soutsas was the first Greek Hamlet, Othello, Julius Caesar and Macbeth. After his death in 1875 he was succeeded by his younger collaborator, Tavoularis, who established his reputation as a Shakespearean actor mainly as Hamlet and Othello. His company moved constantly in and out of the boundaries of the Greek state, using Athens as a base and targeting the Greek audiences at the periphery of the Mediterranean and the diaspora (Tavoularis 136, 140, 141, 150). Alexiadis travelled with his company as far as southern Russia, where he impressed the audiences with his rendering of Othello (Hatzipantazis 2002: 143). Smaller companies occasionally produced various Shakespearean plays at different points in time. The most active during the 1890s was that of Demetrius Kotopoulis with several performances of *Hamlet*, *Othello* and *Macbeth* in both Athens and Constantinople.

The review published after Soutsas's first appearance as Hamlet in Constantinople (5 Dec. 1869) throws ample light on his acting technique. Overtly referring to the European literary and performance history of the play, a reviewer described his impersonation of Hamlet as a 'sarcastic hero', adding in conclusion that 'perhaps, the ethereal self of Hamlet was diminished, but it became more comprehensible and accessible to the majority' (*Neologos*, 11 Dec. 1869). Soutsas was mostly admired – but also criticized – for a boundless energy usually associated with the common practices of romantic acting: loud outbursts of passion, melodramatic postures and abrupt alternations between high and low pitch.

His younger successor, Tavoularis, was very different in both physical appearance and acting style. He was certainly more handsome and elegant, with a calm musical voice, best suited for roles of subdued lyricism and contemplation. Here is how a reviewer compares his impersonation of Hamlet with that of his predecessor: 'Soutsas's Hamlet emits lightning and thunder; that of Tavoularis is a deep sea full of mystery and huge waves without froth or splash – he induces reverie, not terror' (*Rabagas*, 13 August 1881). Coleridge had used the 'lightning' metaphor to describe Edmund Kean's acting: 'To see him act is like reading Shakespeare in flashes of lightning' (Coleridge 13).

The obvious preference of the early Greek audiences for Shakespeare's tragedies stems primarily from their potential for moral edification and their representation of complex dramatic characters. Throughout this period, Shakespeare was staged in Constantinople twice as often as in Athens, with *Othello* as the most popular play in Constantinople and *Hamlet* in Athens. The commentaries of reviewers suggest that the popularity of *Othello* in both cities was due to the familiarity of its Mediterranean setting, the elements of domestic drama, and the vitality of a passionate hero. *Hamlet*'s appeal rested in the interiority and mental complexity of a new kind of hero, of a new tragic experience. In both Athens and Constantinople it was perceived as a 'tragedy of the intellect', a new species of drama with no precedent in the familiar genre of Greek classical tragedy (*Byron*, 1 March 1874). A way to solve this was by domesticating Shakespeare's play: 'Hamlet's situation is similar to Orestes' in the ancient drama – he must revenge the death of his father caused by a treacherous wife and brother', notes the reviewer of the 1869 production of *Hamlet* in Constantinople (*Neologos*, 23 December 1869).

The fact that certain plays did not migrate to the Greek stage or appeared less frequently reveal the political constraints of performance as well as the tastes of the audience. Until the end of the 1870s there was only one performance of *Macbeth* in Athens and none in Constantinople, while *Julius Caesar* appeared once in Athens and three times in Constantinople. It seems that the acting companies hesitated to produce these two plays, because their theme of 'killing the king' could be a possible source of trouble, in view of the presence of an unpopular Bavarian monarch in Athens and the severe censorship of the Ottoman authorities in Constantinople. During the last decades of the century, *The Merchant of Venice* (1882), *King Lear* (1882), *Romeo and Juliet* (1883), *The Comedy of Errors* (1885) and *Richard III* (1897) appeared for the first time with the newly formed company of the actor Nikolaos Lekatsas. Yet, plays with a 'Greek' context – *Pericles, A Midsummer's Night's Dream, Coriolanus, Troilus and Cressida, Timon of Athens, Two Noble Kinsmen* – attracted no interest.

By 1881, the various ideological conflicts had lost their edge: the warm reception for the Greek Shakespearean performances in Constantinople and Smyrna in the previous decade, as well as the gradual improvement of acting practices, helped to establish a better climate in Athens and increased the number of performances in front of full audiences. Moreover, the emergence after 1881 of Nikolaos Lekatsas enriched the stage with new Shakespearean productions and a renewed approach to acting. Lekatsas came to Athens in 1881, after twenty-five years in England and twelve years of an acting career under the stage name A. Nicholas in various theatres of the British provinces, but also at Sadler's Wells and at the Royal Aquarium (Dimitriadis 260, 290): constantly moving between London and the regions he kept himself informed about new developments in the theatre, especially the acting achievements of Henry Irving, the Bancrofts and Samuel Phelps, a former manager of Sadler's Wells. After a variety of secondary roles he was able to play major parts in a classical repertory. At the Royal Theatre of Ryde in the Isle of Wight, he interpreted Romeo 'with all the warmth of a southern temperament, such a Romeo as we do not often see, and which cold English blood is not equal to perform' (*The Isle of Wight Observer*, 25 August 1877).

His first appearance on his return to Athens was with the company of Tavoularis in a bilingual performance of *Hamlet* (27 August 1881), during which he delivered the hero's part in English while the rest of the cast spoke Greek in Pervanoglou's purist translation. He was probably following the lead of Tommaso Salvini who, during his American tour of 1880, had delivered his lines in Italian among an English-speaking cast. Although Lekatsas was not particularly handsome – he was rather short with irregular features – his impersonation of the Danish prince on that night enchanted the Athenian spectators, who applauded with enthusiasm and immediately invested him with the title of future reformer of the Greek theatre.

Lekatsas differed from older actors by his ability to combine traditional ways of acting with a new approach to performance. The reviewers praised his more realistic way of speaking and moving on stage, and the exceptional plasticity of his facial and bodily expressions that vividly set off the psychological depths of the dramatic characters (Dimitriadis 192). The Shakespearean accomplishments of the other Greek actors now appeared deficient compared to 'the naturalness, the truth, the art of Mr. Lekatsas' (*Rabagas*, 2 September 1882). Apart from his acting, Lekatsas may have owed his success to his English background, which brought the air of Europe to the Greek stage. He took great care over the staging of his performances and did not hesitate to cut whole scenes in the manner of Victorian theatre managers (Booth 28). He also showed special concern for historical fidelity: the programme of his *Hamlet* in Athens (7 September 1882) records that he brought from England costumes whose style 'belonged to the specific historical period'. It is quite interesting that the earliest use of the term 'mise en scène' in relation to a Greek production appeared in reviews about Lekatsas's first performances in Athens (Glytzouris 436).

In all of his Shakespeare productions, Lekatsas used the translations of Vikelas, with the exception of *King Lear* – on which no information is available. As Dimitriadis succinctly argues, 'through the immediacy of Vikelas's demotic discourse Lekatsas could lower the tones of the performance and, thus, adjust his speech in line with the realist effects that he privileged in his acting' (228). The play, however, that established Lekatsas's reputation as a superb Shakespearean actor was *The Merchant of Venice,* with fifty-four performances altogether. Characteristically, in a late production of the play a reviewer noted that his rendition of Shylock was the opposite of the Italian actor Rossi, who gave the character a comical hue (*Acropolis*, 14 May 1890), whereas Lekatsas's impersonation of the Jew underlined the tragic dimension of his plight: after the trial scene, as he walks away, 'his breath is heavy and painful, and he clutches with both trembling hands a staff that supports his collapsing body. Miserable and shattered, he exits groping and faltering' (*Estia*, 5 July 1895).

These performances, often attended as they were by royalty and state officials, constituted important social events. A case in point is an 1883 bilingual performance of *Hamlet*, requested by foreign diplomats in Constantinople who wished to see Lekatsas in action:

The theatre was decorated with flags and flower wreaths hanging from either side of the staircase leading to the gallery. Many people gathered there, hours before the time of the opening of the performance – people of all kinds, many Englishmen, Europeans, foreign government representatives, who knew both English and Greek or just the first. Most of the Greeks did not understand English, but they still came, because they desired to hear Lekatsas perform in English.

Neologos, 12 November 1883

Obviously, Lekatsas's immense popularity would produce a number of enemies who sided with the older actors. Some mocked the nasal tone of his voice, his grammatical mistakes and foreign accent when he spoke Greek. Others used Lekatsas to attack the anglophile policies of Prime Minister Tricoupis, who was one of his main supporters. All the same, the discussion of Shakespeare remained alive, while the overall increase in the number of Shakespearean performances in the 1880s must be attributed for the most part to Lekatsas's contribution.

The new era

Fresh theatrical forces and further developments informed the last decade of the century. At this point, major tragedies of Shakespeare appeared side by side with an overwhelming amount of vaudeville, as well as domestic dramas dealing with realistic contemporary situations – represented mainly by Ibsen. The institutionalization of the star-system and the growing commercialization of the theatre in the wake of these changes suggest predominantly the slow yet systematic urbanization of Greek society. The new era was moving steadily towards the development of a civic bourgeois theatre in the next century.[4] The persistence of Shakespeare's plays signals their consolidation as indispensable classics, but also the need for their re-accommodation in a public sphere that advocated change and sought solutions for new problems. The humiliating defeat of the country in the 1897 war with Turkey, which dispersed the former visions of Greek nationalism, kept the theatres closed for several months. Characteristically, the war and the accumulated problems at the turn of the century, prompted a reviewer to suggest that the suffering of the country had transformed it into 'Hamlet-Greece' (*Asty*, 26 October 1897).

In this transitional phase the popularization of Shakespeare and the hyperbolic energies of romantic passion were no longer considered valid signs of modernity; a new reading 'against the grain' was needed to revitalize the interest in Shakespearean productions, as did the androgynous appearance of the actress Evangelia Paraskevopoulou in the role of Hamlet at the turn of the century (1900). A few years earlier, Ekaterini Lekatsa had played the part of Romeo in an 1897 production of *Romeo and Juliet* and received negative reviews for her impudence in cross-dressing. Nevertheless, Paraskevopoulou dared to appear as Hamlet, following the trend established by the example of the famous Sarah Bernhardt. The performance took place at the recently constructed Demotiko Theatre of Athens, with the price of the tickets purposefully lowered in order to attract a larger audience.

On the day of the performance, half of the seats in the pit and the first row boxes remained empty. However, the gallery, where the populace and students usually sat, was overcrowded and vibrating with enthusiasm. The boldness of the endeavour produced ambiguous responses from the reviewers. The luxury of the costumes and scenography made a great impression (*Acropolis*, 21, 23 April, 1900), but not the antiquated language of Pervanoglou's translation – some reviewers questioned this choice, since the demotic text of Vikelas was already available (*Asty*, 23 April 1900). The actress appeared in a black costume and a blond wig, a moustache and beard. According to one reviewer, her posture during 'the moments of doubting and the explosion of revenge' had taken a great deal of study and reflection, but her sex still betrayed her: she recited her lines with wonderful nuances and alterations of tone, in the same sentimental style and voice she had used in her rendering of Margarita in *Tosca* (ibid.).

At the dawn of the twentieth century, after thirty-five years of performance history, the multifaceted process of Shakespeare's early migration to Greece had run its full course. And along the way both actors and spectators had matured, as a reviewer observed: 'At last, now we understand Shakespeare' (*Asty*, 27 October 1897). While this may be true, from 1866 until the end of the century, the Shakespearean performances in the revived Greek theatre drew their vitality and vibrancy from the strengths and limitations of a semi-literate popularizing context of performance and reception. In this dynamic space, the early Greek performances succeeded in reproducing the 'pregnant interplay of varied social and theatrical elements' of the kind that Robert Weimann found so characteristic of Shakespeare's plays (175).

The popular energies of the nascent Greek theatre released Shakespeare's plays from the confines of literariness and reproduced them in a living context with added significations. For the new urban citizens of Greece and the unaccommodated audiences of the diaspora, these performances were a signature of civic progress and live participation in the advanced bourgeois culture of Europe. From a present perspective, the Shakespearean itinerary of the Greek travelling actors forms a narrative that speaks about the collective longings of a people for national consolidation and political integration in the map of nineteenth-century Europe.

Notes

1 All the English translations from Greek sources are mine.
2 In addition to the above, the first Greek translations of Shakespearean plays published in this century include *Julius Caesar*, *Macbeth*, *Othello*, *Romeo and Juliet*, *The Merchant of Venice*, *The Two Gentlemen of Verona*, *Richard III*, *The Comedy*

of *Errors*, *King Lear*, *Twelfth Night*, *Antony and Cleopatra*, *Coriolanus* and *As You Like It*. See Karagiorgos (1995) and Douka-Kambitoglou for more information.

3 The main sources of information about the Greek Shakespearean performances are the nineteenth-century journals and newspapers researched for this project, as well as the works about the Greek theatre by Laskaris (1938–9), Sideris (1964, 1999, 2000), and Hatzipantazis (2002, 2012).

4 The construction of the Greek Royal Theatre took place between 1895 and 1901. For the Shakespeare productions of its initial period see Mouzenidou (375–91).

References

Books and articles

Booth, Michael (1991), *Theatre in the Victorian Age*, Cambridge: Cambridge University Press.

Coleridge, Henry Nelson, ed. [1835] (1836), *Specimens of the Table Talk of Samuel Taylor Coleridge*, London: John Murray.

Damiralis, M. (1890), *Sekspir, Hamlet* (Shakespeare, *Hamlet*), Athens: I. Sideris.

Davis, Tracy C. (1995), 'Reading Shakespeare by "Flashes of Lightning": Challenging the Foundations of Romantic Acting Theory', *ELH* 62(4): 933–54.

Dávidházi, Péter (1998), *The Romantic Cult of Shakespeare. Literary Reception in Anthropological Perspective*, Basingstoke: Palgrave, Macmillan.

Delabastita, Dirk and D'hulst, Lieven, eds, (1993), *European Shakespeares: Translating Shakespeare in the Romantic Age*, Amsterdam/Philadelphia: John Benjamin's.

Dimaras, K. Th. (1947), 'Epafes tis neoteris ellinikis logotechnias me tin aggliki' (Connections of modern Greek literature with the English), *Aggloelliniki Epitheorisi* 3(1): 18–22.

Dimitriadis, Andreas (2006), *Shekspiristis, ara peritos* (Shakespearist, therefore not needed), Heraklion: University of Crete publications.

Douka-Kambitoglou, Ekaterini (1981), *I parousia tou Sekspir ston elliniko horo* (Shakespeare's presence in Greece), Thessalonike.

Glytzouris, Antonis (2001), *I skenothetiki techni stin Ellada* (The art of the director in Greece), Athens: Ellinika Grammata.

Hatzipantazis, Theodoros (2002, 2012), *Apo tou Nilou mehri tou Dounaveos* (From Nile to Danube), Iraklio: The University of Crete Press.

Healy, Thomas (1997), 'Past and Present Shakespeares: Shakespearian Appropriations in Europe', in John J. Joughin ed., *Shakespeare and National Culture*, 206–32, Manchester and New York: Manchester University Press.

Hemmings, Frederic William John (1993), *The Theatre Industry in Nineteenth-Century France*, Cambridge: Cambridge University Press.

Hobsbawm, Eric J. (1990), *Nations and Nationalism Since 1780*, Cambridge: Cambridge University Press.

Jusdanis, Gregory (1991), *Belated Modernity and Aesthetic Culture: Inventing National Literature, Theory and History of Literature*, vol. 81, Minneapolis: University of Minnesota Press.

Karagiorgos, Panos (1976), 'The First Greek Translation of Shakespeare's *Macbeth* by Andreas Theotokis (1819)', *Dodoni*, 5: 223–41.

Karagiorgos, Panos (1995), *Shakespeare Studies*, Thessalonike: Kyriakidis.

Laskaris, Nikolaos (1938–9), *Istoria tou Neoellinikou theatrou* (History of the Modern Greek Theatre). 2 vols, Athens: M. Vasiliou.

Mouzenidou, Agni (2004), 'Skiniki prosegisi tou Sekspir sta kratika theatra: To Oniro kalokerinis nyhtas' (Stage approaches to Shakespeare at the state theatres: *A Midsummer Night's Dream*), *Abstracts of the B' Panhellenic Theatre Conference*, 375–91, Athens: Ergo.

Pervanoglou, Ioannis (1858; 1883), *Amletos tou Sekspirou* (*Hamlet* by Shakespeare), Athens: I. Kostopoulos.

Paulin, Roger (2003), *The Critical Reception of Shakespeare in Germany 1682–1914: Native Literature and Foreign Genius*, Hildesheim, Zurich, and New York: Georg Olms Verlag.

Polylas, Iakovos, trans. [1889] (2000), *Amletos, tragodia Sekspirou* (*Hamlet*, tragedy by Shakespeare), M. Yanni ed., Introduction by D. Polychronakis, Athens: Ideogramma.

Pujante, A. Luis and Hoenselaars, Ton, eds (2003), *Four Hundred Years of Shakespeare in Europe,* Newark: University of Delaware Press /London: Associated University Presses.

Sideris, Yannis (1964–5), 'O Sekspir stin Elladha' (Shakespeare in Greece), *Theatro*, issues 13 to 21.

Sideris, Yannis (1999–2000), *Istoria tou neu ellinikou theatrou (1794-1944)* (History of the Modern Greek theatre), 2 vols, Athens: Kastaniotis.

Stamatopoulou-Vassilakou, Chrysothemis (1994–6), *To elliniko theatro stin Konstantinoupoli ton 19 eona* (The Greek theatre in Constantinople in the nineteenth century), 2 vols, Athens: Neos kyklos Konstadinopoliton.

Tavoularis, Dionysios (1930), *Memoirs*, Introduction by Nikolaos Laskaris, Athens: Pyrsos.

Taylor, George (1999), 'François Delsarte: A Codification of Nineteenth-Century Acting', *Theatre Research International* 24.1: 71–81

Vernardakis, Demetrius (1858), *Maria Doxapatri*, Munich: J. G. Weiss.

Vikelas, Demetrius, trans. (1876), *Sekspirou Tragodie, Meros proto: Romeos ke Ioulieta* (Shakespeare's Tragedies, Part One: *Romeo and Juliet*), Athens: Filokalia.

Weimann, Robert (1978), *Shakespeare and the Popular Tradition in the Theatre: Studies in the Social Dimension of Dramatic Form and Function*, ed. Robert Schwartz, Baltimore: Johns Hopkins University Press.

Williams, Simon [1990] (2004), *Shakespeare on the German Stage*, vol. I: 1586–1914, Cambridge: Cambridge University Press.

Yanni, Mara (2005), *Shakespeare's Travels: Greek Representations of Hamlet in the Nineteenth Century,* University of Athens Monographs, no. 66, Athens.

Nineteenth-century Greek journals and newspapers

Athens: *Acropolis, Asty, Avgi, Byron, Efimeris, Estia, Mi Hanese, Nea Efimeris, Palligensia, Rabagas.*
Constantinople: *Neologos, Tilegragos ke Vyzantis.*
Smyrna: *Velos.*

INDEX

Adamian, Petros 249–56
Alboise, Jules-Edouard 25
Alcalá Galiano, Antonio 222, 228
Aldridge, Ira 12, 159, 166, 239, 268
Alexander I of Russia 20, 163, 179
Alexiadis, Demosthenis 272–3
Algarotti, Francesco 20, 24
Amatuni, Napoleon 249
Amsterdam 4, 11, 96–101, 107, 112, 114
Andrés, Juan 6, 23, 211–12, 218, 228–9
Appia, Adolphe 24
Argental, Charles-Augustin Ferriol, comte d' 27, 121–2
Aristotle 101, 212, 220, 226
Armenia 4, 11–12, 15, 21–3, 233–57, 270
Arteaga, Esteban de 215, 217, 229
Artzruni, Grigor 244, 252
Artzruni, Senekerim 244, 250, 251, 255
Athens 11, 15, 21, 23, 66, 259, 264–78
Austrian Empire 14, 29, 42, 150–1, 157, 160

Bacon, Francis 218
Balbi, Francesco 37
Baretti, Giuseppe xi, 34
Barlaeus, Caspar (Kaspar van Baerle) 100
Baronian, Hagop 240
Basel 81–2
Basili, Basilio 225
Baudissin, Wolf Heinrich von 65–6
Beaumarchais, Pierre Caron de 194, 199
Belinsky, Vissarion 22, 179–80, 184–6, 245, 251, 254–5
Belleforest, François de 98
Bellini, Vincenzo 268
Berio, Francesco 38
Berlin 113, 148
Berlioz, Hector 8, 25, 140
Bernhardt, Sarah 278
Bilderdijk, Willem 107
Bjurbäck, Olof 200
Blanc, Johann von 193
Blanco White, José 223, 229
Bodmer, Johann Jakob 5, 14, 32, 82–8, 91
Bogusławski, Wojciech 12, 21, 151–2
Böhl von Faber, Johann Nikolaus 220–2, 229
Bohuslän 203

Bologna 37, 46, 50
Bouwmeester, Louis 22, 113
Boye, Johannes 190
Bräker, Ulrich 11, 86–7, 91
Brandt, Geeraert 98
Brazil 120, 139, 140, 142
Bredero, Gerbrand 96–8
Bremner, Lisa 248
Brill, E. J. 108, 115–16
Brooke, Henry 197
Browne, Robert 99
Bryan, George 146
Bulgarin, Faddey 177
Bulla, Franz Heinrich 151–2
Burgersdijk, Leendert Alexander Johannes xiv, 16, 108–16
Busino, Orazio 30
Bykowski, Ignacy 151, 165
Byron, George Gordon, Lord 107, 175, 178, 238, 241, 251, 264

Cadalso, José 213, 229
Cadiz 220, 222
Caetano, João 139, 142
Calcutta 234–7, 254
Calderón de la Barca, Pedro 13, 151, 175, 212, 220–4
Calvin, Jean 81, 98, 101
Campbell, Colin 195–6
Carcano, Giulio 45, 49
Carnerero, José María de 218
Caro, Jacob 162–3
Caroline Mathilde 202
Catherine II of Russia 16, 18, 23, 165, 170–1
Cecil, Robert 30
Cervantes, Miguel de 183

Chaadayev, Pyotr 185
Charles I 100
Charles IV of Spain 216, 219
Chateaubriand, François-Auguste-René de 7, 25, 195
Chmshkian, Gevork 244–50, 256
Chmshkian, Satenik 245, 248
Chobanian, Arshag 240
Christian VII of Denmark 202, 207
Cibber, Colley 5
Cibber, Theophilus 131
Cimino, Giorgio Tommaso 46, 53
Cinzio, Giambattista Giraldi 181
Clark, Jaime 227, 231
Clerico, Francesco 37
Coello, Carlos 218
Coleridge, Samuel Taylor 7, 18–19, 25, 59, 107, 182, 223, 273, 280
Constantini, Bartolomeo 148
Constantinople 11–12, 15, 21, 234, 239–41, 249–54, 259, 264, 267–76, 282
Conti, Antonio Schinella, Abbot 5, 20, 25, 30–4, 50–1, 54, 83–4, 91
Copeau, Jacques 24
Corneille, Pierre 6, 9, 31–2, 61, 83–4, 101, 121–2, 126, 129, 132
Coster, Samuel 96–7
Craig, Edward Gordon 24
Crowne, John 17
Cyprus 11, 270

Czartoryska, Izabela 149–50
Czartoryski, Adam 150

Dahlgren, Carl Fredric 205
Damiralis, Michael 268, 280
Dante Alighieri 10, 32–3, 37,
    39, 88, 107, 127–8, 175,
    183, 238, 241
Davenant, William 17
De la Calle, Teodoro 218–19
De la Cruz, Ramón 13, 212
De la Vega, Ventura 226–7
Delacroix, Eugène 8, 140
Delavigne, Casimir 224
Delius, Nicolaus 109
Delvig, Anton 179
Denmark 22, 34, 58, 190–1,
    201–3, 207–8, 251
Desgarcins, Louise 135
Diaz, José María 218, 224
Diderot, Denis 133, 140
Dingelstedt, Franz 72, 76
Dresden 57, 146, 148
Dryden, John 17–18, 84, 122,
    142
Du Lac 22, 25
Ducis, Jean-François xiv, 5,
    12–13, 16–17, 23, 35–8,
    49, 51–2, 112, 119–43,
    148, 152, 170, 183,
    190–1, 197, 212–13,
    218, 224, 228, 231, 234,
    265
Dumas, Alexandre 8, 25,
    241
Duncombe, William 20
Duval, Alexandre 226–7

Edward I 157
Egypt 11, 270

Ehrenberg, Gustaw 163–4,
    165
Ekroth, Nathanael 197
Ekshian, Stephan 239
Elbląg 3, 147
Elizabeth I 30
Elsinore 146, 191, 202, 263
Emerson, Ralph Waldo 227
Emin, Joseph Hovsep 235–6,
    254–5
England 4–7, 11, 14, 17–19,
    26, 30–5, 58–9, 62, 65,
    69, 72, 81–2, 93, 98,
    104–5, 109, 119, 122,
    140, 147–8, 150, 157,
    186, 191–7, 201–5, 213,
    222, 231, 241, 259, 271,
    275, 279
Erfurt 20
Eschenburg, Johann Joachim
    18, 63, 85–6, 92, 148–9,
    151, 171
Euripides 238, 262

Ferdinando I of Sicily 47
Ferdinand VII 221–2
Finland 190, 208
Florence 11, 34, 37, 43
Fontenelle, Bernard le Bouyer
    de 32
Foppa, Giuseppe Maria 37
Foxe, John 81
France 2–5, 8–9, 12–14, 17,
    20–1, 32, 37, 59, 65, 80,
    106, 119–43, 148, 154,
    168, 173, 188, 192,
    196–9, 201, 209–10,
    213, 222–3, 259, 269,
    271, 281
Frey, Johann Ludwig 82

Fulda, Ludwig 73, 76
Funke, G. L. 107–8
Füssli, Johann Heinrich
    (Henry Fuseli) 5, 23,
    85–8, 92

Galdós, Benito Pérez 219
Gantajian, Astghik 249
Gantajian, Siranush 249
Garagashian, Vergine 249
Garagashian, Yearanuhi 249
Garcia de Villalta, José 224
Garcia Suelto, Manuel 218
Garrick, David 6, 16–18, 26,
    88, 122–3, 126, 130–1,
    136, 197, 202, 218, 236
Gasparini, Francesco 34
Gautier, Théophile 8, 140, 142
Gdańsk 3, 146–7, 152, 166
Geijer, Erik Gustaf 204–5
Geneva 15, 59, 81, 89
Germany 2–7, 9–10, 14, 19,
    23, 32, 38, 55–78, 80,
    88, 91, 96, 107, 109,
    141, 164, 168, 171–3,
    259, 263, 269, 281
Gil y Carrasco, Enrique 225,
    229
Goethe, Johann Wofgang von
    7, 14, 16, 18, 20, 25, 26,
    56, 63–4, 70–1, 76–7,
    90, 92, 107, 176, 241,
    250
Gollancz, Israel 73, 76
Gómez Hermosilla, José 221,
    230
Gothenburg 4, 22, 189–205
Gottlieb, Maurycy 152, 161
Gottsched, Johann Christoph
    6–7, 60–1, 83

Gouges, Olympe de 137–8
Gramsbergen, Matthus 98
Greece viii, xiv, 5, 11, 14, 15,
    22–4, 38, 48–9, 73, 89,
    214, 239, 241, 243,
    259–82
Greene, John 57, 99, 147
Greene, Robert 146
Grimaldi, Jean (Juan) 219, 229
Gritti, Francesco 13, 35–7,
    51–2, 123
Grynäus, Johann Jakob 82
Grynäus, Simon 84–5
Gryphius, Andreas 58
Guizot, François 8–9, 25,
    176–7
Gundolf, Friedrich 72–3, 76
Gustav III 138, 201–4, 207

Hauptmann, Gerhart 72, 76
Hazlitt, William 18, 107, 182
Heinsius, Daniel 101
Herder, Johann Gottfried 7,
    59, 63–4, 76–7, 107,
    172–3
Herzen, Alexander 184
Hołowiński, Ignacy 153
Homer 14, 87, 168, 238, 241,
    262
Hooft, Pieter Corneliszoon
    96–8, 100
Horn, Franz 74, 76
Hovhannisian, Richard 241,
    256
Hovhannisyan, Lyudmila 236,
    256
Hugo, François-Victor 242–3,
    255
Hugo, Victor 8–10, 21, 26, 140,
    176, 179, 222–3, 241

Huygens, Constantijn Jr 96–8
Huygens the Elder, Sir
 Constantijn 98

Ibsen, Henryk 277
Iceland 190, 206
India 4, 195–6, 206, 208, 235,
 238, 257, 271
Irving, Henry 275, 141
Italy 5, 7–8, 10–1, 14–16,
 19–20, 22–3, 29–54, 80,
 83–4, 123–4, 140–2,
 148, 181, 227, 228, 230,
 241–2, 263, 267–8,
 275–6

James I 30, 98
Jankowski, Placyd 154
Jew, Jewish 22–3, 46–7, 50,
 113, 157–61, 241, 242,
 246–8, 276
Johnson, Samuel 16, 18, 34,
 47, 63, 67, 85, 149, 165,
 220
Jovellanos, Gaspar Melchor de
 214–15, 219, 230
Juliane Marie 202

Kamiński, Jan Nepomucen
 152
Karamzin, Nikolai 14, 21,
 172–3, 177, 179, 187
Kavafis, Konstandinos 263
Kean, Edmund 22, 107, 273
Kemble, Charles 8, 135,
 139–40
Kempe, William 95–6, 146
Kipiani, Kote 246–7
Kitt, Johann Jakob 85, 91
Koberstein, August 72, 77

Kok, Abraham Seyne 107–8
Komierowski, Jan 154
Königsberg 4, 147–8
Kontopoulos, Nikolaos 268
Korzeniowski, Apollo 154
Korzeniowski, Józef 154
Kossakowski, Józef 151
Kotopoulis, Demetrius 273
Kozintsev, Grigori 22
Kozitsky, Grigoriy 170
Koźmian, Andrzej 158, 166
Koźmian, Stanisław 157–9
Koźmian, Stanisław Egbert
 154, 158
Krakow 4, 147, 156–8, 160–1,
 163
Krasicki, Ignacy 150, 165
Kruseman, A. C. 107
Kurz, Felix 148
Kyd, Thomas 99

La Harpe, Jean-François 175
La Place, Pierre-Antoine de 12,
 121, 123, 124–5, 134,
 142, 168–9
La Tocnaye, Jacques-Louis de
 Bougrenet de 196, 206
Lach-Szyrma, Krystyn 150
Lagerström, Magnus 196, 206
Lagrenée, Louis-Jean-François
 138
Lamb, Charles 18
Lambros, Spyridon 264
Laroche, Benjamin 246, 248
Larra, Mariano José de 222–3
Le Tourneur, Pierre-Prime-
 Félicien 6, 18, 26, 43,
 63, 121, 124, 134,
 141–2, 150, 170–1, 176,
 183, 217, 265

Leclercq, Pieter 105
Leicester, Robert Dudley, Earl of 95–6
Leiden 96, 108
Lekatsa, Ekaterini 278
Lekatsas, Nikolaos 267, 274–7
Lensky, Aleksandr 250
Lenz, Jakob Michael Reinhold 64–5, 77, 172
Leoni, Michele 14, 20, 30, 41–5, 47–9, 50, 51–2
Leopold, Carl Gustaf af 6, 200–1
Lermontov, Mikhail 185
Lessing, Gotthold Ephraim 5, 7, 56, 59–62, 65, 77, 141
Leti, Gregorio 30
Lichtenberg, Georg Christoph 17, 26
Lidner, Bengt 198
Loffelt, Anton Cornelis 110–13, 115, 116
Lofthuus, Christian Jensen 202
London 5, 11, 17, 19, 20, 30, 34, 51, 87–8, 96–8, 107, 110–11, 113, 135, 141, 146–7, 149, 171, 195, 197, 202, 222, 224, 235–6, 241, 259, 266, 275
Lope de Vega y Carpo, Félix 13, 97, 212
Lucerne 89
Lucini, Francesco 225
Luzán, Ignacio de 211–12, 230
Lvov 151–2, 156–7, 159–61

Macquet, Jan D. 106
Madrid 13, 120, 212, 215–16, 225
Magalhães, Domingos 139
Maghakian, Petros 239
Máiquez, Isidoro 139, 219
Malone, Edmond 67
Marlowe, Christopher 204
Massalski, Ignacy 150
Matkowsky, Adalbert 268
Mavromichalis, Ioannis 264
Mazzini, Giuseppe 44–5, 52
Mekhitar of Sebaste 234
Mendelssohn, Moses 61
Mercier, Louis-Sébastien 16, 151, 174
Meursio, Giovanni 34
Meyerhold, Vsevolod 24
Michelangelo Buonarroti 29–30, 48–9
Mickiewicz, Adam 155
Middleton, Thomas 97
Milan 15, 19, 22, 23, 29, 37, 42, 45, 49, 51
Milton, John 7, 10, 32, 53, 82–4, 87–8, 90, 91, 103, 168
Mkrtchian, Martiros 236
Mochalov, Pavel 183–4, 187, 251, 255
Modena, Gustavo 49, 51
Molé, François-René 133, 138
Molière (Jean-Baptiste Poquelin) 151, 175, 182, 241, 242
Molineri, Giuseppe Cesare 45–6, 52
Moniuszko, Stanisław 161
Montagu, Lady Mary Wortley 32

Montbrun, Louis 148
Mora, José Joaquín de 221
Moraitidis, Alexander 264
Moratín, Leandro Fernández de 6, 215–18, 225–8, 229, 230
Mortara, Edgardo 46
Moscow 170–4, 177, 178–9, 183–6, 250–2
Mounet-Sully, Jean 268
Munich 161, 263, 265
Muralt, Béat Louis de 82, 92

Nalbandian, Mikael 247
Naples 11, 29, 34, 49, 227
Napoleon I 14, 18–19, 20, 42, 138, 153, 174, 198–9, 207, 222, 229
Netherlands 3, 4, 6, 10, 15, 22–3, 95–117, 136
Newton, Isaac 30, 32, 102, 218
Nicolai, Friedrich 61
Nicholas I 179, 185
Nipho, Francisco Mariano 209–11, 230
Nodier, Charles 8, 23
Norway 190, 202, 203
Novelli, Ermete 46
Novikov, Nikolai 173

Ochoa, Eugenio de 223, 230
Odessa 176, 250, 252
Osiński, Ludwik 12, 152
Ostrowski, Krysty 154, 160, 166
Otto I 259, 265
Ottoman Empire 15, 21, 148, 233, 240, 241–3, 253, 267, 269–70, 274

Otway, Thomas 127–8, 130–1, 142

Padua 6, 15, 30
Palamas, Kostis 263
Papazian, Arusiak 239
Papazian, Sargis 242, 204, 212
Paraskevopoulou, Evangelia 278–9
Pariati, Pietro 34, 54
Paris 8, 22, 127, 138, 139, 149, 160, 240
Paszkowski, Józef 154–6, 168
Paul I 170
Pervanoglou, Ioannis 265–8, 275, 278, 281
Peter I the Great 23, 182
Peter III 21, 170, 173
Petrossian, Gevork 248
Pforta 72, 77
Phelps, Samuel 107, 275
Pichot, Amédée 176
Pinsuti, Ciro 46, 50, 53
Platter, Thomas 81, 93
Plesheev, Mikhail 10, 171–2
Pług, Adam 154
Poland 3–4, 5, 8, 11, 13–14, 21, 23, 89, 120, 145–66, 207
Polevoy, Nikolai 183
Polylas, Iakovos 265, 281
Pomerantsev, Vasiliy 174
Poniatowski, Stanisław 21, 149–50, 165
Pontano, Giovanni 34
Pope, Alexander 30, 102, 151, 168, 220
Pope, Thomas 146
Portugal 120
Poznan 152

Prague 148
Pushkin, Alexander 7–9, 14, 19, 23, 167, 170, 172, 175–83, 185–6, 187–8

Racine, Jean 6, 9, 27, 30, 61, 121–2, 151, 175–6
Radziwiłł, Bogusław 148
Rangavis, Kleon 264
Rayevsky, Nikolai, Jr 178
Regulski, Stanisław 152
Reynolds, Sir Joshua 88
Riga 4, 147
Rodenburgh, Theodore 'Dirk' 97
Roe, William 96
Rolli, Paolo 10, 32–4, 51, 53
Romania 120
Rome 19, 20, 23, 24, 30–1, 38, 43–4, 61, 88, 180, 214, 224, 237
Rossi, Ernesto 22, 45–6, 50–3, 108, 250–1, 268, 276
Rössing, Johan Herman 109, 112
Rossini, Gioacchino 38, 268
Rousseau, Jean-Jacques 89, 133–4, 142
Rowe, Nicholas 47, 226, 228
Rusconi, Carlo 48
Russia 2, 5–11, 12–14, 16, 20–2, 45, 120, 150, 153, 156, 159, 167–88, 203, 233, 238, 243–8, 250–3, 254, 259, 270, 273

Sakellarios, Georgios 265
Saint Petersburg 149, 170, 171, 183, 185, 245, 250, 252
Salvini, Tommaso 250–1, 268, 275
San Miguel, Evaristo 226, 231
Santi, Pietro 45
Saviñón, Antonio de 218
Schepkin, Mikhail 183
Schiller, Friedrich 2, 14, 63, 69, 89–90, 92–3, 107, 152, 172, 204–5, 241, 264
Schlegel, August Wilhelm von 7–8, 19, 26, 42, 47, 52, 55–7, 59, 65–70, 73, 77–8, 92, 107, 152, 176, 220, 229, 265–6
Schlegel, Friedrich von 68
Schröder, Friedrich Ludwig 148–9, 151
Schwenter, Daniel 57–8
Seuerling, Carl Gottfried 190, 193
Sevumian, Ovi 248
Shakespeare, WIlliam
  Antony and Cleopatra 82, 280
  As You Like It 107
  Coriolanus 85, 91, 113, 210, 274, 280
  Cymbeline 45, 66, 111, 123, 134, 263
  Hamlet xi, xii, 4, 6, 8, 10–13, 17, 21–3, 33, 35–7, 41, 51, 53, 57–8, 67, 71, 76, 78, 79, 85, 88, 92, 98, 103–5, 107, 113, 119–40, 142, 143
  Julius Caesar 6–7, 16, 19–22, 31–1, 38–41, 43–5, 53, 57, 60–1, 81, 85, 90, 113–14, 149,

172–3, 211, 238, 272, 274, 279
King Henry IV 38
King Henry V 89, 167, 180
King John 154, 224
King Lear 18, 23, 57, 280
King Richard II 16, 27, 45, 154
King Richard III 23, 62, 104, 107, 113, 159, 180, 202, 224, 226, 253, 274, 279
Love's Labour's Lost 65, 167
Macbeth xii, 11–12, 23, 37–8, 51, 54, 66, 85–8, 105, 113–14, 115, 121, 123–7, 132, 134–9, 151–3, 155–8, 167, 197, 204–5, 211, 224–5, 229, 230, 234, 239–40, 253, 264–8, 270–4, 279, 281
Measure for Measure 113, 167, 181, 236–7
The Merchant of Venice 22–3, 45–7, 50, 57, 113, 157–62, 243, 245–7, 255, 256, 266, 268, 274, 276, 279
The Merry Wives of Windsor 57, 123, 171, 173
A Midsummer Night's Dream xiv, 23–4, 45, 57, 66, 85, 88, 98, 113–14, 236–7, 274, 281
Much Ado about Nothing 66, 113, 236
Othello 11, 12, 23, 37–8, 41, 43, 49, 51, 104–5, 123–5, 129–30, 134–41, 152, 156–7, 174, 182, 198, 211, 218–19, 227, 229, 236, 239, 245, 248–9, 252–3, 256, 263–6, 268, 270, 272–4, 279
Pericles 274
The Rape of Lucrece 180
Romeo and Juliet xii, 16, 23, 26, 37, 45, 52, 57, 66, 70, 76, 77, 84–5, 91, 92, 112–13, 123–34, 140, 148, 151, 156, 174, 181–3, 190–1, 197, 242–3, 256, 263–6, 274–5, 278–9, 282
The Taming of the Shrew 45, 66, 99, 113, 115, 148, 157, 250
The Tempest 45, 163, 173, 263, 265
Timon of Athens 66, 274
Titus Andronicus 11, 57, 99, 147, 196, 208, 245
Troilus and Cressida 122, 274
Twelfth Night 109, 113–14, 163, 236, 280
The Two Gentlemen of Verona 66, 147, 236, 279
Two Noble Kinsmen 274
The Winter's Tale 23, 66, 98, 113–14, 145, 162–4, 167
Sheffield, John, Duke of Buckingham 17–20, 30, 32

Shermazanian, Galoust 244
Siddons, Sarah 136
Sidney, Sir Philip 95–7
Sienkiewicz, Karol 150
Słowacki, Juliusz 14, 155
Smyrna 11, 15, 23, 234, 241–3, 254, 256, 270, 274
Solís, Antonio de 212
Solomos, Dionysios 263
Soutsas, Pantelis 11–12, 268, 272–3
Spain 3, 6, 9, 13–14, 23, 31, 49, 95, 97, 136, 139–40, 209–31
Staël-Holstein, Germaine de v, 8–9, 18–19, 26, 42–3, 48, 53, 59, 69, 78, 139, 142, 176
Steele, Richard 4, 84, 91, 102
Steevens, George 18, 63, 67, 85
Stendhal (Henri Beyle) 9–10, 21, 25, 27, 176
Stephanie, Johann Gottlieb 152
Stockholm 4, 191–2, 199–202, 205–6
Stratford-upon-Avon ix, 56, 96, 113, 150
Sulchasiantz, Stepanos 252
Sumarokov, Alexander 168–70, 187, 188
Surenyantz, Vardgez 253
Sweden 4–6, 9, 22, 120, 138, 189–208
Switzerland 4, 8–9, 11, 14–15, 32, 63, 75, 79–93, 173
Sybant, Abraham 99

Talma, François-Joseph 20, 26, 130, 135–9
Tamayo y Baus, Manuel 227
Tate, Nahum 17–18, 27, 142
Tavoularis, Dionysos 268, 272–5, 282
Ter-Grigorian, Vano 247
Teteyan, Aram Karapet 23, 241–3, 256
Thaliadian, Mesrovb David 21, 237–8
Theobald, Lewis 16, 26–7, 39
Theocharidis, Themistocles 264
Theotokis, Andreas 265, 281
Tieck, Dorothea 7, 55–7, 65–7
Tieck, Ludwig 7, 19, 55–7, 65–7, 69–70, 77–8
Tiflis 23, 234, 243–5, 248–50, 253–4
Trediakovsky, Vasiliy 169

Üchtritz, Friedrich von 66, 78
Ulrich, Leon 154–6
Utrecht 95–6, 99

Valentini, Domenico 16, 38–41, 54
Valera, Juan 227, 231
Van den Bergh, Adriaen 99
Van den Bergh, Ariane 99
Van den Bergh, Laurent 107, 115
Van Effen, Justus 10, 27, 101–6, 116, 117
Van den Vondel, Joost 97–8, 100–1
Vardovian, Hagop 239–40
Vassiliadis, Spyridon 264
Velyaminov, Ivan 12–13, 174 174

Venice 13, 15, 29–30, 34–5, 38, 120, 133, 138, 161, 182, 234–8
Verdi, Giuseppe 37–8, 51, 54, 267–8
Vernardakis, Demetrios 14, 263–4, 282
Verri, Alessandro 41, 50
Veselovski, Alexei 250
Vestris, Madame (Françoise-Marie-Rosette Gourgaud) 135
Vienna 45, 113, 148, 151–2, 181
Vigny, Alfred de 8, 14, 124, 140
Vikelas, Demetrius 266–7, 276, 278, 282
Villiers de l'Isle Adam, Auguste 23
Vilnius 4, 13, 147, 150–2, 155
Voltaire (Jean-François-Marie Arouet) xiv, 5–12, 17–20, 25–7, 30–5, 41, 54, 83, 85, 93, 103, 106, 119–23, 140–1, 142–3, 151, 168–9, 171–2, 175, 195–8, 210, 215, 217, 222, 231, 241
Vos, Jan 11, 99–101, 106, 115
Vossius, Gerardus (Gerrit Janszoon Vos) 101
Vyazemsky, Pyotr 176

Wallenberg, Jacob 8, 197
Warsaw 4, 12, 147–52, 156–7, 161
Weimar 16, 20, 26, 56, 70, 89–90
Weinberg, Peter 248, 252
Weisse, Felix Christian 148
Weyerman, Jacob Campo 105–6, 115
Widebäck, Anna Catharina 195–6
Widerberg, Andreas 190–5, 198–9, 201–5
Wieland, Christoph Martin 5, 10–11, 18, 63, 67, 78, 85–6, 93, 151
William III 96, 98, 105
Wiselius, Samuel 108
Wollstonecraft, Mary 195–6, 208
Wrocław (Breslau) 4, 147, 152

Yarishkin, Aleksandr Ivanovich 250–1, 256
Yeritsian, Alexander 245
Young, Edward 62

Zarian, Ruben 250–2, 257
Zellweger, Laurenz 82
Zeno, Apostolo 11, 34, 54
Zimovit III 162–3
Zumel, Enrique 227
Zurich 5, 10, 15, 18, 81–2, 85, 87–8

www.ingramcontent.com/pod-product-compliance
Lightning Source LLC
Chambersburg PA
CBHW072124290426
44111CB00012B/1766